Oxford Primary Atlas

D0245868

Editorial Adviser
Dr Patrick Wiegand

OXFORD
UNIVERSITY PRESS

Great Clarendon Street, Oxford OX2 6DP
Oxford University Press is a department of the University of Oxford.
It furthers the University's objective of excellence in research, scholarship, and education by publishing worldwide in

Oxford New York

Auckland Cape Town Dar es Salaam Hong Kong Karachi Kuala Lumpur Madrid Melbourne Mexico City Nairobi New Delhi Shanghai Taipei Toronto

With offices in

Argentina Austria Brazil Chile Czech Republic France Greece Guatemala Hungary Italy Japan Poland Portugal Singapore South Korea Switzerland Thailand Turkey Ukraine Vietnam

First published 2011

ISBN 978 0 19 848016 7 (hardback)

ISBN 978 0 19 848017 4 (paperback)

3 5 7 9 10 8 6 4 2

Printed in Singapore by KHL Printing Co. Pte Ltd.

Acknowledgments

The publisher and author would like to thank the following:

p5br: ICP/Alamy; **p8t:** Robert Harding Picture Library Ltd/Alamy; **p8tc:** The Photolibrary Wales/Alamy; **p8c:** Geogphotos/Alamy; **p8bc:** Ivan J Belcher/Worldwide Picture Library/ Alamy; **p8b:** Chinch Gryniewicz/Corbis; **p9tr:** Jonathan Dorey - Scotland/Alamy; **p9cl:** Andy Stothert/Britain on View/Photolibrary.com; **p9bl:** Graham Oliver/Alamy; **p9br:** Realimage/ Alamy; **p10tl:** Jason Hawkes Aerial Photography; **p10tr:** Sefton Samuels/Rex Features; **p10cr:** David Goddard/Getty Images; **p10bl:** Derek Rees/Photolibrary Wales; **p10br:** Steve Benbow Photolibrary Wales; **p11tl:** Planetary Visions Ltd/Science Photo Library; **p11tr:** Roger Ressmeyer/Corbis; **p11bl:** NASA/age Fotostock/Photolibrary.com; **p11br:** NASA; **p12:** PlanetObserver/Science Photo Library; **p16:** PlanetObserver/Science Photo Library; **p17:** James McNie; **p18t:** Tomasz Szatewicz/ Alamy; **p18b:** Michael David Murphy/Alamy; **p19:** North News; **p20:** Russell Kord/Alamy; **p21br:** Simon Margetson/Alamy; **p21bl:** Ingolf Pompe 5/Alamy; **p21br:** Pakimon/Shutterstock; **p23:** Pawel Osinski/iStockphoto.com; **p24:** Superstock Inc/ Photolibrary.com; **p26:** Liquid Light/Alamy; **p29:** John Boud/Alamy; **p30:** Philip Fenton/Britain on View /Photolibrary.com; **p32t:** David Crausby/Alamy; **p32c:** Elmtree Images/Alamy; **p32b:** Patrick Ingrand/Stone/Getty Images; **p33t:** Clynt Garnham Renewable Energy/ Alamy; **p33c:** Pixtal Images/Photolibrary.com; **p33b:** Neil lee Sharp/Alamy; **p34t:** Brenton West/Alamy; **p34b:** Digital Vision/Getty Images; **p35tr:** Tony Page/Stone/Getty Images; **p35cr:** Jon Arnold Images Ltd/Alamy; **p35bl:** Chris Demetriou/Frank Lane Picture Agency; **p35cl:** Ian Thraves/Alamy; **p36l:** David Martyn Hughes/Alamy; **p36c:** Jason Hawkes Aerial Photography; **p36r:** G P Bowater/Alamy; **p37t:** Martin Jones/Corbis; **p37tc:** The Trustees Of The British Museum/British Museum Images; **p37bc:** Herbert Kehrer/imagebroker.net/ Photolibrary.com; **p37b:** Richard Cooke/Taxi/Getty Images; **p40:** Phil Dunne/Alamy; **p42:** Carmen Sedano/Alamy; **p46:** Jagadeesh/Reuters/Corbis; **p49:** Emma Sklar/Rex Features; **p52:** Yann Arthus-Bertrand/ Corbis; **p53:** Daryl Balfour/ABPL/Animals Animals/ Photolibrary.com; **p57:** James Randklev/ Photographer's Choice/Getty Images; **p60:** Pascal Rondeau/Stone/Getty Images; **p64l:** Image Makers/The Image Bank/Getty Images; **p64r:** NPA/Stone/Getty Images; **p65l:** Earth Satellite Corporation/Science Photo Library; **p65r:** Planetary Visions Ltd/Science Photo Library; **p68cl:** Mediacolor's/Alamy; **p68tl:** Radius Images/Photolibrary.com; **p68tr:** Ron Watts/Corbis; **p68bl:** Ashfordplatt/Alamy; **p68br:** Charles & Josette Lenars/Corbis; **p69tl:** John Warburton-Lee Photography/Photolibrary.com; **p69tr:** Richard A. Cooke/Documentary Value/Corbis; **p69bl:** Wolfgang Kaehler/Corbis; **p69bc:** Galen Rowell/Terra/Corbis; **p69br:** Frans Lemmens/The Image Bank/Getty Images; **p70bl:** Jan Krimmer/imagebroker.net/ Photolibrary.com; **p70br:** Christian Heinrich/imagebroker RF/Photolibrary.com; **p71bl:** Ben Osborne/Stone/Getty Images; **p71br:** Fawzan Husain/Photolibrary.com; **p71cr:** Neale Clarke/Robert Harding Travel/ Photolibrary.com

Images sourced by Pictureresearch.co.uk

Illustrations by Mark Brierley p66 (icons); Mark Duffin p5 (compass), p59; Gary Hincks p8, p9; Harry Venning p66

Cover photo by Magskyphoto/Shutterstock. Cover globe by Jan Rysavy/iStockphoto

Contents

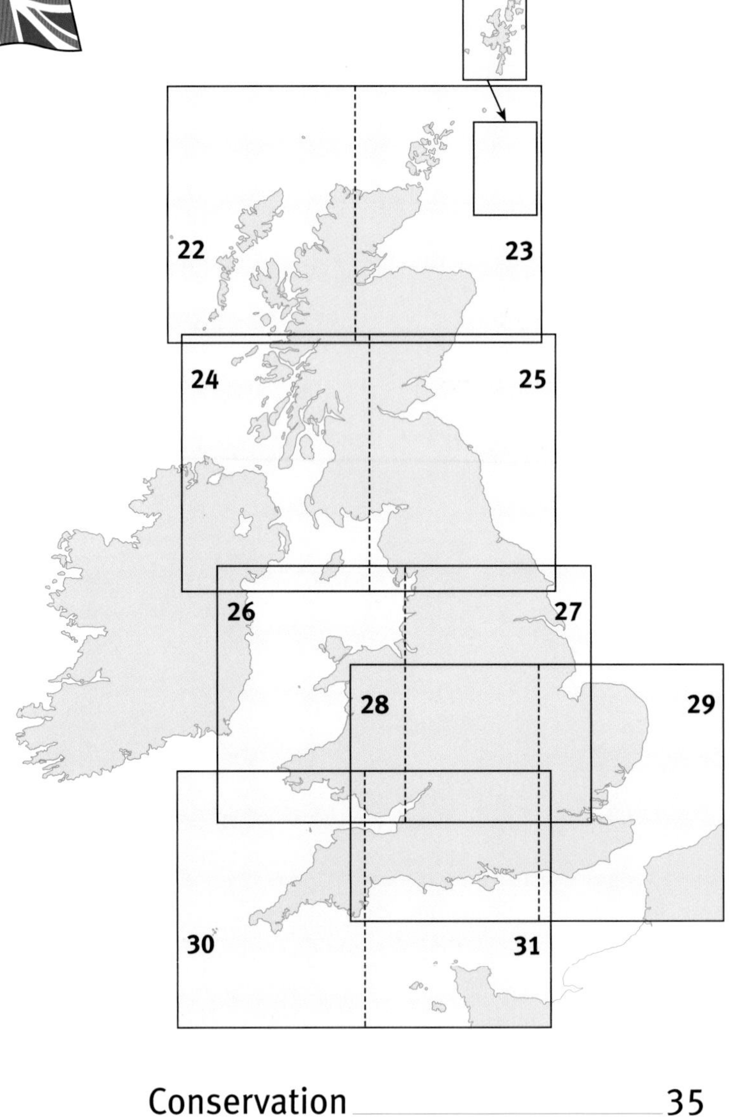

22
23
24
25
26
27
28
29
30
31

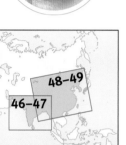

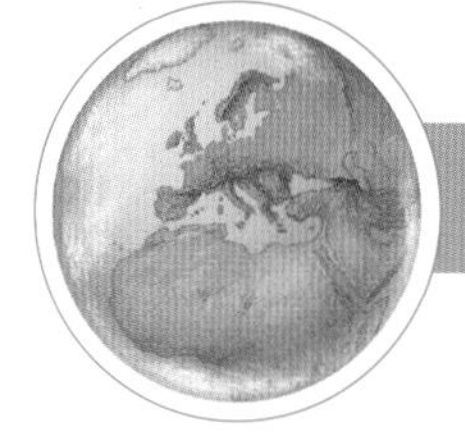

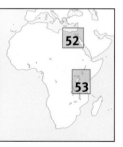

Europe

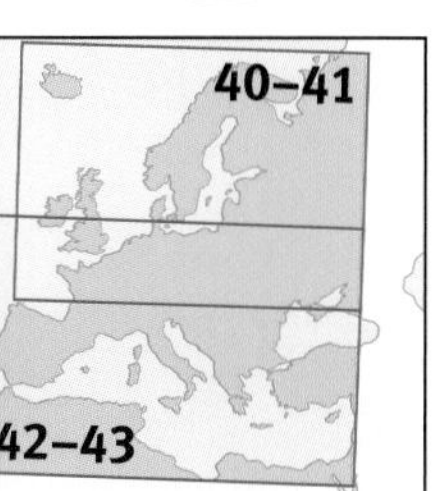

40–41
42–43

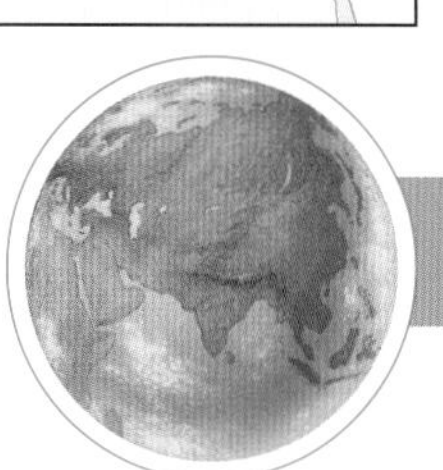

Asia

48–49
46–47

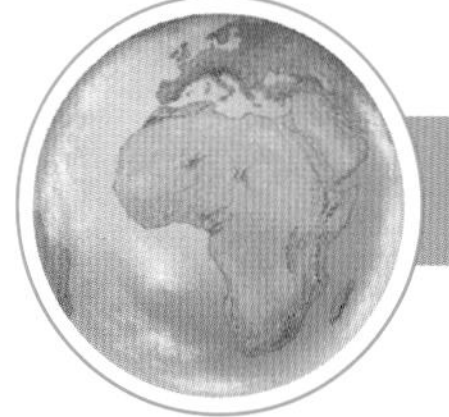

Africa

52
53

North America

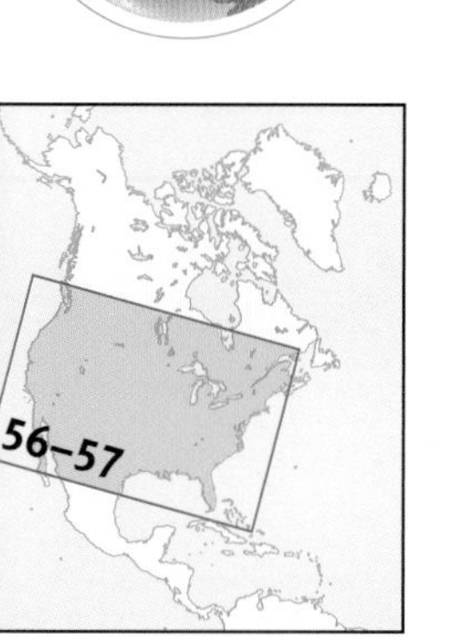

56–57

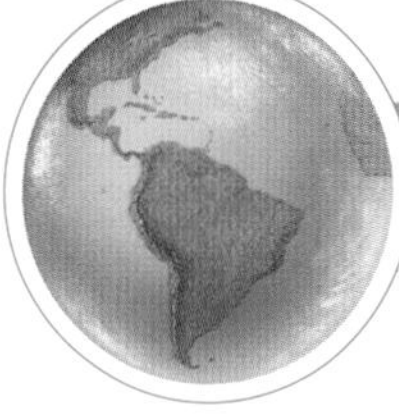

South America

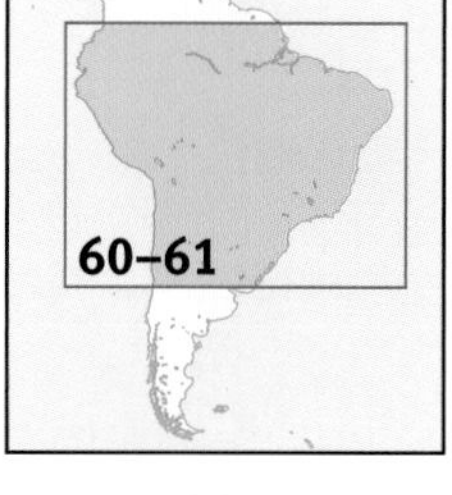

60–61

Oceania

The Poles

World

Understanding the Earth

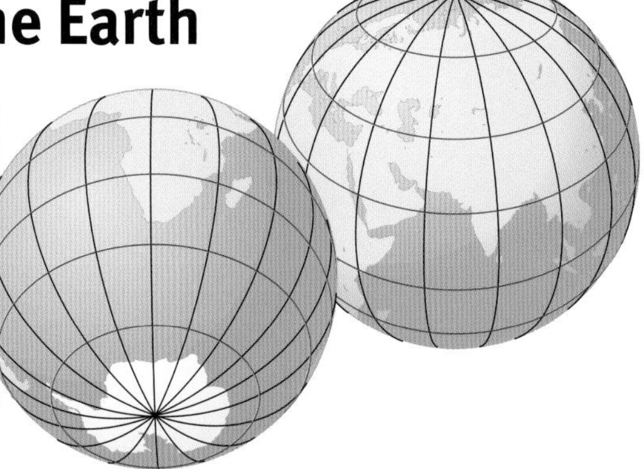

The Earth is a planet in space. It is a sphere. Two sets of imaginary lines help us describe where places are on the surface of the Earth.

Longitude

Lines of longitude measure distance east or west of the Prime Meridian.

The **Prime Meridian** (also called the Greenwich Meridian) is at longitude 0°.

The **International Date Line** (on the other side of the Earth) is based on longitude 180°.

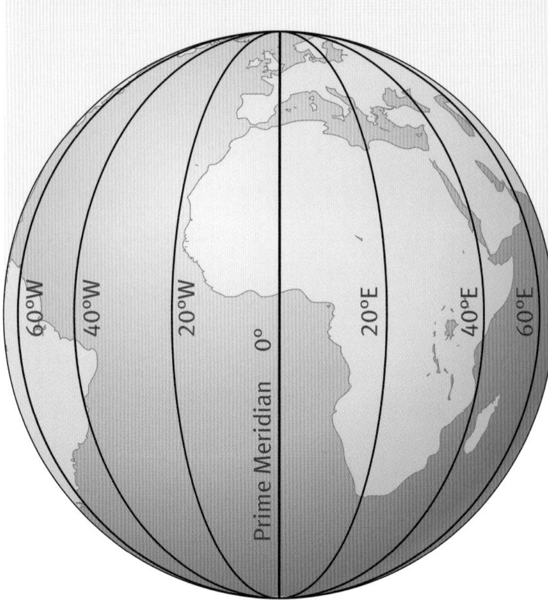
60°W
40°W
20°W
Prime Meridian 0°
20°E
40°E
60°E

Latitude

Lines of latitude measure distance north or south of the equator.

The **Equator** is at latitude 0°.

The **Poles** are at latitude 90°N and 90°S.

North Pole
Arctic Circle
60°N
40°N
Tropic of Cancer
20°N
0° Equator
20°S
Tropic of Capricorn
40°S
60°S
Antarctic Circle
South Pole

Can you find the **Equator**, the **Prime Meridian** and the **International Date Line** on a globe? ?

There are many ways of showing the spherical Earth on a flat world map.

Map projections

How a world map looks depends on where it is going to be used.

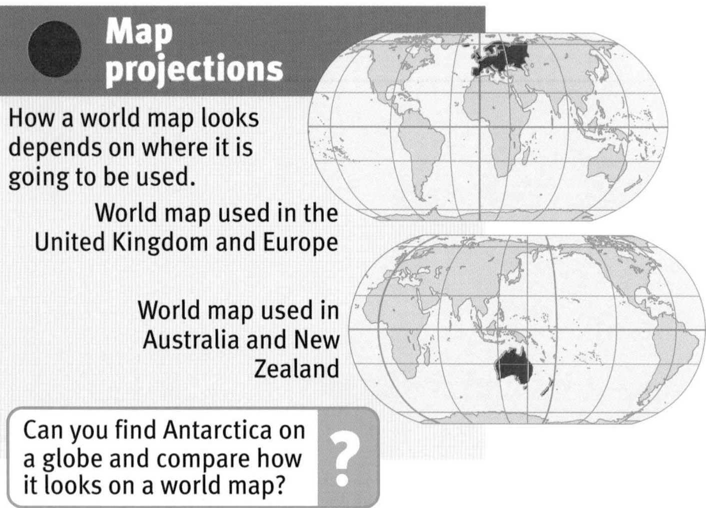

World map used in the United Kingdom and Europe

World map used in Australia and New Zealand

Can you find Antarctica on a globe and compare how it looks on a world map? ?

Grid codes

In this atlas, the lines of latitude and longitude are used to make a grid.

The columns of the grid have letters.

The rows of the grid have numbers.

Numbers and letters together make a **grid code** that can be used to describe where places are on the Earth.

Can you name the city at gridcode **B2**? ?

A B C D
5 4 3 2 1
MEDITERRANEAN SEA
Casablanca
MOROCCO
ALGERIA
Tripoli
LIBYA
Cairo
EGYPT
Tropic of Cancer
MALI
NIGER
CHAD
Khartoum
SUDAN
ETHIOPIA
Monrovia
Abuja
Mogadishu
Equator
KENYA
DEMOCRATIC REPUBLIC OF CONGO
TANZANIA
Dodoma
ATLANTIC OCEAN
INDIAN OCEAN
Prime Meridian
Luanda
ANGOLA
ZAMBIA
MADAGASCAR
Tropic of Capricorn
NAMIBIA
BOTSWANA
REPUBLIC OF SOUTH AFRICA
Durban
Cape Town
SOUTHERN OCEAN
20°W 0° 20°E 40°E

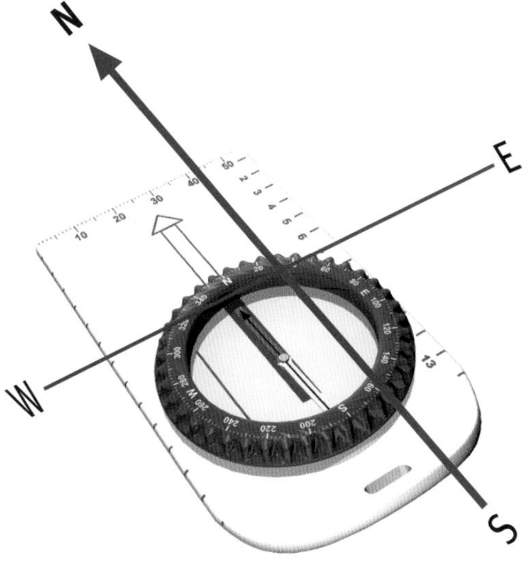
N
E
W
S

A compass is used for finding direction. The needle of a compass always points north.

Which way is North?

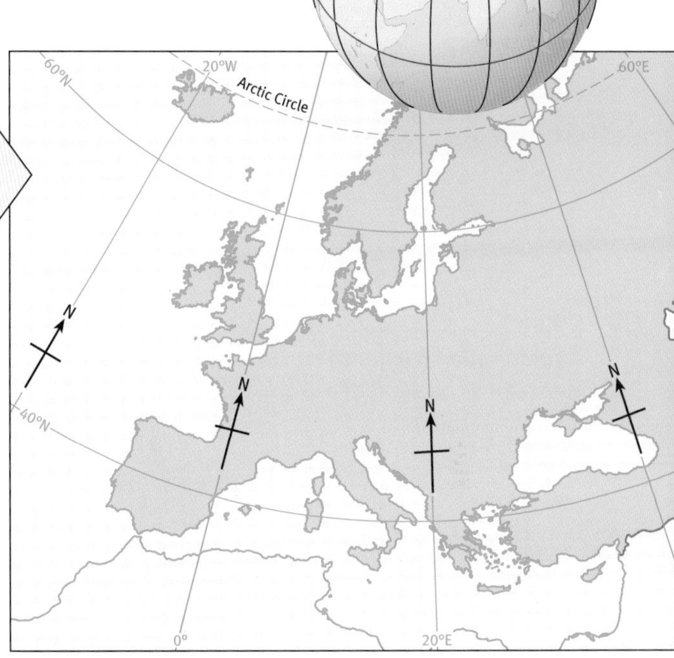
20°W
60°N
Arctic Circle
60°E
N
40°N
0°
20°E

North on atlas maps follows the lines of longitude.

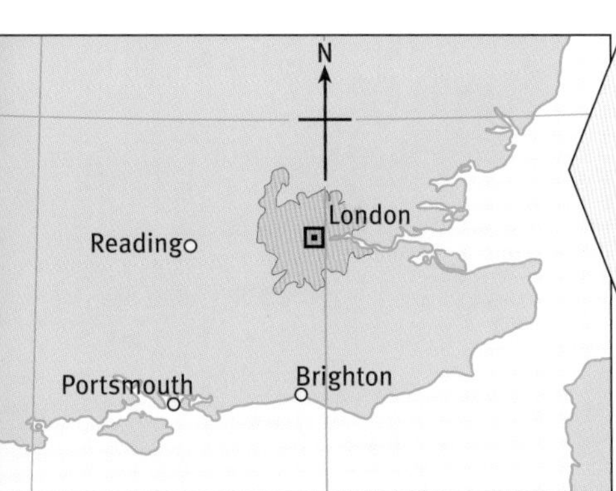
N
London
Reading
Portsmouth
Brighton

London is north of Brighton.

Brighton is south of London.

Reading is west of London.

Portsmouth is south west of London.

Using a compass, can you find which direction north is from where you are?

Global Positioning System (GPS) satellites send signals to equipment on the ground. When a GPS receiver, such as SatNav in a car, picks up signals from several satellites it can work out where it is and give directions to where you want to go.

How does SatNav work?

Twenty four GPS satellites orbit the Earth at a height of 12 000 miles.

A SatNav receiver has to be able to 'see' at least four satellites to work out where it is.

A4 Piccadilly Circus
30
0.35
Street
Regent Street
Air Street
Eagle Place
Picadilly Place
Church Place
A4 Piccadilly
210
yards
3.9
0:13
3:00
tomtom

Tell SatNav where you want to go and it gives you directions. This one has a moving map as well as voice instructions.

6 Understanding maps

Special words are used to describe parts of maps.

Map language

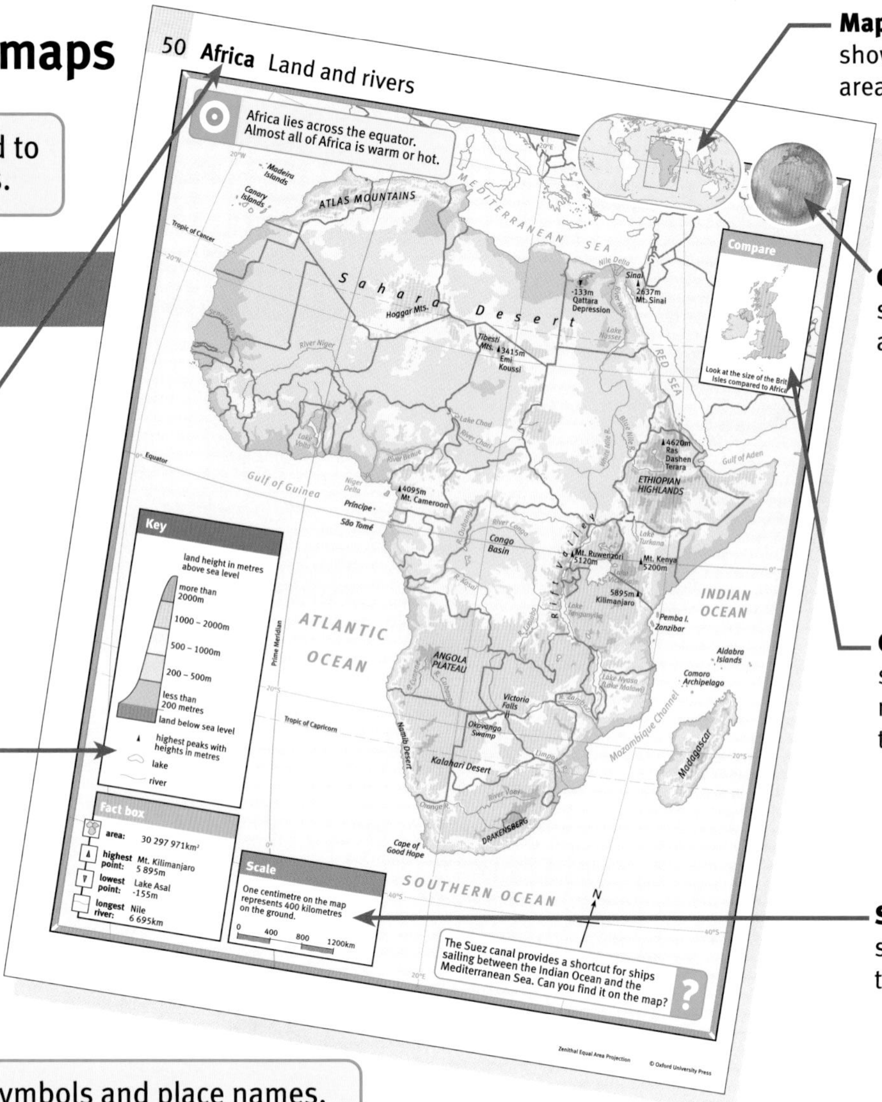

50 Africa Land and rivers
Africa lies across the equator. Almost all of Africa is warm or hot.
Key
Fact box
Scale
One centimetre on the map represents 400 kilometres on the ground.
Compare
The Suez canal provides a shortcut for ships sailing between the Indian Ocean and the Mediterranean Sea. Can you find it on the map?

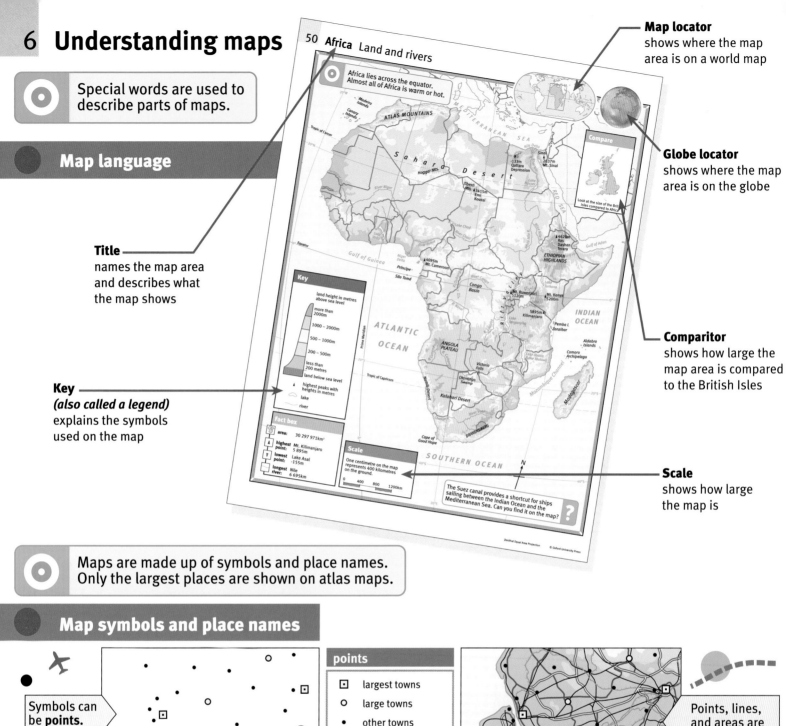

Title names the map area and describes what the map shows

Key *(also called a legend)* explains the symbols used on the map

Map locator shows where the map area is on a world map

Globe locator shows where the map area is on the globe

Comparitor shows how large the map area is compared to the British Isles

Scale shows how large the map is

Maps are made up of symbols and place names. Only the largest places are shown on atlas maps.

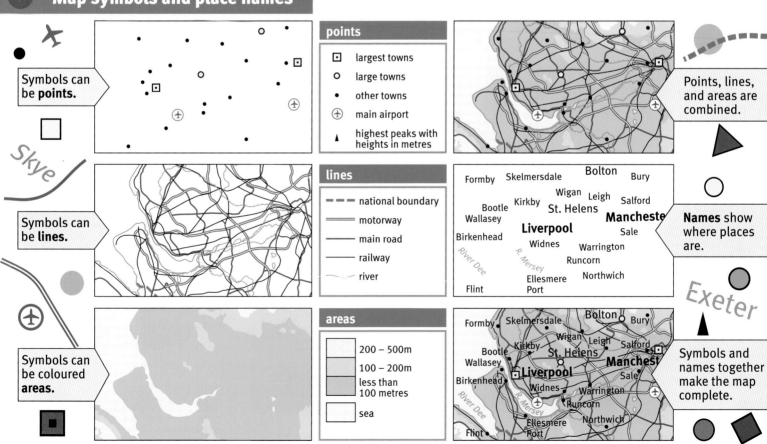

Map symbols and place names

Symbols can be **points**.

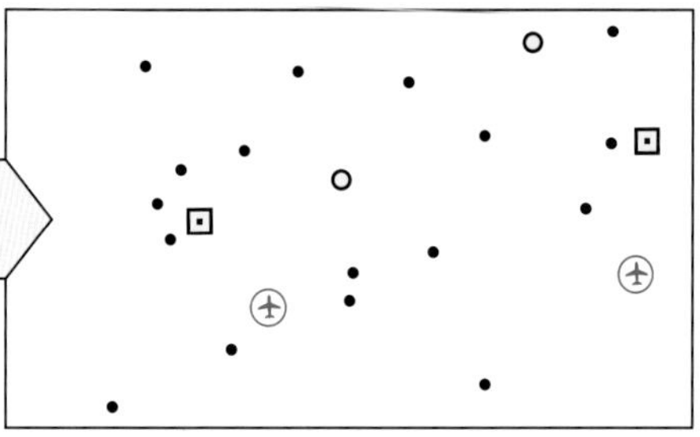

points

- largest towns
- large towns
- other towns
- main airport
- highest peaks with heights in metres

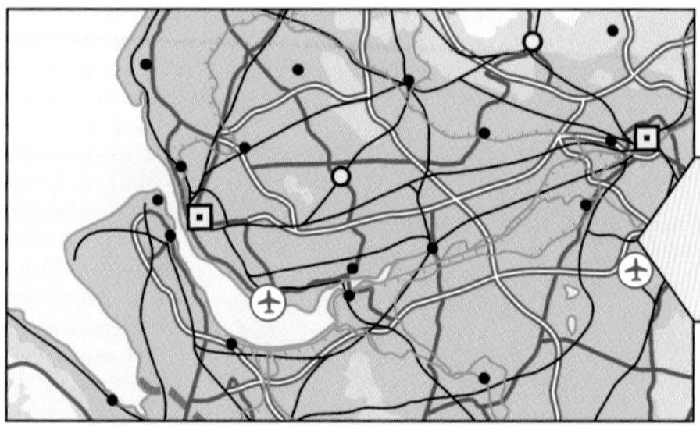

Points, lines, and areas are combined.

Symbols can be **lines**.

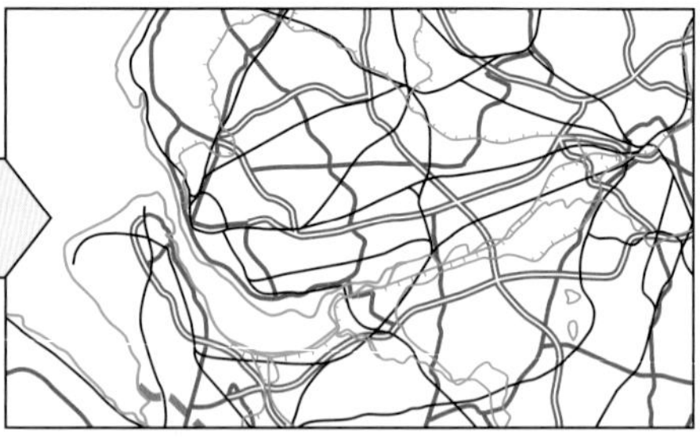

lines

- national boundary
- motorway
- main road
- railway
- river

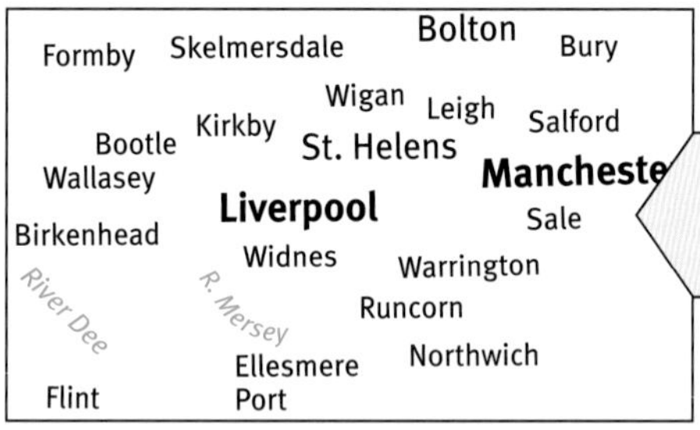

Formby
Skelmersdale
Bolton
Bury
Wigan
Leigh
Salford
Bootle
Kirkby
St. Helens
Wallasey
Manchester
Liverpool
Sale
Birkenhead
Widnes
Warrington
River Dee
R. Mersey
Runcorn
Northwich
Ellesmere Port
Flint

Names show where places are.

Symbols can be coloured **areas.**

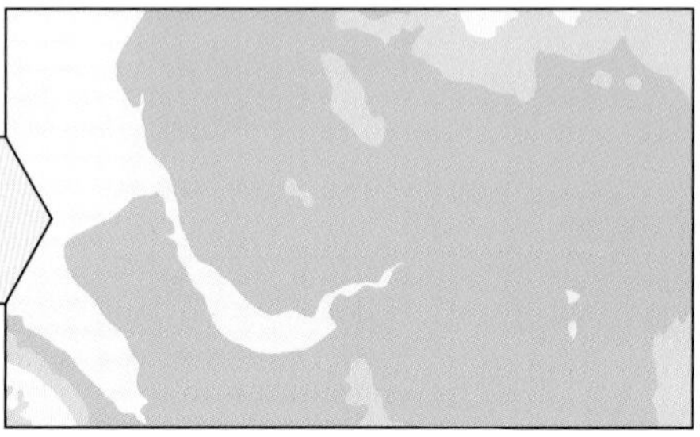

areas

- 200 – 500m
- 100 – 200m
- less than 100 metres
- sea

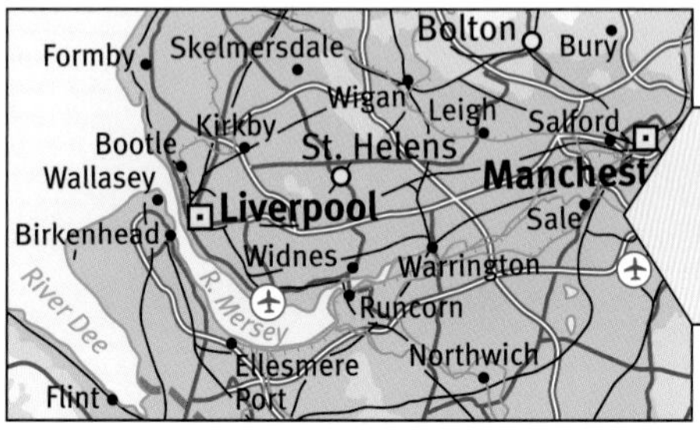

Symbols and names together make the map complete.

Ben Nevis
GRAMPIAN MOUNTAINS
NORTH SEA
SCOTLAND
UNITED KINGDOM
NORTHERN IRELAND
PENNINES
York
Ireland
REPUBLIC OF IRELAND
Manchester
Snowdon
ENGLAND
WALES
Great Britain
Dover
English Channel

The way names are printed on maps gives an important clue to what sorts of places they describe.

Type on maps

AbCDe

Great Britain *Ireland*	islands
UNITED KINGDOM **REPUBLIC OF IRELAND**	countries
ENGLAND **SCOTLAND** **WALES** **NORTHERN IRELAND**	parts of the United Kingdom
PENNINES *GRAMPIAN MOUNTAINS*	physical features
Ben Nevis Snowdon	mountain peaks
NORTH SEA *English Channel*	sea areas
Manchester York Dover	settlements

An abbreviation is a shortened version of a word or a group of words.

R. River
Mt. Mount
Is. Islands
Pen. Peninsula

Map abbreviations

Some country names are abbreviated using the first letters of each word

UK	United Kingdom
USA	United States of America
UAE	United Arab Emirates

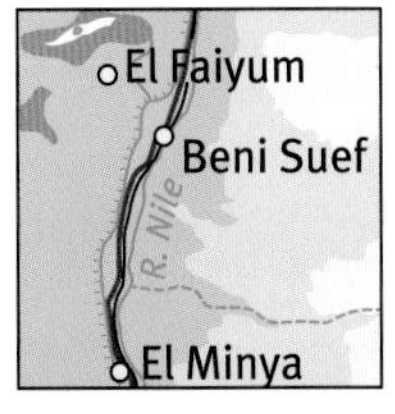
El Faiyum
Beni Suef
R. Nile
El Minya

Lhaze
Mt. Everest 8848m
Kathmandu
Shiliguri

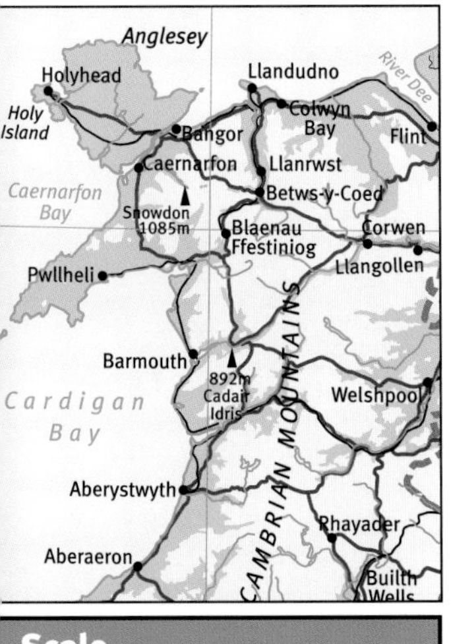
Anglesey
Holyhead
Holy Island
Llandudno
Colwyn Bay
Bangor
Flint
Caernarfon
Llanrwst
Caernarfon Bay
Betws-y-Coed
Snowdon 1085m
Blaenau Ffestiniog
Corwen
Llangollen
Pwllheli
Barmouth
892m Cadair Idris
CAMBRIAN MOUNTAINS
Cardigan Bay
Welshpool
Aberystwyth
Rhayader
Aberaeron
Builth Wells

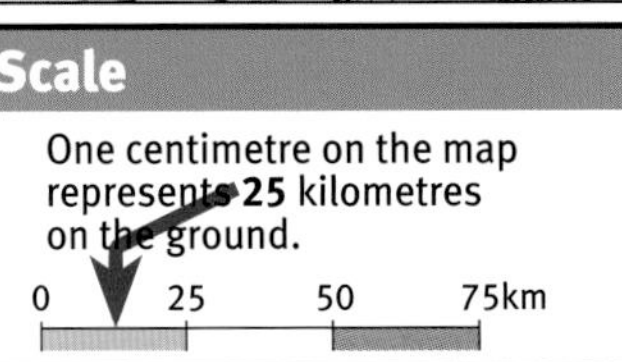
Scale
One centimetre on the map represents 25 kilometres on the ground.
0 25 50 75km

The distance between Bangor and Betws-y-Coed is about 25km

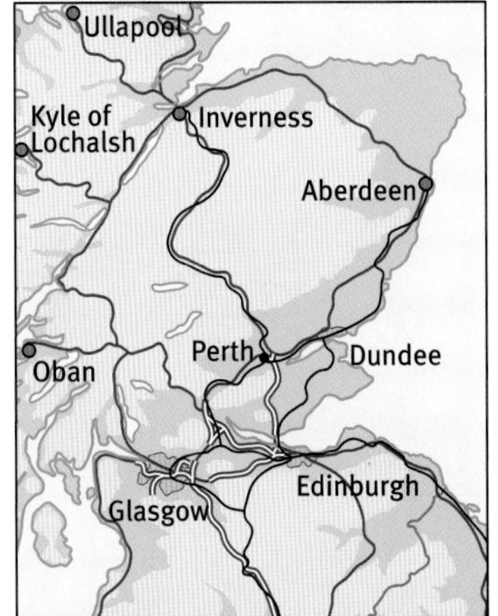
Ullapool
Kyle of Lochalsh
Inverness
Aberdeen
Oban
Perth
Dundee
Glasgow
Edinburgh

Scale

One centimetre on the map represents **50** kilometres on the ground.

0 50 100 150km

The distance between Perth and Edinburgh is about 50km

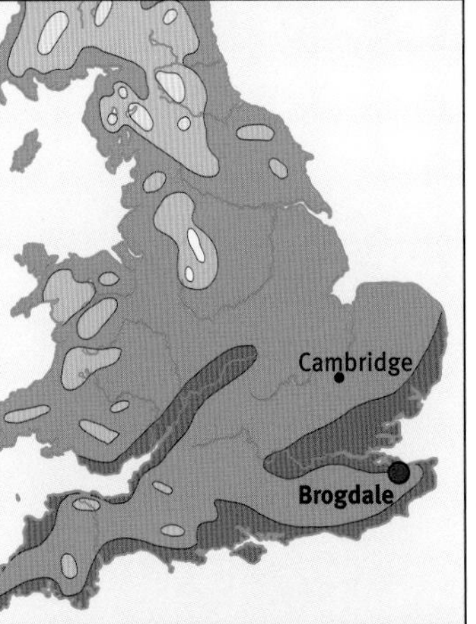
Cambridge
Brogdale

Scale

One centimetre on the map represents **100** kilometres on the ground.

0 100 200 300km

The distance between Cambridge and Brogdale is about 100km

Larger scale smaller area more detail

Smaller scale larger area less detail

Atlas maps are much, much smaller than the places they show. A few centimetres on the map stand for very many kilometres on the ground.

Scale

Each division on the scale line is one centimetre. The scale line shows how many kilometres are represented by one centimetre.

0 25 50 75 100 125km

0 1 2 3 4 5 6
CENTIMETRES

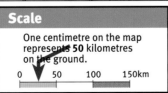

Choose a map from this atlas. Can you use a ruler to work out the distance in kilometres between two places?

?

8 Understanding land height

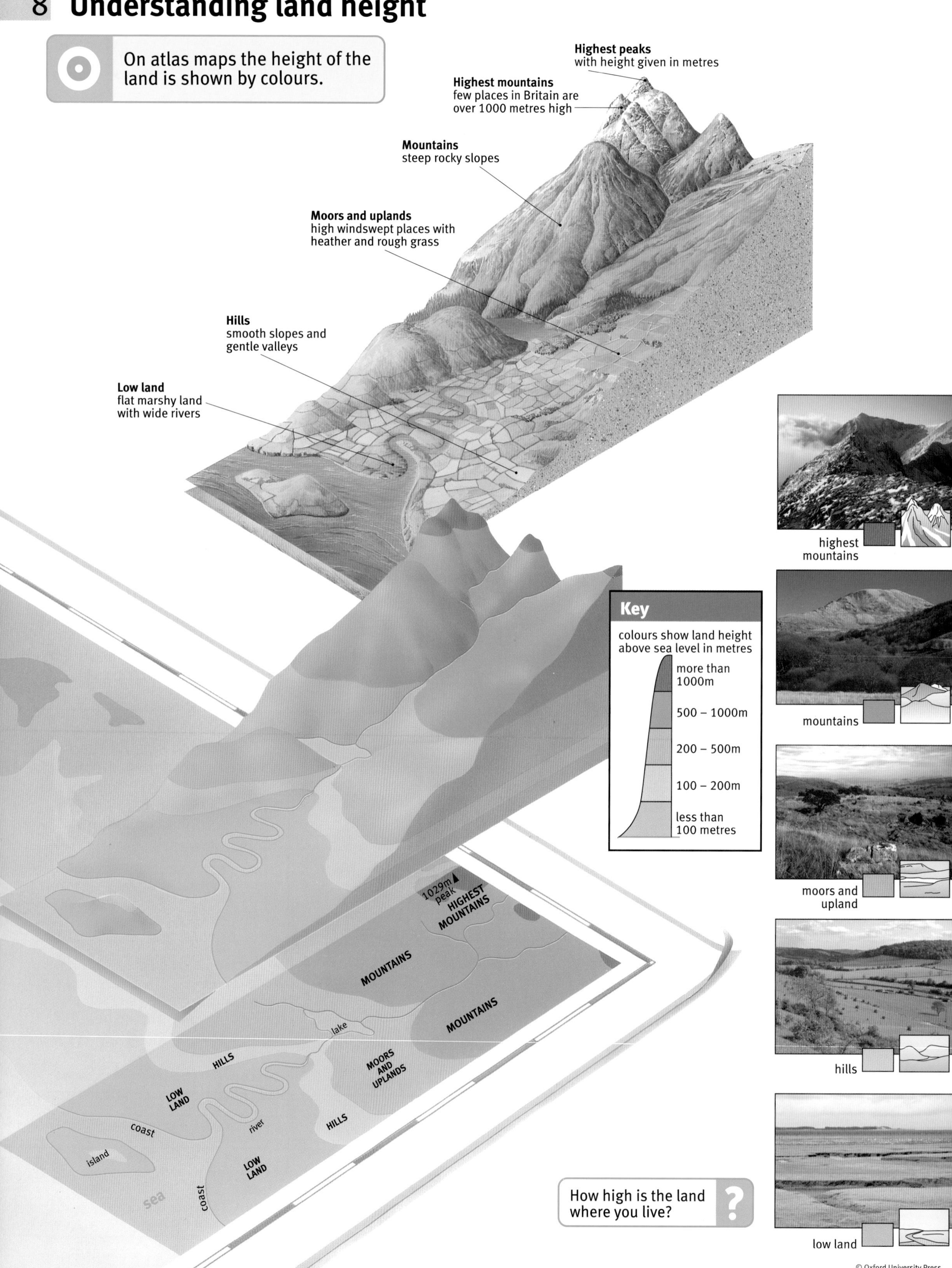

On atlas maps the height of the land is shown by colours.
Highest peaks
with height given in metres
Highest mountains
few places in Britain are over 1000 metres high
Mountains
steep rocky slopes
Moors and uplands
high windswept places with heather and rough grass
Hills
smooth slopes and gentle valleys
Low land
flat marshy land with wide rivers
Key
colours show land height above sea level in metres
more than 1000m
500 – 1000m
200 – 500m
100 – 200m
less than 100 metres
1029m peak
HIGHEST MOUNTAINS
MOUNTAINS
MOUNTAINS
lake
HILLS
MOORS AND UPLANDS
LOW LAND
coast
river
HILLS
island
LOW LAND
sea
coast
highest mountains
mountains
moors and upland
hills
low land
How high is the land where you live?

Understanding rivers

Most landscapes in the British Isles have been shaped by rivers.

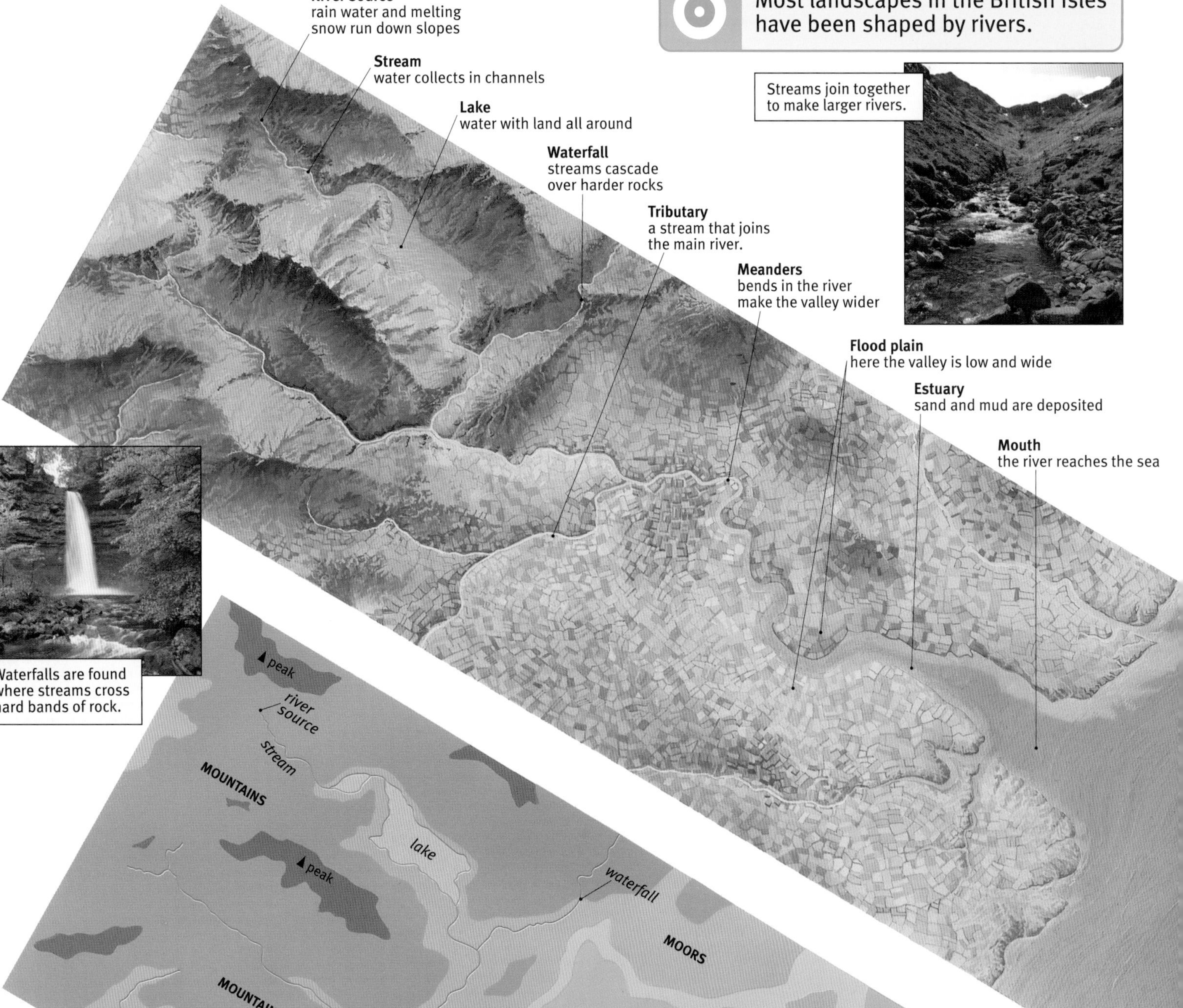

River source
rain water and melting snow run down slopes

Stream
water collects in channels

Lake
water with land all around

Waterfall
streams cascade over harder rocks

Tributary
a stream that joins the main river.

Meanders
bends in the river make the valley wider

Flood plain
here the valley is low and wide

Estuary
sand and mud are deposited

Mouth
the river reaches the sea

Streams join together to make larger rivers.

Waterfalls are found where streams cross hard bands of rock.

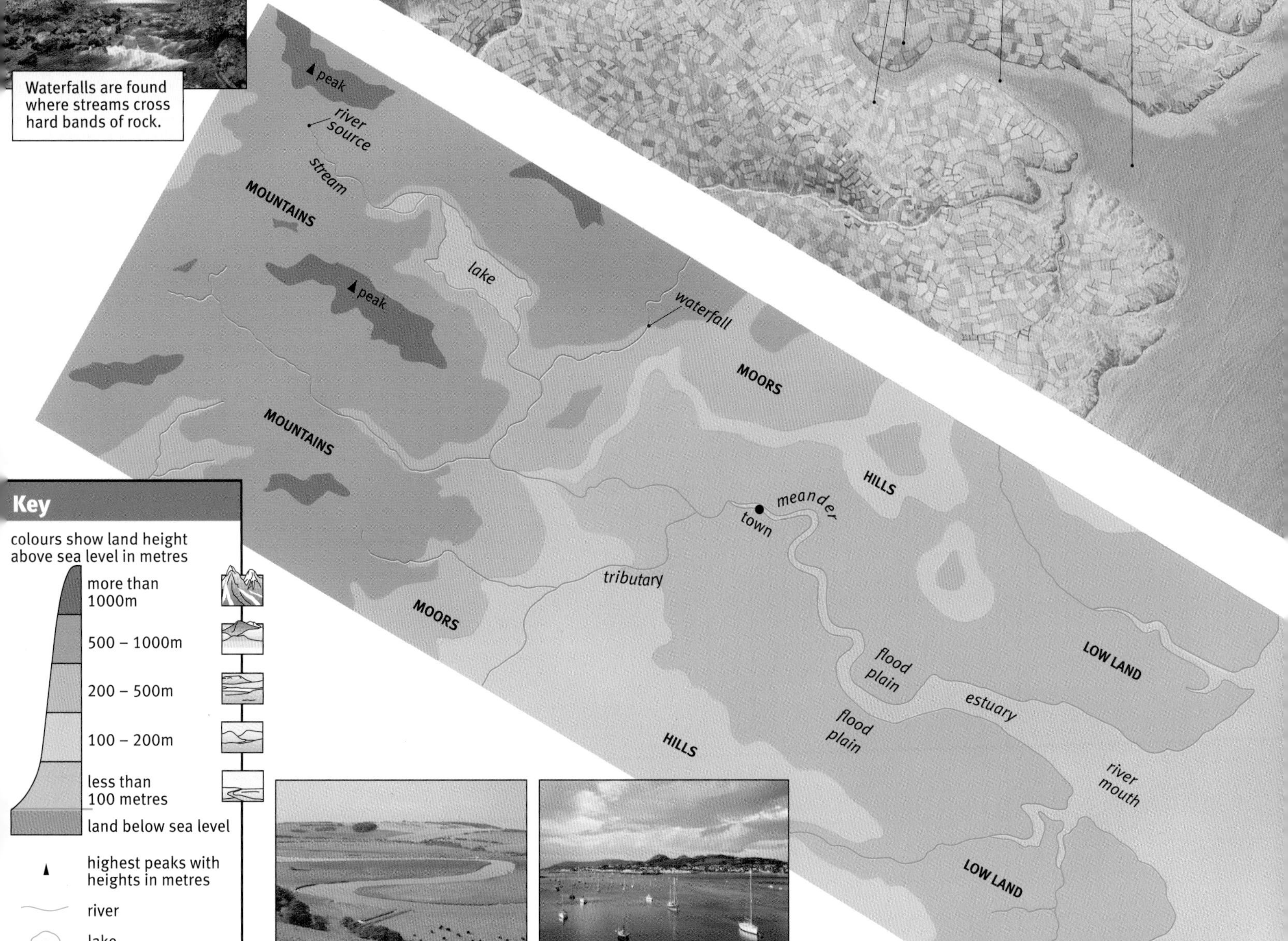

peak
river source
stream
MOUNTAINS
lake
peak
waterfall
MOORS
MOUNTAINS
HILLS
meander
town
tributary
MOORS
flood plain
estuary
flood plain
LOW LAND
HILLS
river mouth
LOW LAND

Key

colours show land height above sea level in metres

- more than 1000m
- 500 – 1000m
- 200 – 500m
- 100 – 200m
- less than 100 metres
- land below sea level
- highest peaks with heights in metres
- river
- lake

Meanders are large bends in the river.

An estuary is where a river meets the sea.

Understanding settlements

People live in settlements of different sizes. Most people in Britain live in towns and cities.

Kirkby
St. He
Liverpool
Widnes
R. Mersey
Tamworth
Walsall
Sutton Coldfield
Birmingham
Warley
Solihull
Kenilworth
Bromsgrove
Woodstock
Kidlington
Oxford
Abingdon
Plynlimon
752m
Aberystwyth
W A

Largest towns
Very tall office buildings mark the centre of the largest towns.

Largest built-up areas
Several towns and cities have grown together to make one continuous built up area.

Large towns
Larger settlements have more shops and services than smaller ones.

Villages
Very small towns and villages are not shown on atlas maps.

Other towns
In smaller towns the countryside is never far away from the centre.

What size of settlement do you live in?

Understanding satellite images

Satellite images are pictures of the Earth taken from space. They help us understand the weather, our environment and the Earth itself.

Hundreds of working satellites orbit the Earth. There are also thousands that don't work any more, called 'space junk'.

During the year many wet weather fronts pass over the British Isles whilst France and Spain stay warm and dry. Compare this satellite image with the maps on pages 38 and 39.

A snow-covered volcano explodes in the Aleutian Islands, Alaska. The cloud of ash was three miles high. Can you find the Aleutian islands on the world map on page 64?

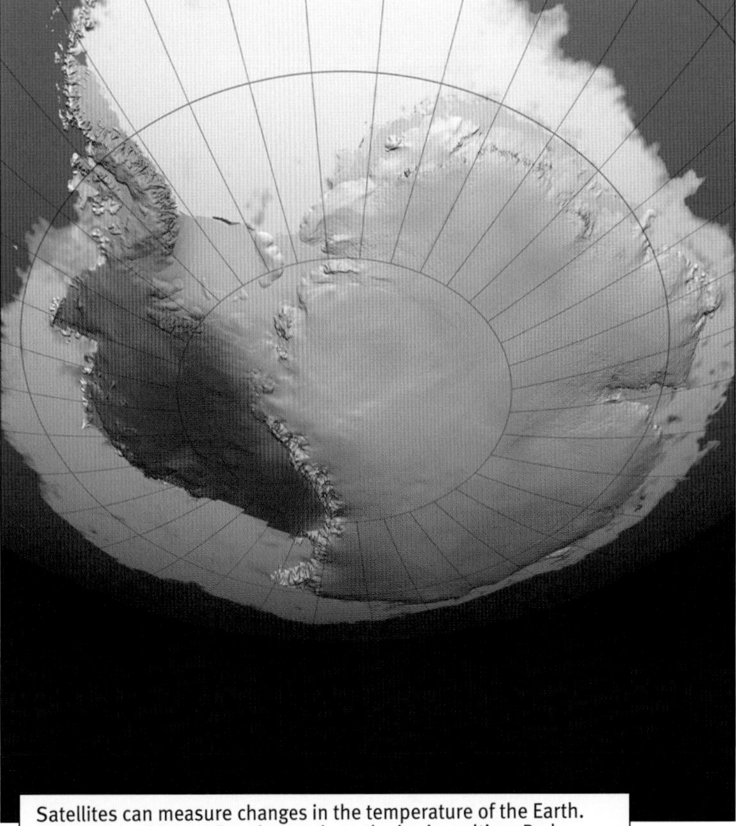

Satellites can measure changes in the temperature of the Earth. This image of Antarctica shows where the ice is melting. Red shows where the ice is melting most. Compare this satellite image with the map on page 63.

World Satellite image

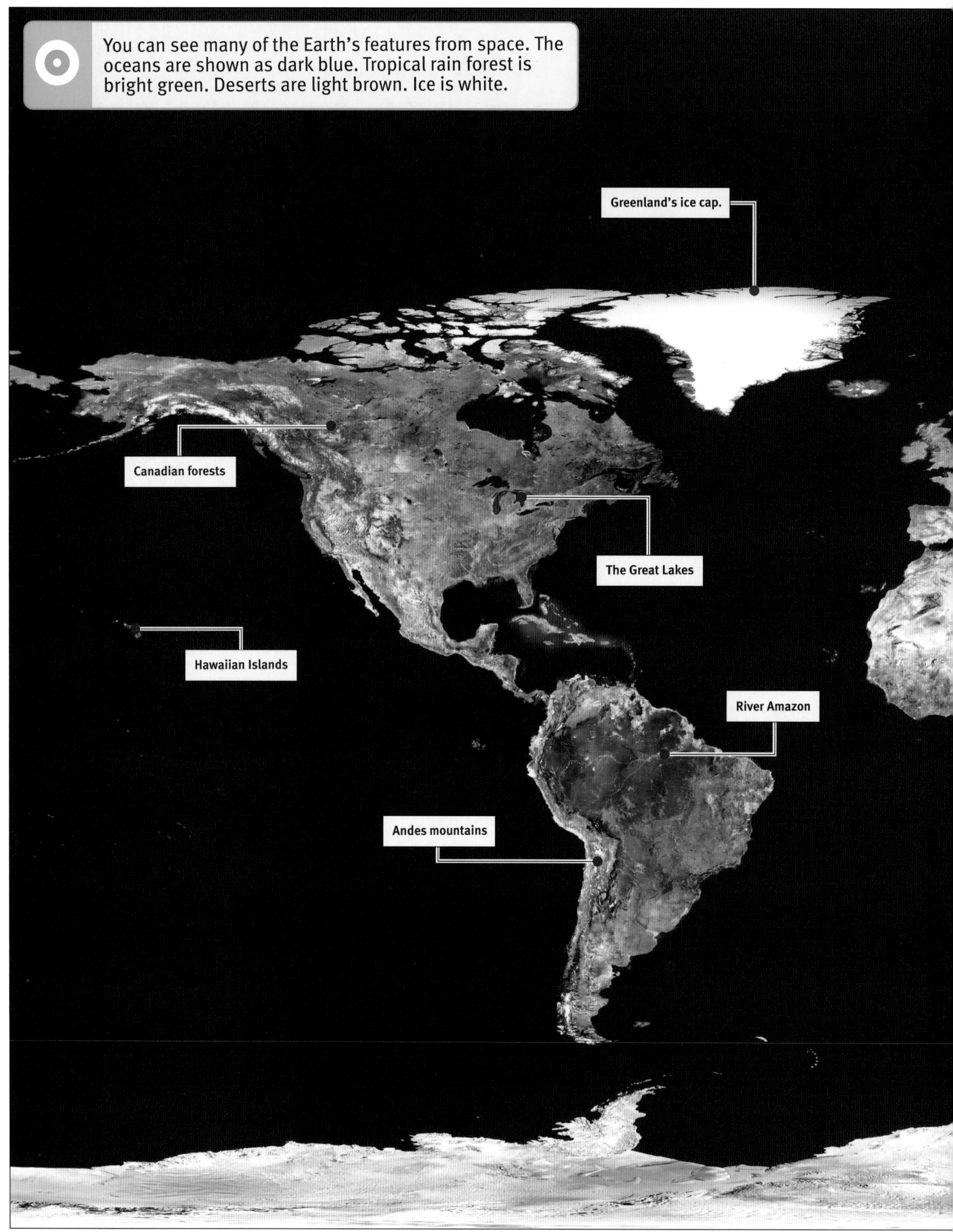
You can see many of the Earth's features from space. The oceans are shown as dark blue. Tropical rain forest is bright green. Deserts are light brown. Ice is white.
Greenland's ice cap.
Canadian forests
The Great Lakes
Hawaiian Islands
River Amazon
Andes mountains

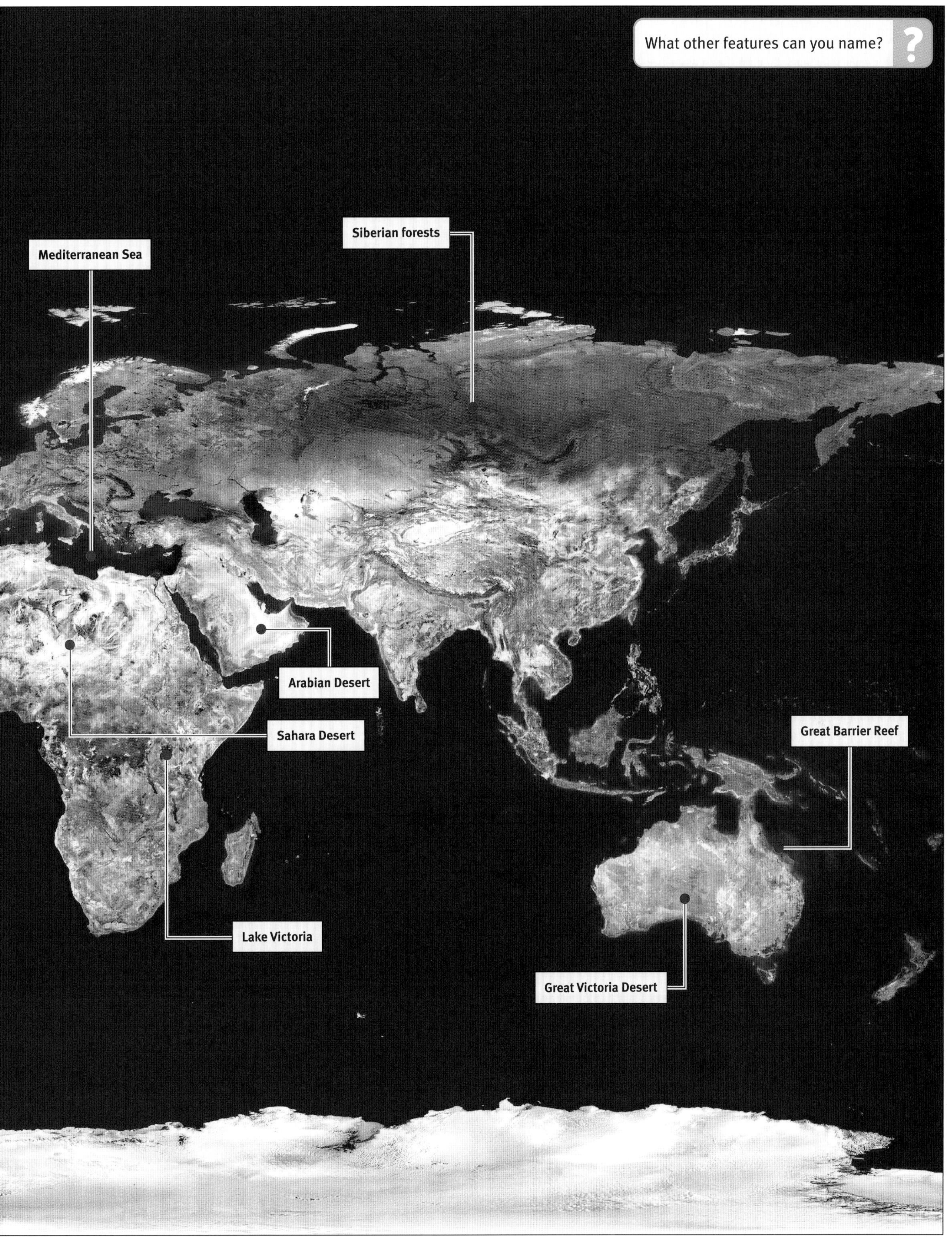
What other features can you name?
?
Siberian forests
Mediterranean Sea
Arabian Desert
Sahara Desert
Great Barrier Reef
Lake Victoria
Great Victoria Desert

World Countries and continents

A country is a land with its own people and its own laws. A capital city is the most important city in a country. It is where the government meets.

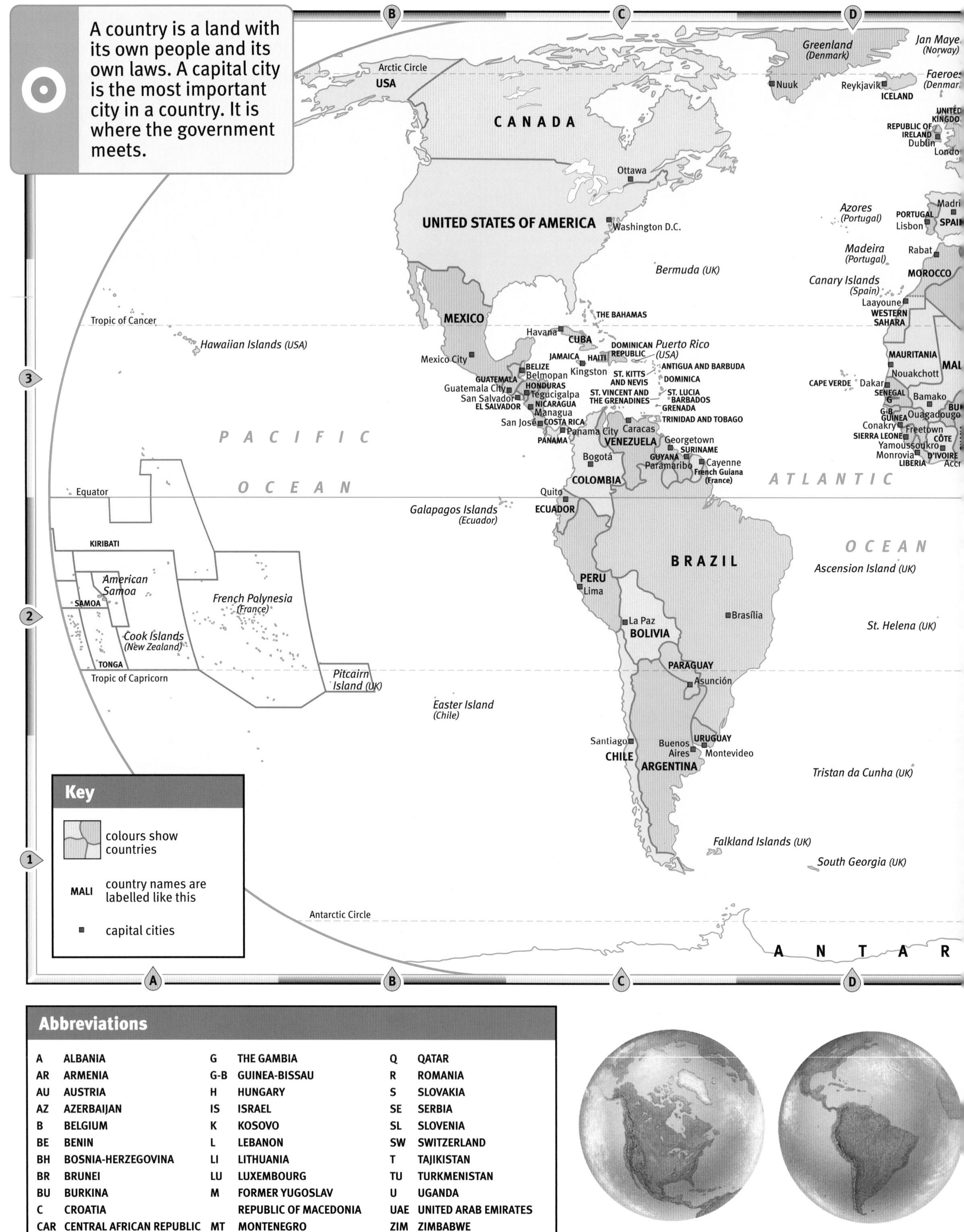

Arctic Circle
USA
CANADA
Greenland (Denmark)
Nuuk
Jan Mayen (Norway)
Faeroes (Denmark)
Reykjavik
ICELAND
REPUBLIC OF IRELAND
Dublin
Ottawa
UNITED STATES OF AMERICA
Washington D.C.
Azores (Portugal)
PORTUGAL
Lisbon
SPAIN
Madeira (Portugal)
Rabat
MOROCCO
Bermuda (UK)
Canary Islands (Spain)
Laayoune
WESTERN SAHARA
Tropic of Cancer
Hawaiian Islands (USA)
MEXICO
Mexico City
THE BAHAMAS
Havana
CUBA
DOMINICAN REPUBLIC
Puerto Rico (USA)
JAMAICA
HAITI
Kingston
BELIZE
Belmopan
GUATEMALA
Guatemala City
HONDURAS
Tegucigalpa
San Salvador
EL SALVADOR
NICARAGUA
Managua
San José
COSTA RICA
Panama City
PANAMA
ST. KITTS AND NEVIS
ANTIGUA AND BARBUDA
DOMINICA
ST. VINCENT AND THE GRENADINES
ST. LUCIA
BARBADOS
GRENADA
TRINIDAD AND TOBAGO
MAURITANIA
Nouakchott
CAPE VERDE
Dakar
SENEGAL
G
Bamako
G-B
GUINEA
Ouagadougou
Conakry
Freetown
SIERRA LEONE
Yamoussoukro
Monrovia
LIBERIA
CÔTE D'IVOIRE
PACIFIC OCEAN
Caracas
VENEZUELA
Georgetown
SURINAME
GUYANA
Paramaribo
Cayenne
French Guiana (France)
Bogotá
COLOMBIA
ATLANTIC OCEAN
Equator
Quito
ECUADOR
Galapagos Islands (Ecuador)
KIRIBATI
BRAZIL
Ascension Island (UK)
American Samoa
SAMOA
French Polynesia (France)
PERU
Lima
Brasília
St. Helena (UK)
La Paz
BOLIVIA
Cook Islands (New Zealand)
TONGA
Tropic of Capricorn
Pitcairn Island (UK)
PARAGUAY
Asunción
Easter Island (Chile)
Santiago
CHILE
Buenos Aires
URUGUAY
Montevideo
ARGENTINA
Tristan da Cunha (UK)
Falkland Islands (UK)
South Georgia (UK)
Antarctic Circle
ANTAR
A
B
C
D
1
2
3

Key

- colours show countries
- **MALI** country names are labelled like this
- ▪ capital cities

Abbreviations

A	ALBANIA	G	THE GAMBIA	Q	QATAR
AR	ARMENIA	G-B	GUINEA-BISSAU	R	ROMANIA
AU	AUSTRIA	H	HUNGARY	S	SLOVAKIA
AZ	AZERBAIJAN	IS	ISRAEL	SE	SERBIA
B	BELGIUM	K	KOSOVO	SL	SLOVENIA
BE	BENIN	L	LEBANON	SW	SWITZERLAND
BH	BOSNIA-HERZEGOVINA	LI	LITHUANIA	T	TAJIKISTAN
BR	BRUNEI	LU	LUXEMBOURG	TU	TURKMENISTAN
BU	BURKINA	M	FORMER YUGOSLAV REPUBLIC OF MACEDONIA	U	UGANDA
C	CROATIA			UAE	UNITED ARAB EMIRATES
CAR	CENTRAL AFRICAN REPUBLIC	MT	MONTENEGRO	ZIM	ZIMBABWE
CZ	CZECH REPUBLIC	N	NETHERLANDS		

North America **South America**

Eckert IV Projection

Can you name three countries that are larger than the United Kingdom and three that are smaller?

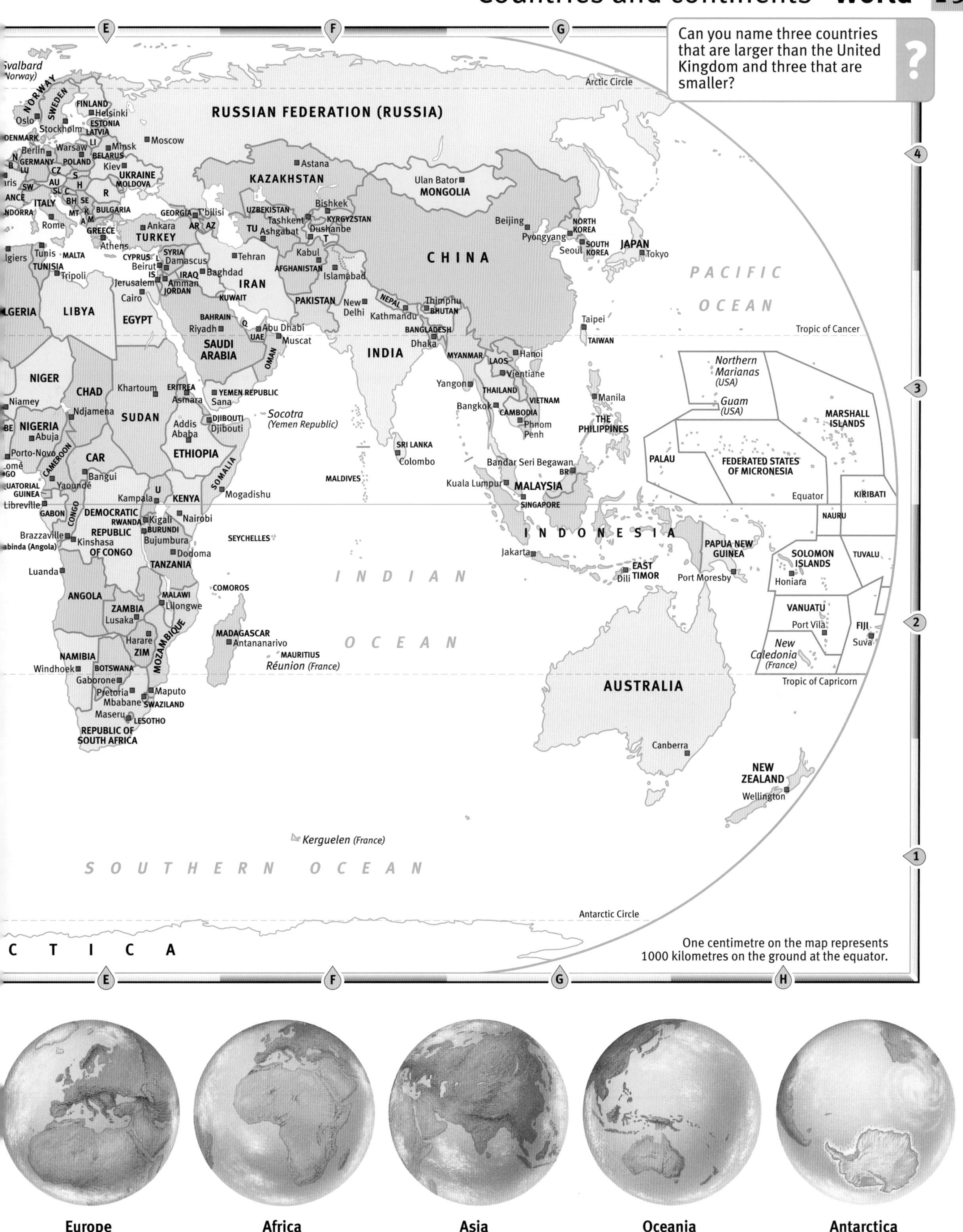
E
F
G
H
1
2
3
4
Svalbard (Norway)
Arctic Circle
RUSSIAN FEDERATION (RUSSIA)
NORWAY
SWEDEN
FINLAND
Helsinki
Oslo
Stockholm
ESTONIA
LATVIA
LI
DENMARK
Moscow
Minsk
Warsaw
BELARUS
Berlin
GERMANY
POLAND
Kiev
CZ
S
UKRAINE
MOLDOVA
AU
H
SL
C
R
ITALY
BH
SE
BULGARIA
MT
K
M
A
Rome
GREECE
Athens
GEORGIA
T'bilisi
AR
AZ
Ankara
TURKEY
Astana
KAZAKHSTAN
UZBEKISTAN
Tashkent
KYRGYZSTAN
Bishkek
TU
Ashgabat
Dushanbe
T
Ulan Bator
MONGOLIA
Beijing
NORTH KOREA
Pyongyang
SOUTH KOREA
Seoul
JAPAN
Tokyo
CHINA
PACIFIC OCEAN
Tunis
MALTA
TUNISIA
Tripoli
CYPRUS
L
SYRIA
Beirut
Damascus
IS
Jerusalem
IRAQ
Baghdad
Amman
JORDAN
Tehran
IRAN
Kabul
AFGHANISTAN
Islamabad
PAKISTAN
KUWAIT
Cairo
LIBYA
EGYPT
ALGERIA
BAHRAIN
Q
Riyadh
UAE
Abu Dhabi
Muscat
SAUDI ARABIA
OMAN
New Delhi
NEPAL
Kathmandu
Thimphu
BHUTAN
BANGLADESH
Dhaka
INDIA
Taipei
TAIWAN
Tropic of Cancer
MYANMAR
LAOS
Hanoi
Vientiane
Yangon
THAILAND
Bangkok
VIETNAM
CAMBODIA
Phnom Penh
Manila
THE PHILIPPINES
Northern Marianas (USA)
Guam (USA)
MARSHALL ISLANDS
PALAU
FEDERATED STATES OF MICRONESIA
NIGER
CHAD
Khartoum
ERITREA
Asmara
YEMEN REPUBLIC
Sana
Niamey
Ndjamena
SUDAN
DJIBOUTI
Djibouti
Socotra (Yemen Republic)
NIGERIA
Abuja
Addis Ababa
ETHIOPIA
SRI LANKA
Colombo
Porto-Novo
CAMEROON
CAR
Bangui
SOMALIA
MALDIVES
Bandar Seri Begawan
BR
Yaoundé
EQUATORIAL GUINEA
U
KENYA
Kampala
Mogadishu
Kuala Lumpur
MALAYSIA
SINGAPORE
Equator
KIRIBATI
Libreville
GABON
CONGO
DEMOCRATIC REPUBLIC OF CONGO
RWANDA
Kigali
Nairobi
BURUNDI
NAURU
Brazzaville
Kinshasa
Bujumbura
SEYCHELLES
INDONESIA
Cabinda (Angola)
Dodoma
TANZANIA
Jakarta
PAPUA NEW GUINEA
SOLOMON ISLANDS
TUVALU
EAST TIMOR
Dili
Port Moresby
Honiara
Luanda
INDIAN OCEAN
COMOROS
ANGOLA
MALAWI
ZAMBIA
Lilongwe
Lusaka
VANUATU
Port Vila
FIJI
Suva
Harare
ZIM
MOZAMBIQUE
MADAGASCAR
Antananarivo
New Caledonia (France)
NAMIBIA
MAURITIUS
Réunion (France)
Windhoek
BOTSWANA
Gaborone
Tropic of Capricorn
AUSTRALIA
Pretoria
Maputo
Mbabane
SWAZILAND
Maseru
LESOTHO
REPUBLIC OF SOUTH AFRICA
Canberra
NEW ZEALAND
Wellington
Kerguelen (France)
SOUTHERN OCEAN
Antarctic Circle
ANTARCTICA
One centimetre on the map represents 1000 kilometres on the ground at the equator.

Europe

Africa

Asia

Oceania

Antarctica

British Isles Satellite image

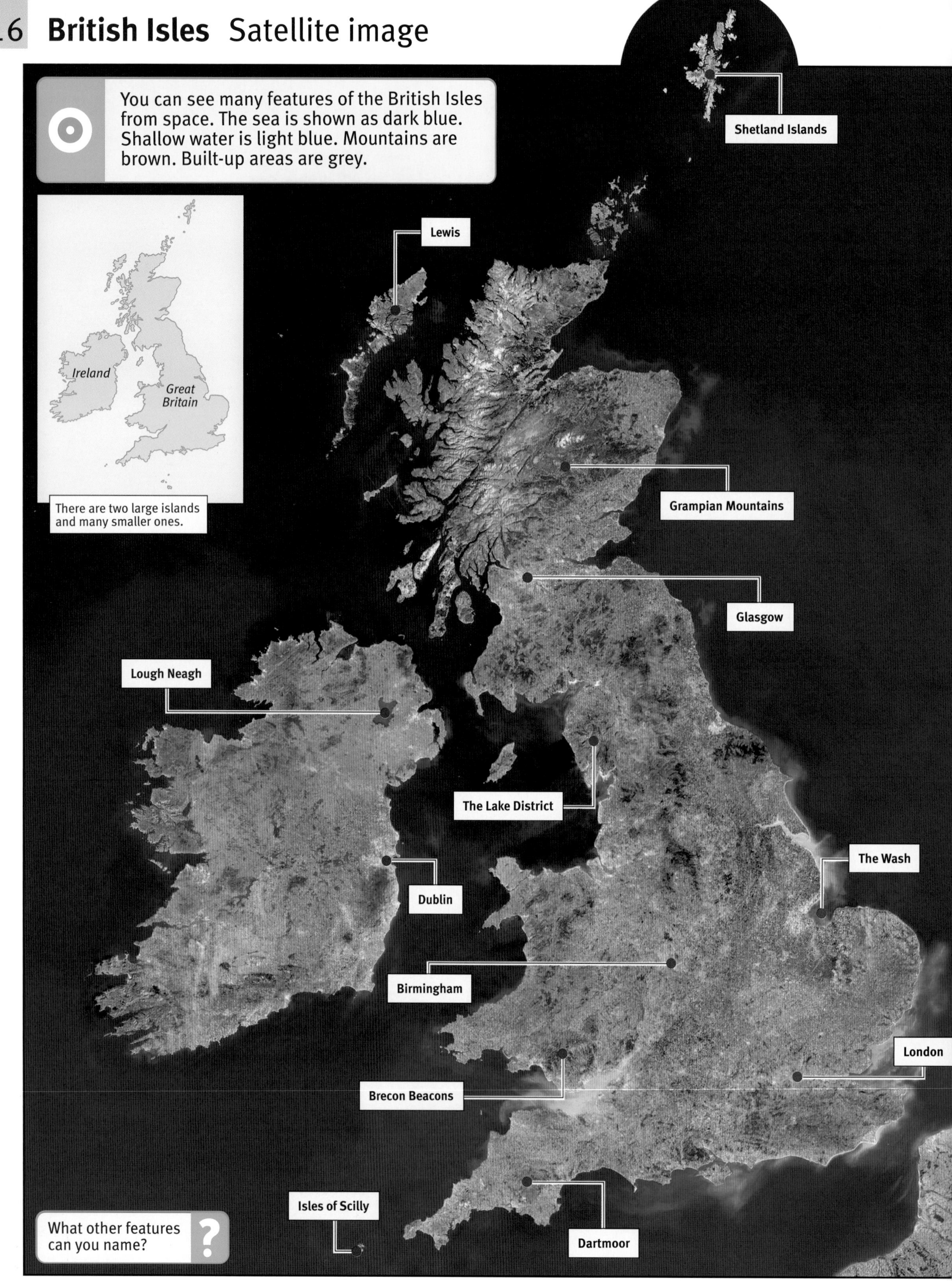

You can see many features of the British Isles from space. The sea is shown as dark blue. Shallow water is light blue. Mountains are brown. Built-up areas are grey.
Ireland
Great Britain
There are two large islands and many smaller ones.
Shetland Islands
Lewis
Grampian Mountains
Glasgow
Lough Neagh
The Lake District
The Wash
Dublin
Birmingham
London
Brecon Beacons
Isles of Scilly
Dartmoor
What other features can you name?

British Isles Geography

This map shows the height of the land, where the largest towns and cities are and how they are joined by motorways, major roads and main railway lines.

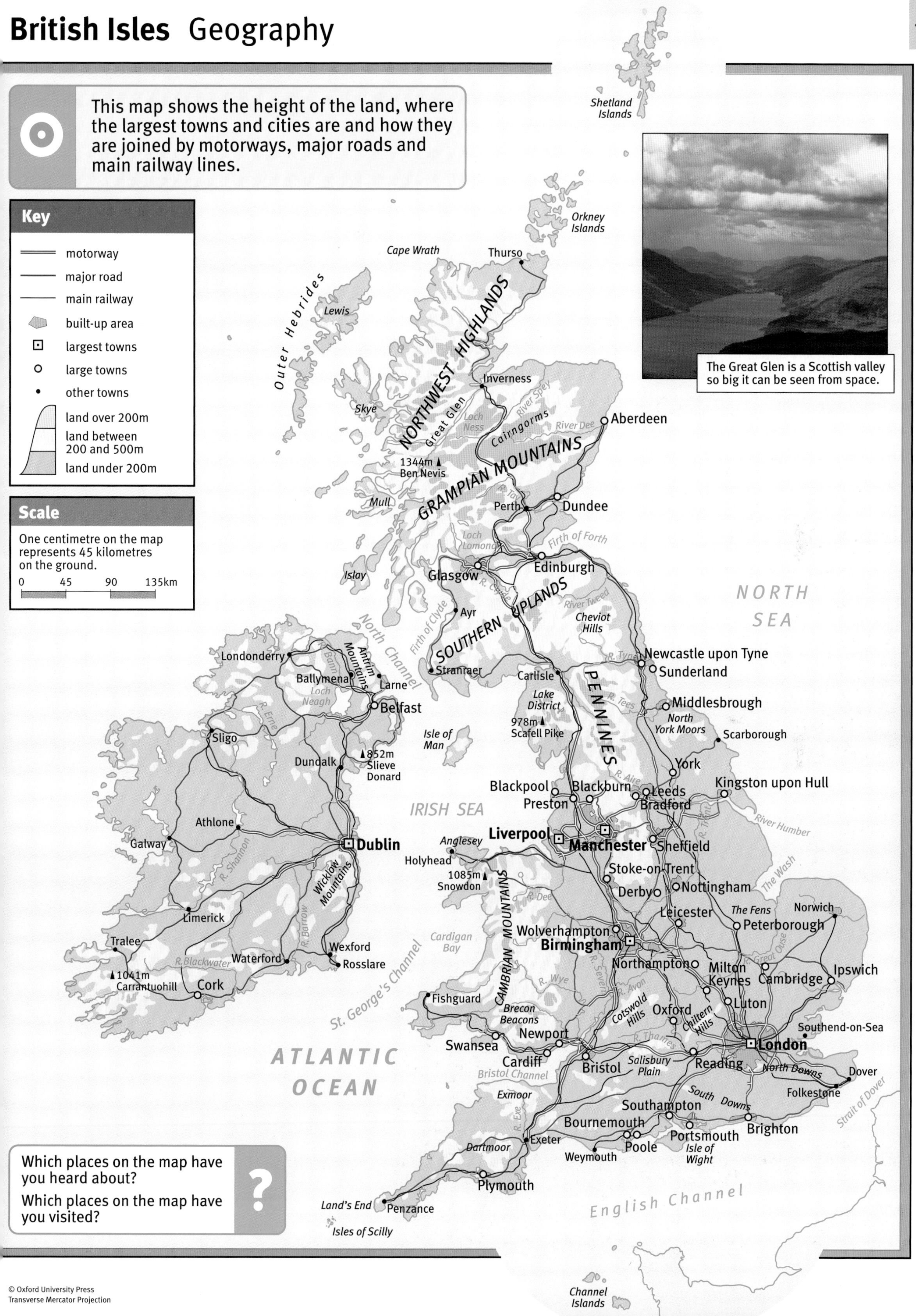

Key

- motorway
- major road
- main railway
- built-up area
- largest towns
- large towns
- other towns
- land over 200m
- land between 200 and 500m
- land under 200m

Scale

One centimetre on the map represents 45 kilometres on the ground.

0 45 90 135km

The Great Glen is a Scottish valley so big it can be seen from space.

Shetland Islands
Orkney Islands
Cape Wrath
Thurso
Outer Hebrides
Lewis
NORTHWEST HIGHLANDS
Skye
Inverness
Great Glen
Loch Ness
River Spey
Cairngorms
River Dee
Aberdeen
GRAMPIAN MOUNTAINS
1344m Ben Nevis
Mull
R. Tay
Perth
Dundee
Loch Lomond
Firth of Forth
Islay
Glasgow
Edinburgh
R. Clyde
SOUTHERN UPLANDS
River Tweed
Cheviot Hills
Ayr
Firth of Clyde
North Channel
SOUTHERN
Stranraer
NORTH SEA
Londonderry
R. Bann
Antrim Mountains
Ballymena
Larne
Lough Neagh
Belfast
R. Erne
Sligo
Carlisle
Lake District
978m Scafell Pike
R. Tyne
Newcastle upon Tyne
Sunderland
PENNINES
R. Tees
Middlesbrough
North York Moors
Scarborough
Isle of Man
Dundalk
852m Slieve Donard
IRISH SEA
York
R. Aire
Blackpool
Preston
Blackburn
Leeds
Bradford
Kingston upon Hull
Athlone
Dublin
Galway
R. Shannon
Wicklow Mountains
Anglesey
Holyhead
Liverpool
Manchester
Sheffield
R. Trent
River Humber
1085m Snowdon
Stoke-on-Trent
Derby
Nottingham
The Wash
R. Dee
Limerick
R. Barrow
Tralee
R. Blackwater
Waterford
Wexford
Rosslare
1041m Carrantuohill
Cork
Cardigan Bay
CAMBRIAN MOUNTAINS
Leicester
The Fens
Norwich
Peterborough
Wolverhampton
Birmingham
R. Severn
R. Wye
Great Ouse
Northampton
Milton Keynes
Cambridge
Ipswich
St. George's Channel
Fishguard
Brecon Beacons
R. Avon
Cotswold Hills
Oxford
Chiltern Hills
Luton
Southend-on-Sea
ATLANTIC OCEAN
Swansea
Newport
Cardiff
R. Thames
London
Bristol
Salisbury Plain
Reading
North Downs
Dover
Bristol Channel
Exmoor
Folkestone
Strait of Dover
South Downs
Southampton
R. Exe
Bournemouth
Exeter
Dartmoor
Poole
Portsmouth
Brighton
Weymouth
Isle of Wight
Plymouth
English Channel
Land's End
Penzance
Isles of Scilly
Channel Islands

Which places on the map have you heard about?

Which places on the map have you visited?

?

Transverse Mercator Projection

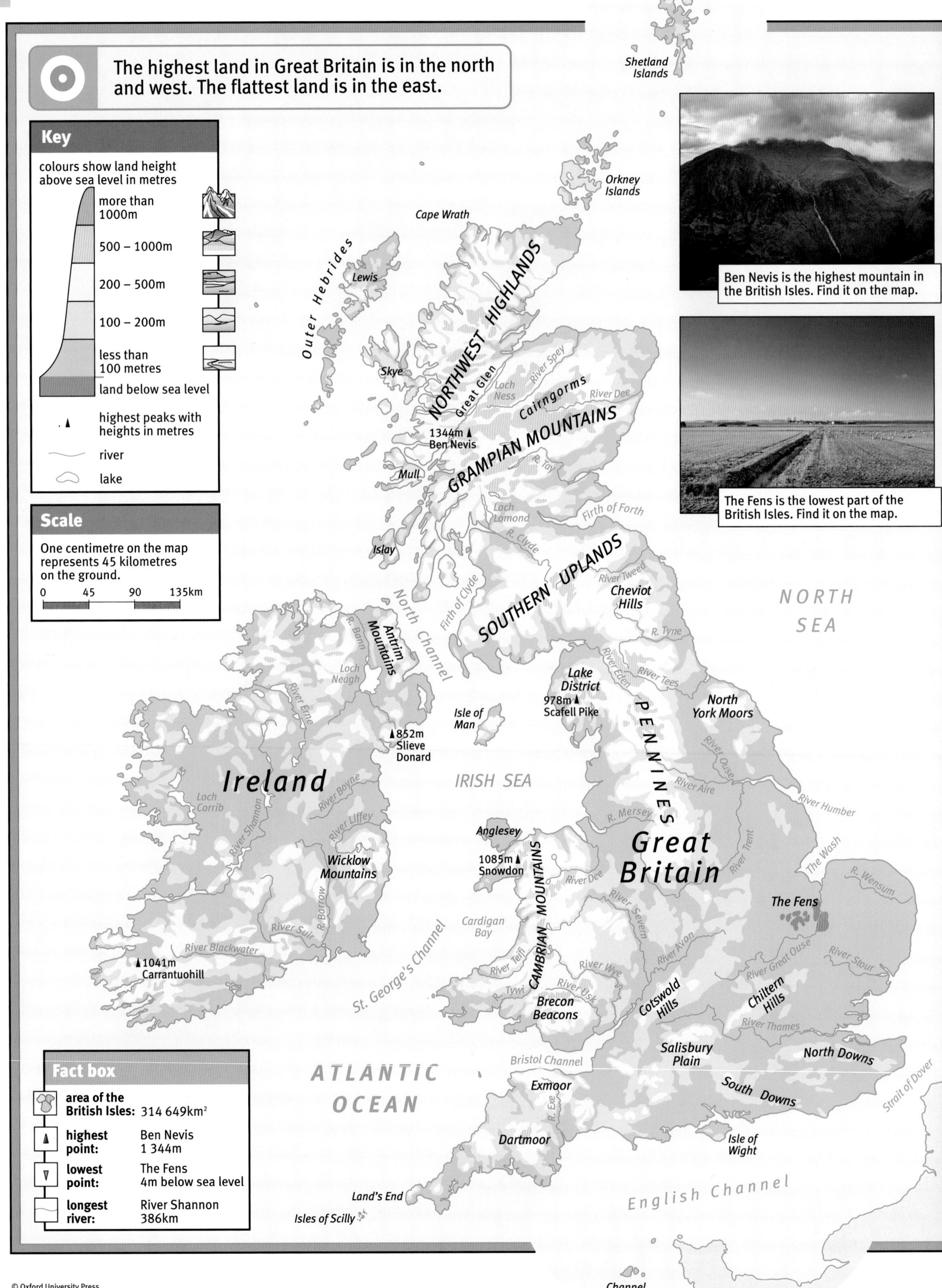
The highest land in Great Britain is in the north and west. The flattest land is in the east.
Key
colours show land height above sea level in metres
more than 1000m
500 – 1000m
200 – 500m
100 – 200m
less than 100 metres
land below sea level
highest peaks with heights in metres
river
lake
Scale
One centimetre on the map represents 45 kilometres on the ground.
0 45 90 135km
Shetland Islands
Orkney Islands
Cape Wrath
Outer Hebrides
Lewis
Skye
NORTHWEST HIGHLANDS
Great Glen
Loch Ness
River Spey
Cairngorms
River Dee
GRAMPIAN MOUNTAINS
1344m Ben Nevis
Mull
R. Tay
Loch Lomond
Firth of Forth
R. Clyde
Islay
SOUTHERN UPLANDS
River Tweed
Cheviot Hills
Firth of Clyde
North Channel
NORTH SEA
R. Tyne
R. Bann
Antrim Mountains
Loch Neagh
River Erne
Lake District
978m Scafell Pike
River Eden
River Tees
PENNINES
North York Moors
Isle of Man
852m Slieve Donard
River Ouse
Ireland
IRISH SEA
River Aire
River Humber
Loch Corrib
River Boyne
River Liffey
River Shannon
R. Mersey
Anglesey
Great Britain
River Trent
The Wash
1085m Snowdon
CAMBRIAN MOUNTAINS
River Dee
R. Wensum
Wicklow Mountains
River Severn
The Fens
R. Barrow
Cardigan Bay
River Suir
River Blackwater
St. George's Channel
River Avon
River Great Ouse
River Stour
1041m Carrantuohill
River Teifi
River Wye
R. Tywi
River Usk
Brecon Beacons
Cotswold Hills
Chiltern Hills
River Thames
Bristol Channel
Salisbury Plain
North Downs
ATLANTIC OCEAN
Exmoor
South Downs
Strait of Dover
R. Exe
Dartmoor
Isle of Wight
Land's End
Isles of Scilly
English Channel
Channel Islands
Fact box
area of the British Isles: 314 649km²
highest point: Ben Nevis 1 344m
lowest point: The Fens 4m below sea level
longest river: River Shannon 386km

Ben Nevis is the highest mountain in the British Isles. Find it on the map.

The Fens is the lowest part of the British Isles. Find it on the map.

Transverse Mercator Projection

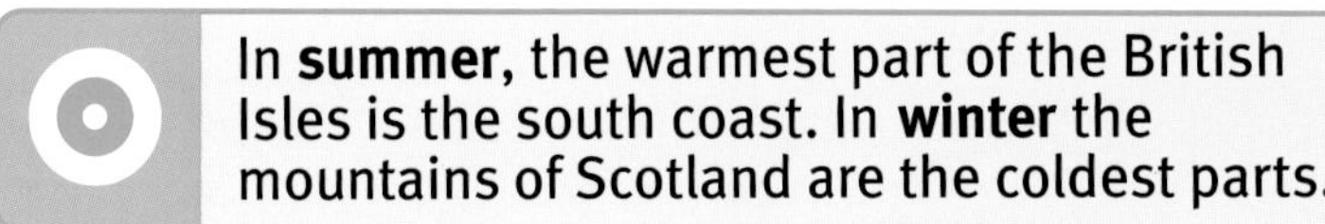

In **summer,** the warmest part of the British Isles is the south coast. In **winter** the mountains of Scotland are the coldest parts.

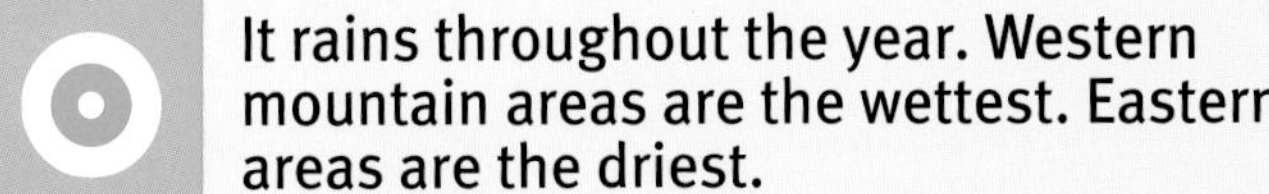

It rains throughout the year. Western mountain areas are the wettest. Eastern areas are the driest.

Extreme rainfall in November 2009 caused flooding in Cumbria.

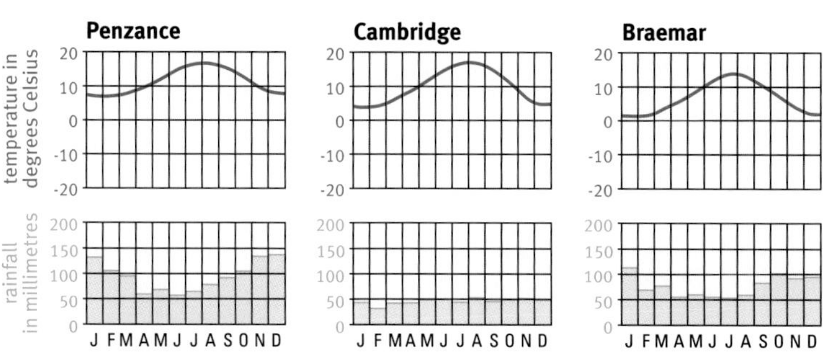
Penzance
Cambridge
Braemar
temperature in degrees Celsius
rainfall in millimetres
J F M A M J J A S O N D

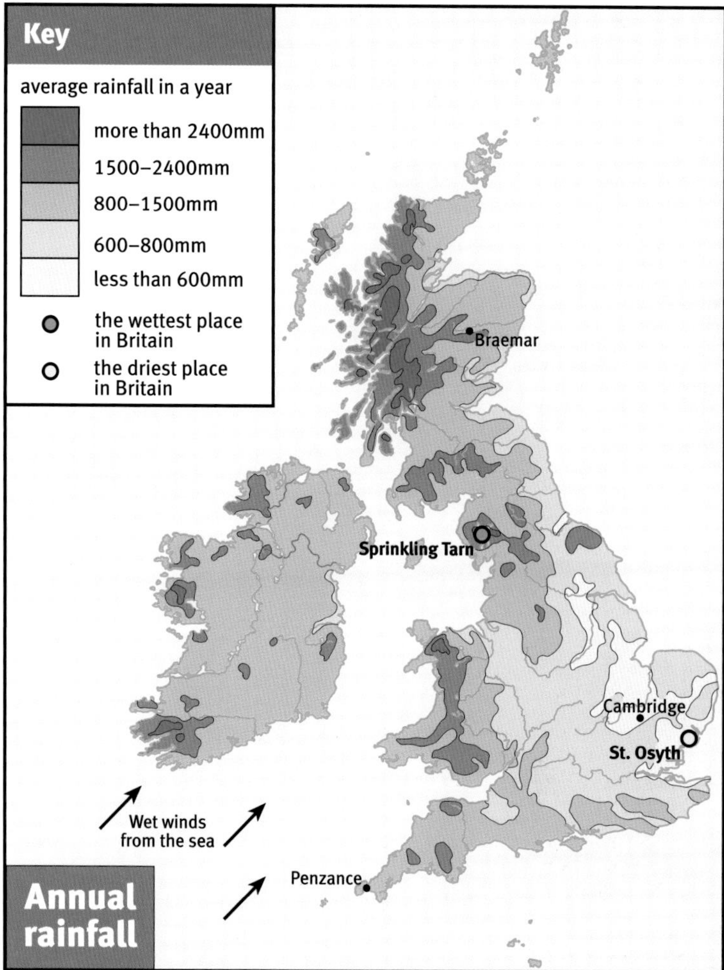
Key
average rainfall in a year
more than 2400mm
1500–2400mm
800–1500mm
600–800mm
less than 600mm
the wettest place in Britain
the driest place in Britain
Braemar
Sprinkling Tarn
Cambridge
St. Osyth
Wet winds from the sea
Penzance
Annual rainfall

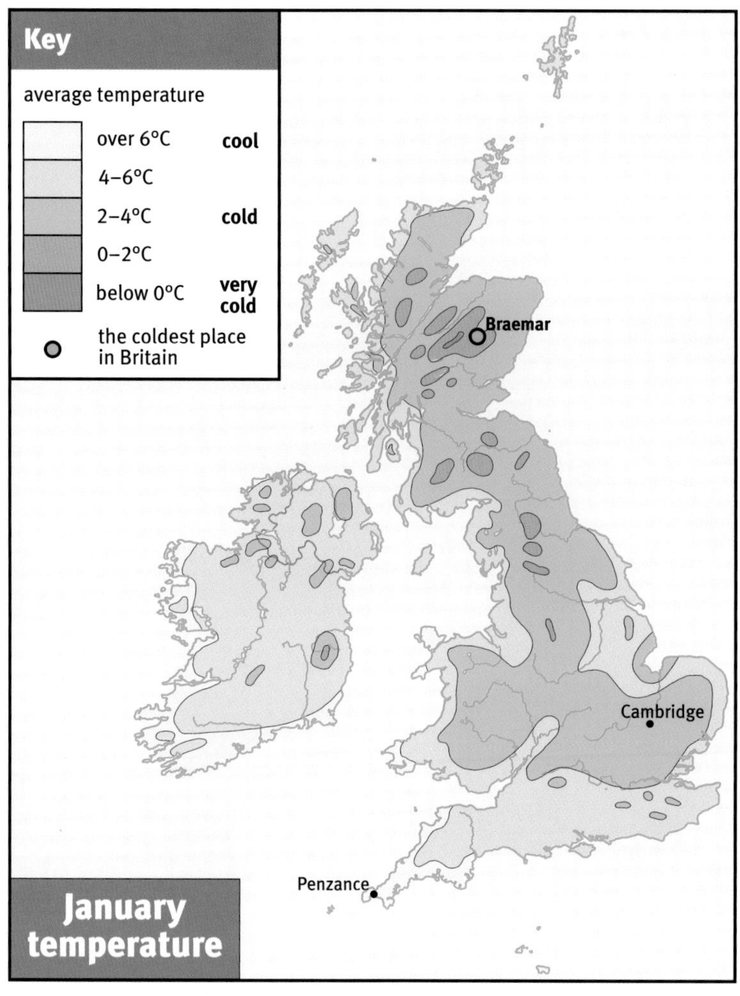
Key
average temperature
over 6°C cool
4–6°C
2–4°C cold
0–2°C
below 0°C very cold
the coldest place in Britain
Braemar
Cambridge
Penzance
January temperature

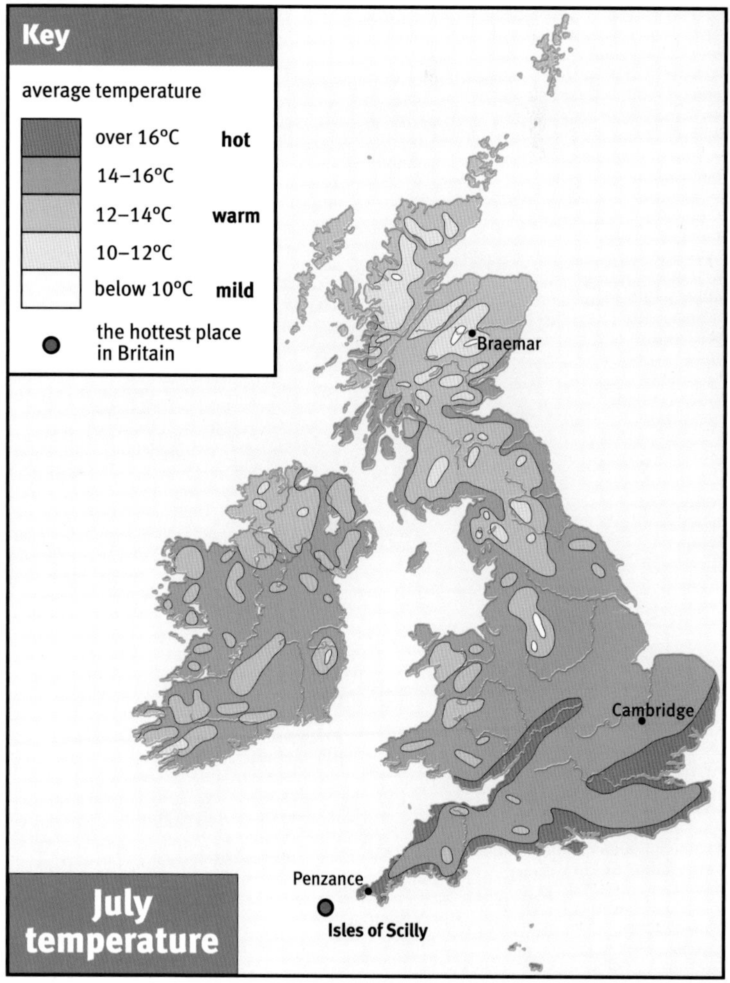
Key
average temperature
over 16°C hot
14–16°C
12–14°C warm
10–12°C
below 10°C mild
the hottest place in Britain
Braemar
Cambridge
Penzance
Isles of Scilly
July temperature

England, Scotland and Wales, together with Northern Ireland make the **United Kingdom**.

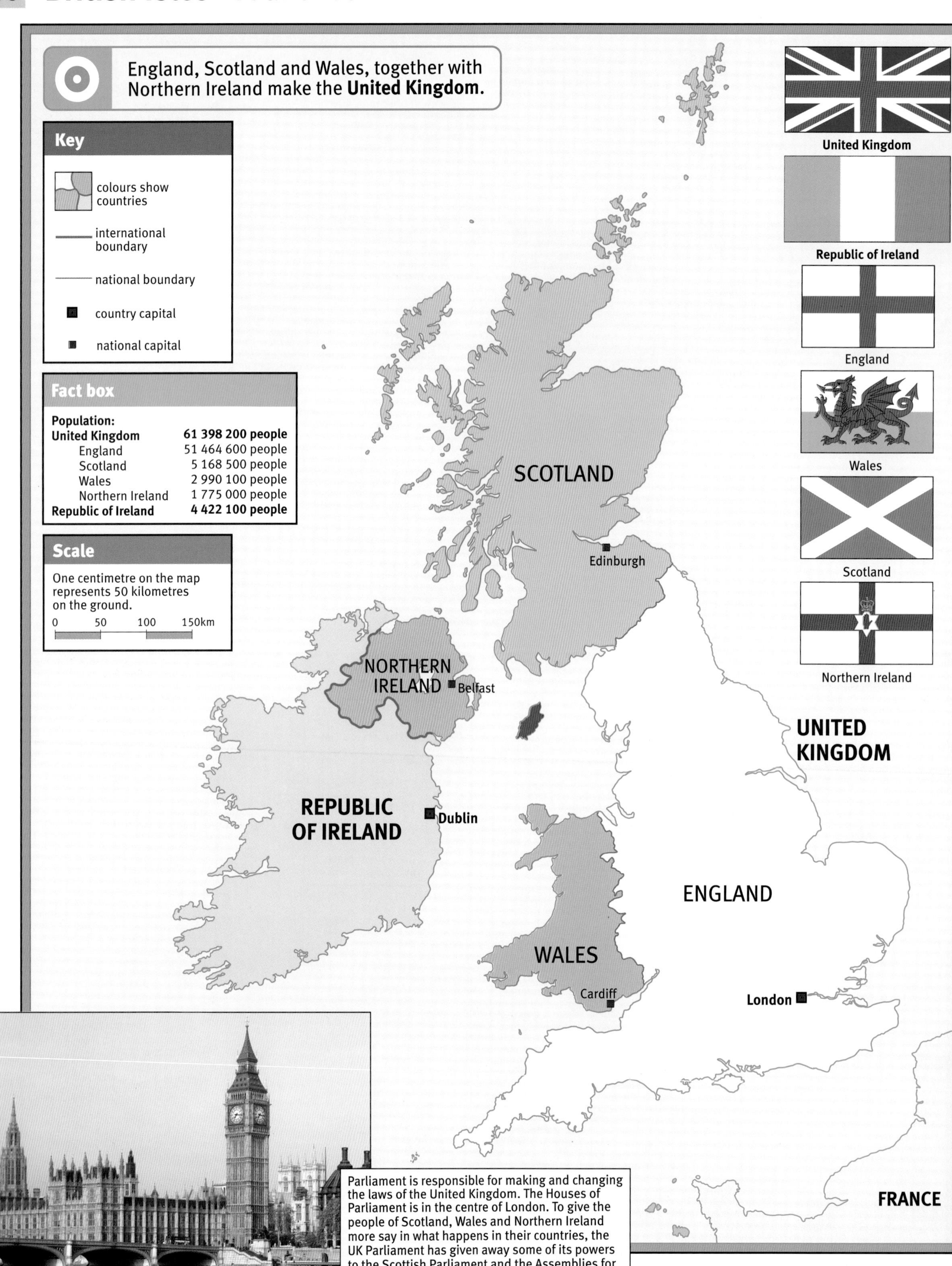

Key
colours show countries
international boundary
national boundary
country capital
national capital
SCOTLAND
Edinburgh
NORTHERN IRELAND
Belfast
REPUBLIC OF IRELAND
Dublin
WALES
Cardiff
ENGLAND
London
UNITED KINGDOM
FRANCE
United Kingdom
Republic of Ireland
England
Wales
Scotland
Northern Ireland

Fact box

Population:	
United Kingdom	**61 398 200 people**
England	51 464 600 people
Scotland	5 168 500 people
Wales	2 990 100 people
Northern Ireland	1 775 000 people
Republic of Ireland	**4 422 100 people**

Scale

One centimetre on the map represents 50 kilometres on the ground.

0 50 100 150km

Parliament is responsible for making and changing the laws of the United Kingdom. The Houses of Parliament is in the centre of London. To give the people of Scotland, Wales and Northern Ireland more say in what happens in their countries, the UK Parliament has given away some of its powers to the Scottish Parliament and the Assemblies for Wales and Northern Ireland.

Transverse Mercator Projection

The United Kingdom and the European Union

The European Union (EU) was set up in 1957 so that its people could live in peace and have a better quality of life. Since then it has grown from six member countries to twenty-seven. Other countries hope to join.

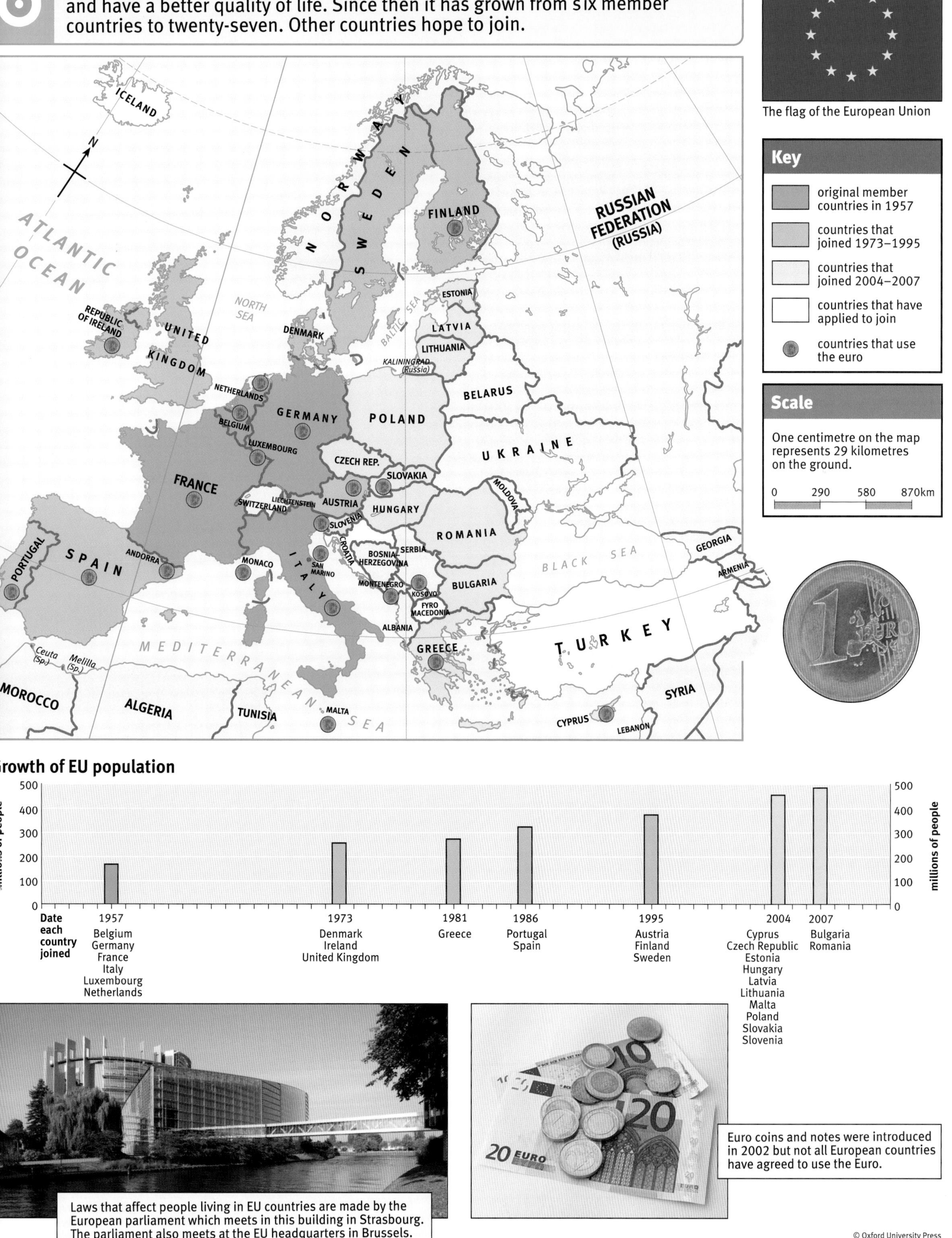

ICELAND
N
ATLANTIC OCEAN
NORWAY
SWEDEN
FINLAND
RUSSIAN FEDERATION (RUSSIA)
NORTH SEA
BALTIC SEA
ESTONIA
LATVIA
LITHUANIA
KALININGRAD (Russia)
REPUBLIC OF IRELAND
UNITED KINGDOM
DENMARK
NETHERLANDS
BELGIUM
LUXEMBOURG
GERMANY
POLAND
BELARUS
UKRAINE
CZECH REP.
SLOVAKIA
MOLDOVA
FRANCE
SWITZERLAND
LIECHTENSTEIN
AUSTRIA
HUNGARY
SLOVENIA
ROMANIA
CROATIA
BOSNIA-HERZEGOVINA
SERBIA
SAN MARINO
MONTENEGRO
KOSOVO
BULGARIA
FYRO MACEDONIA
ALBANIA
PORTUGAL
SPAIN
ANDORRA
MONACO
ITALY
GREECE
BLACK SEA
GEORGIA
ARMENIA
TURKEY
MEDITERRANEAN SEA
Ceuta (Sp.)
Melilla (Sp.)
MOROCCO
ALGERIA
TUNISIA
MALTA
CYPRUS
LEBANON
SYRIA
Key
original member countries in 1957
countries that joined 1973–1995
countries that joined 2004–2007
countries that have applied to join
countries that use the euro
Scale
One centimetre on the map represents 29 kilometres on the ground.
0 290 580 870km
Growth of EU population
millions of people
0 100 200 300 400 500
Date each country joined
1957 Belgium Germany France Italy Luxembourg Netherlands
1973 Denmark Ireland United Kingdom
1981 Greece
1986 Portugal Spain
1995 Austria Finland Sweden
2004 Cyprus Czech Republic Estonia Hungary Latvia Lithuania Malta Poland Slovakia Slovenia
2007 Bulgaria Romania
EURO
20 EURO
10
20

The flag of the European Union

Laws that affect people living in EU countries are made by the European parliament which meets in this building in Strasbourg. The parliament also meets at the EU headquarters in Brussels.

Euro coins and notes were introduced in 2002 but not all European countries have agreed to use the Euro.

Conical Orthomorphic Projection

Northern Scotland

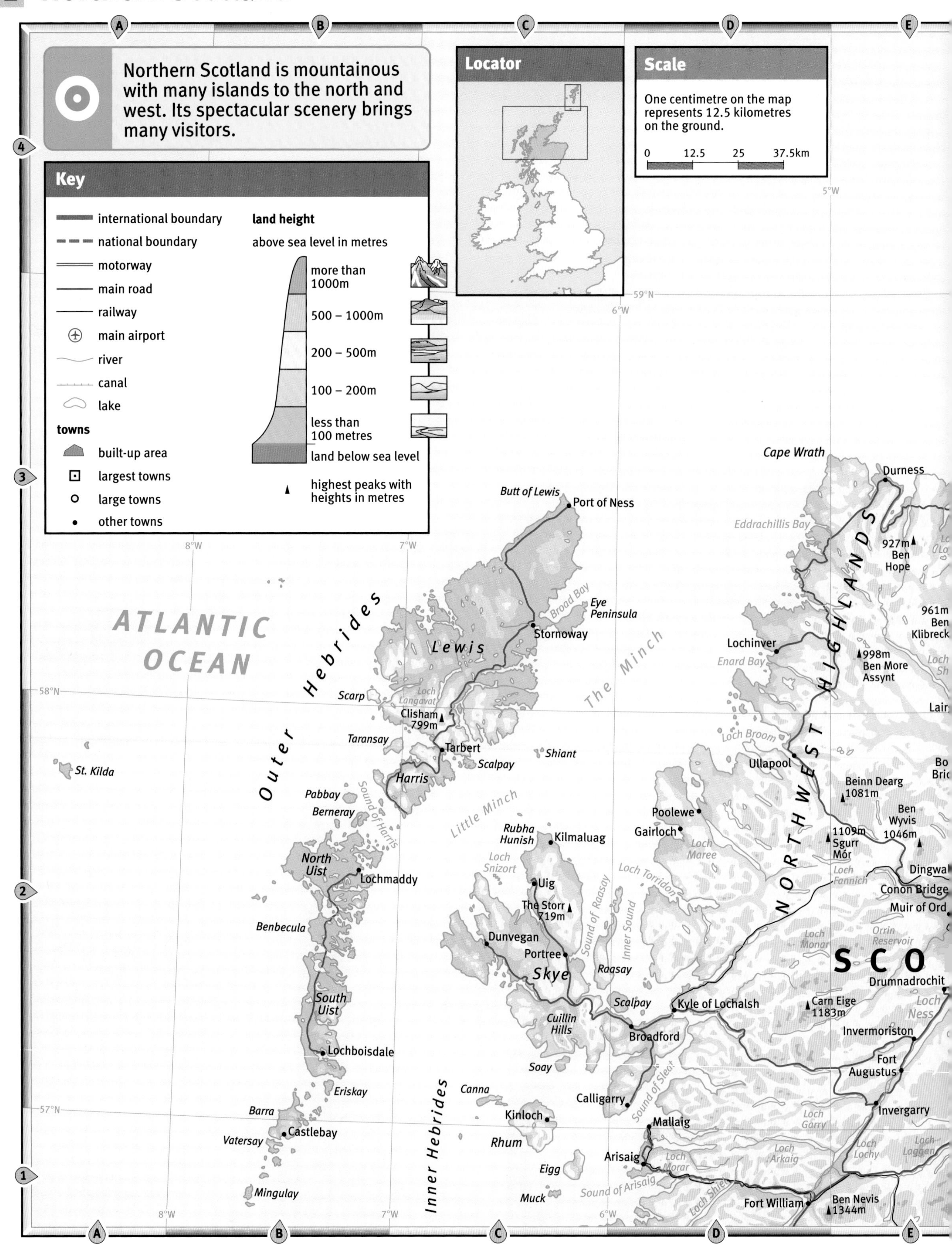
Northern Scotland is mountainous with many islands to the north and west. Its spectacular scenery brings many visitors.
Locator
Scale
One centimetre on the map represents 12.5 kilometres on the ground.
0 12.5 25 37.5km
Key
international boundary
national boundary
motorway
main road
railway
main airport
river
canal
lake
towns
built-up area
largest towns
large towns
other towns
land height
above sea level in metres
more than 1000m
500 – 1000m
200 – 500m
100 – 200m
less than 100 metres
land below sea level
highest peaks with heights in metres
A
B
C
D
E
1
2
3
4
5°W
6°W
7°W
8°W
59°N
58°N
57°N
ATLANTIC OCEAN
Outer Hebrides
Inner Hebrides
Butt of Lewis
Port of Ness
Eye Peninsula
Broad Bay
Stornoway
Lewis
Loch Langavat
Scarp
Clisham 799m
Taransay
Tarbert
Scalpay
Shiant
Harris
St. Kilda
Pabbay
Berneray
Sound of Harris
Little Minch
The Minch
North Uist
Lochmaddy
Benbecula
South Uist
Lochboisdale
Eriskay
Barra
Castlebay
Vatersay
Mingulay
Rubha Hunish
Kilmaluag
Loch Snizort
Uig
The Storr 719m
Dunvegan
Portree
Skye
Sound of Raasay
Inner Sound
Raasay
Scalpay
Cuillin Hills
Broadford
Soay
Canna
Kinloch
Rhum
Eigg
Muck
Calligarry
Sound of Sleat
Mallaig
Arisaig
Sound of Arisaig
Loch Morar
Loch Shiel
Fort William
Ben Nevis 1344m
Cape Wrath
Durness
Eddrachillis Bay
927m Ben Hope
961m Ben Klibreck
Lochinver
Enard Bay
998m Ben More Assynt
NORTHWEST HIGHLANDS
Loch Broom
Ullapool
Beinn Dearg 1081m
Ben Wyvis 1046m
Poolewe
Gairloch
Loch Maree
Loch Torridon
1109m Sgurr Mór
Loch Fannich
Dingwall
Conon Bridge
Muir of Ord
Loch Monar
Orrin Reservoir
SCO
Drumnadrochit
Kyle of Lochalsh
Carn Eige 1183m
Loch Ness
Invermoriston
Fort Augustus
Invergarry
Loch Garry
Loch Arkaig
Loch Lochy
Loch Laggan

Transverse Mercator Projection

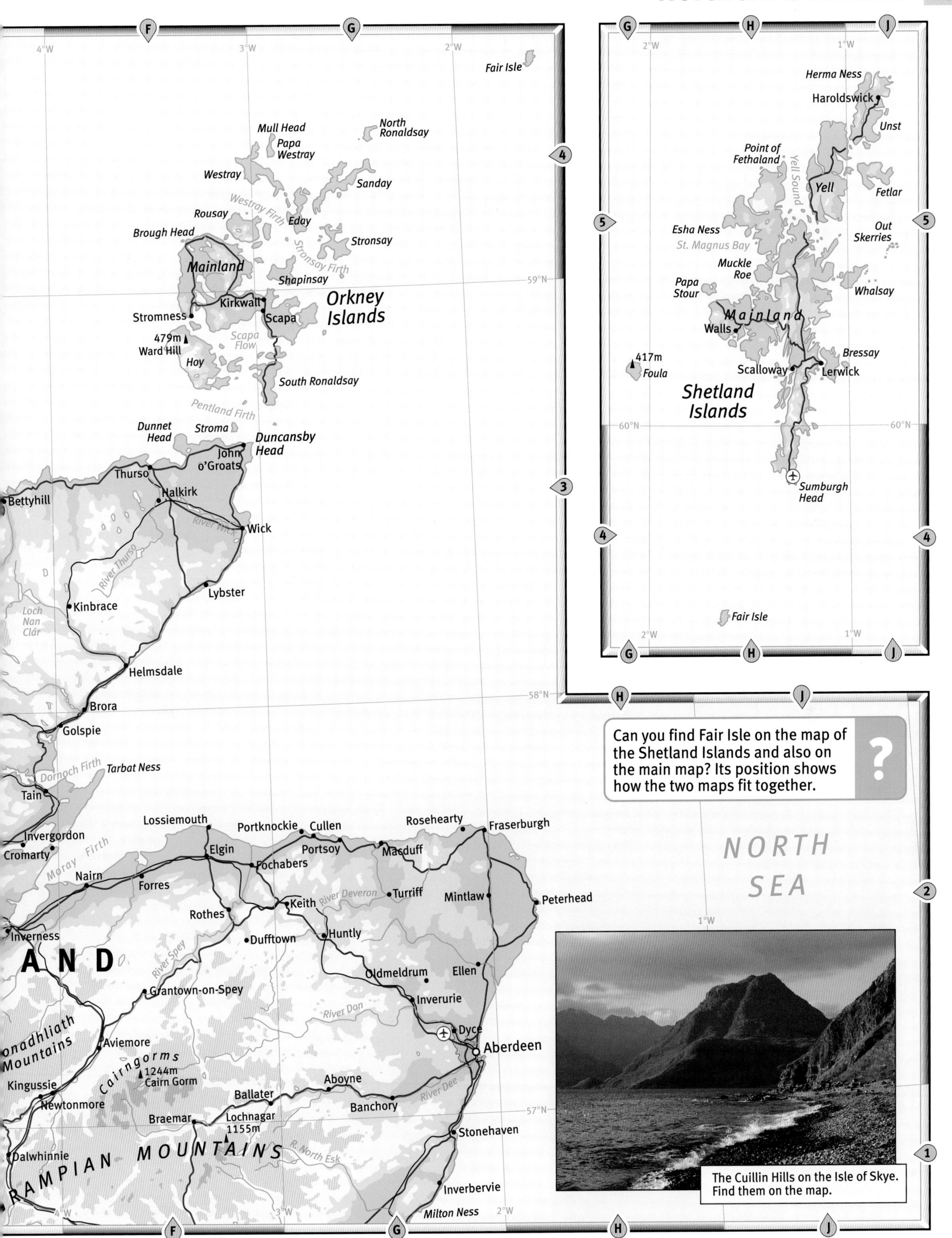
Fair Isle
Mull Head
North Ronaldsay
Papa Westray
Westray
Sanday
Westray Firth
Rousay
Eday
Brough Head
Stronsay
Stronsay Firth
Mainland
Shapinsay
Orkney Islands
Kirkwall
Stromness
Scapa
479m
Ward Hill
Scapa Flow
Hoy
South Ronaldsay
Pentland Firth
Dunnet Head
Stroma
Duncansby Head
John o'Groats
Thurso
Bettyhill
Halkirk
River Wick
Wick
River Thurso
Lybster
Kinbrace
Loch Nan Clár
Helmsdale
Brora
Golspie
Dornoch Firth
Tarbat Ness
Tain
Lossiemouth
Portknockie
Cullen
Rosehearty
Fraserburgh
Invergordon
Cromarty
Moray Firth
Elgin
Portsoy
Macduff
Nairn
Fochabers
Forres
Keith
River Deveron
Turriff
Mintlaw
Peterhead
Rothes
Inverness
Dufftown
Huntly
AND
River Spey
Oldmeldrum
Ellen
Grantown-on-Spey
Inverurie
River Don
onadhliath Mountains
Aviemore
Dyce
Aberdeen
Cairngorms
1244m
Cairn Gorm
Kingussie
Aboyne
Newtonmore
Ballater
Banchory
River Dee
Braemar
Lochnagar
1155m
Stonehaven
Dalwhinnie
RAMPIAN MOUNTAINS
R. North Esk
Inverbervie
Milton Ness
Herma Ness
Haroldswick
Unst
Point of Fethaland
Yell Sound
Yell
Fetlar
Esha Ness
St. Magnus Bay
Out Skerries
Muckle Roe
Papa Stour
Whalsay
Mainland
Walls
417m
Foula
Scalloway
Lerwick
Bressay
Shetland Islands
Sumburgh Head
Fair Isle
NORTH SEA
59°N
58°N
57°N
60°N
4°W
3°W
2°W
1°W

Can you find Fair Isle on the map of the Shetland Islands and also on the main map? Its position shows how the two maps fit together.

The Cuillin Hills on the Isle of Skye. Find them on the map.

In the centre of Northern Ireland lies Lough Neagh, the largest lake in the British Isles.
Locator
On the north coast of Northern Ireland, black basalt rock forms the Giant's Causeway. Find it on the map.
A
B
C
D
1
2
3
8°W
7°W
6°W
5°W
56°N
55°N
54°N
SCOTLAND
SOUTHERN
NORTHERN IRELAND
GRAMPIAN MOUNTAINS
Muck
Coll
Tiree
Tobermory
Lochaline
Sound of Mull
Ulva
Craignure
Lismore
967m Ben More
Mull
Kerrera
Iona
Fionnphort
Ross of Mull
Firth of Lorn
Loch Shiel
Fort William
1344m Ben Nevis
Blackwater Reservoir
Kinlochleven
Loch Rannoch
Loch Linnhe
Loch Etive
Ben Lawers 1214m
Loch Lyon
River Orchy
Tyndrum
Oban
1124m Ben Cruachan
Crianlarich
Ben More 1174m
Lochearnhead
Loch Earn
Callander
Inveraray
Loch Awe
Furnace
Strachur
974m Ben Lomond
Loch Lomond
River Forth
Scarba
Colonsay
Scalasaig
Oronsay
Jura
Sound of Jura
Lochgilphead
Loch Fyne
Loch Long
Garelochhead
Helensburgh
Campsie Fells
Greenock
Dumbarton
Kirkintilloch
Dunoon
Port Glasgow
Clydebank
Bearsden
Coatbridge
Glasgow
Johnstone
Paisley
Barrhead
Hamilton
Newton Mearns
East Kilbride
Port Askaig
Craighouse
Tarbert
Rothesay
Kennacraig
Bute
Sound of Bute
Firth of Clyde
Largs
Islay
Portnahaven
Gigha
Clachan
Lochranza
Goat Fell 874m
Ardrossan
Saltcoats
Irvine
Stewarton
Darvel
Kilmarnock
Mull of Oa
Port Ellen
Kintyre
Kilbrannan Sound
Brodick
Arran
Prestwick
Ayr
River Ayr
Cumnock
New Cumnock
Campbeltown
Maybole
River Doon
Rathlin Island
Rathlin Sound
Mull of Kintyre
Southend
Ailsa Craig
Girvan
Malin Head
Lough Swilly
Inishowen Peninsula
615m Slieve Snaght
Giant's Causeway
Portrush
Bushmills
Ballycastle
Fair Head
Antrim Mountains
North Channel
Creeslough
Buncrana
Lough Foyle
Coleraine
R. Bush
Ballymoney
Ballantrae
New Galloway
Kilmacrenan
Limavady
Corsewall Point
Letterkenny
Londonderry
River Foyle
River Bann
R. Main
Carnlough
Cairnryan
Newton Stewart
Dungiven
Stranraer
Gatehouse of Fleet
Wigtown
Glenluce
Kirkcudbright
Ballybofey
Lifford
Strabane
Sperrin Mountains
683m Sawel
Maghera
Ballymena
Larne
Island Magee
R. Finn
R. Derg
Magherafelt
Randalstown
Newtownstewart
Antrim
Carrickfergus
Whithorn
Donegal
Drummore
Newtownabbey
Belfast Lough
Bangor
Donaghadee
Lough Derg
Omagh
Cookstown
Lough Neagh
Crumlin
Belfast
Newtownards
Mull of Galloway
Coalisland
Dungannon
Lisburn
Strangford Lough
Ards Peninsula
Lower Lough Erne
Irvinestown
Aughnacloy
Portadown
Lurgan
Craigavon
Dromore
Saintfield
R. Blackwater
R. Lagan
Point of Ayre
Manorhamilton
Enniskillen
Armagh
Banbridge
River Bann
Ramsey
Monaghan
Downpatrick
Kirk Michael
Snaefell 620m
R. Shannon
Lisnaskea
Keady
Upper Lough Erne
Newtownhamilton
Newcastle
St. John's Point
Peel
Isle of Man
Clones
852m Slieve Donard
Newry
Mourne Mtns.
Douglas
Castleblayney
Warrenpoint
Port Erin
Crossmaglen
Kilkeel
Calf of Man
Castletown
Cavan

Transverse Mercator Projection

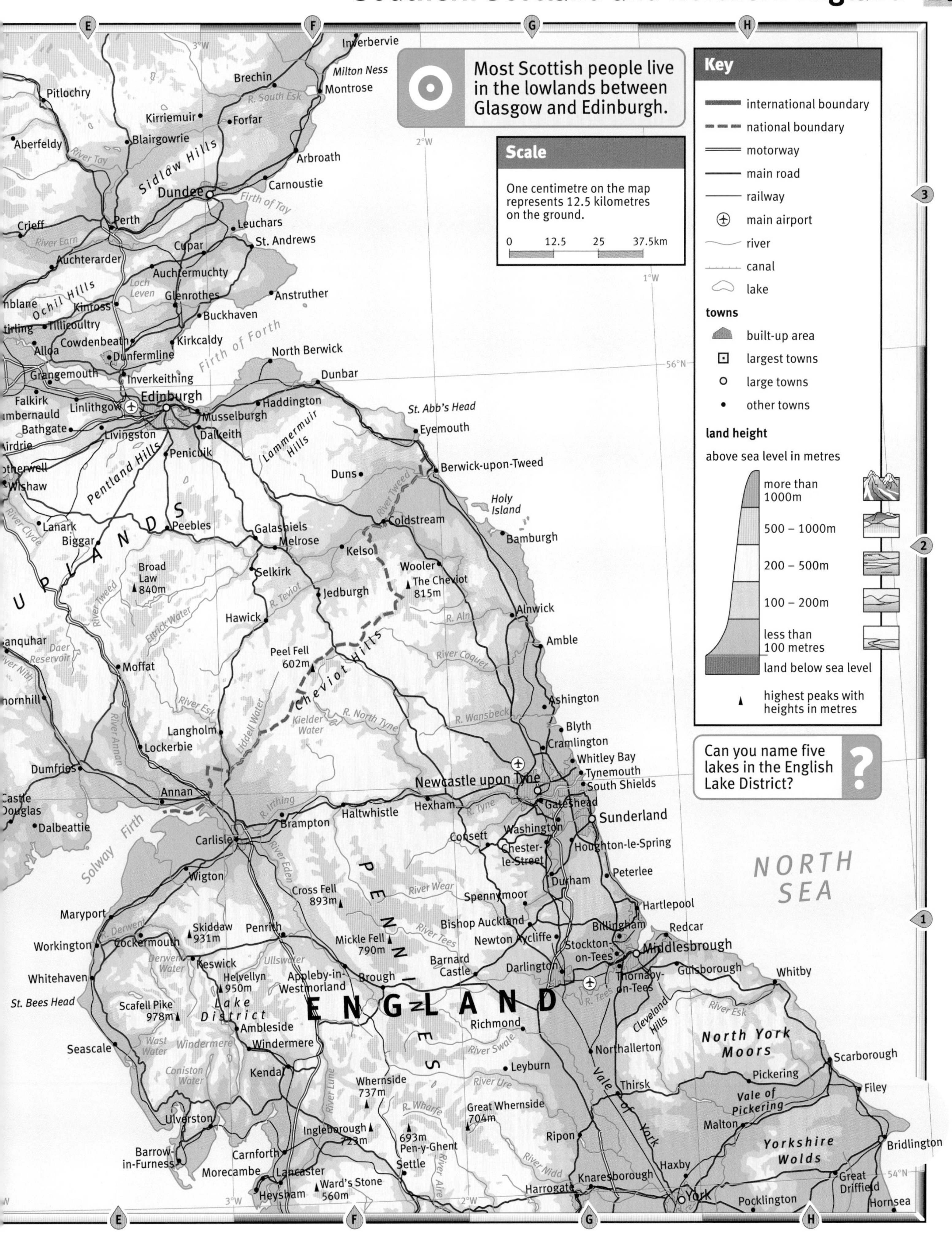
Most Scottish people live in the lowlands between Glasgow and Edinburgh.
Scale
One centimetre on the map represents 12.5 kilometres on the ground.
0 12.5 25 37.5km
Key
international boundary
national boundary
motorway
main road
railway
main airport
river
canal
lake
towns
built-up area
largest towns
large towns
other towns
land height
above sea level in metres
more than 1000m
500 – 1000m
200 – 500m
100 – 200m
less than 100 metres
land below sea level
highest peaks with heights in metres
Can you name five lakes in the English Lake District?
NORTH SEA
ENGLAND
UPLANDS
PENNINES
Inverbervie
Milton Ness
Montrose
Brechin
R. South Esk
Pitlochry
Kirriemuir
Forfar
Aberfeldy
Blairgowrie
River Tay
Sidlaw Hills
Arbroath
Dundee
Carnoustie
Firth of Tay
Crieff
Perth
Leuchars
St. Andrews
River Earn
Cupar
Auchterarder
Auchtermuchty
Ochil Hills
Loch Leven
Kinross
Glenrothes
Anstruther
Tillicoultry
Buckhaven
Cowdenbeath
Kirkcaldy
Alloa
Dunfermline
Firth of Forth
North Berwick
Grangemouth
Inverkeithing
Dunbar
Falkirk
Linlithgow
Edinburgh
Haddington
Musselburgh
St. Abb's Head
Bathgate
Livingston
Dalkeith
Lammermuir Hills
Eyemouth
Penicuik
Pentland Hills
Duns
Berwick-upon-Tweed
Wishaw
River Tweed
Holy Island
River Clyde
Lanark
Peebles
Galashiels
Coldstream
Bamburgh
Biggar
Melrose
Kelso
Broad Law 840m
Selkirk
Wooler
The Cheviot 815m
R. Teviot
Jedburgh
Alnwick
Hawick
R. Aln
Ettrick Water
Amble
Daer Reservoir
Peel Fell 602m
River Coquet
Moffat
Cheviot Hills
River Esk
Ashington
Kielder Water
R. North Tyne
R. Wansbeck
Blyth
Langholm
Liddell Water
River Annan
Cramlington
Lockerbie
Whitley Bay
Dumfries
Tynemouth
Newcastle upon Tyne
South Shields
Annan
Dalbeattie
Solway Firth
R. Irthing
Hexham
R. Tyne
Gateshead
Sunderland
Brampton
Haltwhistle
Carlisle
Consett
Washington
River Eden
Houghton-le-Spring
Chester-le-Street
Wigton
Durham
Peterlee
Cross Fell 893m
River Wear
Spennymoor
Maryport
Hartlepool
R. Derwent
Skiddaw 931m
Penrith
Bishop Auckland
Billingham
Redcar
Cockermouth
Workington
Mickle Fell 790m
River Tees
Newton Aycliffe
Stockton-on-Tees
Middlesbrough
Derwent Water
Keswick
Ullswater
Barnard Castle
Darlington
Thornaby-on-Tees
Guisborough
Whitby
Whitehaven
Helvellyn 950m
Appleby-in-Westmorland
Brough
R. Tees
St. Bees Head
Scafell Pike 978m
Lake District
Cleveland Hills
River Esk
Richmond
Ambleside
North York Moors
Seascale
Wast Water
Windermere
Windermere
River Swale
Northallerton
Scarborough
Kendal
Leyburn
Coniston Water
River Lune
Whernside 737m
River Ure
Vale of York
Thirsk
Pickering
Filey
R. Wharfe
Great Whernside 704m
Vale of Pickering
Ulverston
Malton
Ingleborough 723m
693m Pen-y-Ghent
Ripon
Yorkshire Wolds
Bridlington
Barrow-in-Furness
Carnforth
River Aire
Morecambe
Lancaster
Settle
River Nidd
Haxby
Great Driffield
Heysham
Ward's Stone 560m
Harrogate
Knaresborough
York
Pocklington
Hornsea
3°W
2°W
1°W
56°N
54°N
E
F
G
H
1
2
3

Most of Wales is mountainous. The largest towns and cities are in the south.
Wales is wet. Can you name two Welsh reservoirs?
?
A
B
C
D
E
1
2
3
4
5°W
4°W
3°W
6°W
53°N
52°N
IRISH SEA
Isle of Man
Port Erin
Castletown
Calf of Man
Barrow-in-Furness
Morecambe
Heysham
Lancaster
Carnforth
560m Ward's Stone
Fleetwood
Thornton
Blackpool
Preston
Lytham St. Anne's
Leyland
Darwen
Southport
Formby
Skelmersdale
Wigan
Kirkby
St. Helens
Bootle
Wallasey
Liverpool
Birkenhead
Widnes
Warring
Runcorn
River Dee
R. Mersey
Ellesmere Port
Holywell
Flint
Connah's Quay
Mold
Chester
Winsford
Balbriggan
Swords
Dublin
Dún Laoghaire
Bray
Wicklow
Arklow
Cahore Point
Carmel Head
Amlwch
Holyhead
Anglesey
Holy Island
Llangefni
Menai Bridge
Bangor
Bethesda
Caernarfon
Caernarfon Bay
Snowdon 1085m
Llandudno
Conwy
Colwyn Bay
Prestatyn
Rhyl
R. Conwy
Denbigh
R. Clwyd
Llanrwst
Betws-y-Coed
Llyn Brenig
Ruthin
Wrexham
Nantwich
Ruabon
Chirk
Whitchu
Lleyn Peninsula
Porthmadog
Pwllheli
Blaenau Ffestiniog
Corwen
R. Dee
Llangollen
Bala
Bala Lake
Harlech
Oswestry
Llyn Vyrnwy
R. Vyrnwy
Bardsey Island
Dolgellau
Barmouth
892m Cadair Idris
R. Dyfi
Shrewsbury
Wellingt
407m The Wrekin
Welshpool
R. Severn
Tywyn
Machynlleth
Montgomery
Cardigan Bay
Plynlimon 752m
Newtown
Wenlock Edge
Aberystwyth
Llanidloes
CAMBRIAN MOUNTAINS
WALES
Ludlow
Knighton
Rhayader
River Teme
Aberaeron
New Quay
Claerwen Reservoir
Llandrindod Wells
Kington
Leominste
Llyn Brianne Reservoir
Builth Wells
St. George's Channel
Cemaes Head
Lampeter
Mynydd Eppynt
R. Wye
Strumble Head
Newport
Cardigan
River Teifi
Hay-on-Wye
Hereford
Newcastle Emlyn
Fishguard
Black Mountains
Preseli Mountains
Llandovery
Brecon
St. David's Head
R. Tywi
River Usk
Ross-on-Wye
Carmarthen
886m
Llandeilo
Brecon Beacons
St. Brides Bay
St. Clears
Abergavenny
Cinderf
Ammanford
Monmouth
Milford Haven
Cross Hands
Tredegar
Ebbw Vale
R. Neath
Merthyr Tydfil
Abertillery
Kidwelly
Saundersfoot
Aberdare
Pembroke Dock
Tenby
Burry Port
Llanelli
Pontardulais
Mountain Ash
Pontypool
Cwmbran
Pembroke
Carmarthen Bay
Gorseinon
Neath
Rhondda
Gelligaer
Chepstow
Swansea
Maesteg
Newport
Gower
Port Talbot
Pontypridd
Caerphilly
Worms Head
R. Taff
River Severn
Porthcawl
Bridgend
Cardiff
Mangotsfield
Clevedon
Bristol
Bristol Channel
Barry
Penarth
Keynsha
Weston-super-Mare

The Millennium Stadium, Cardiff. Find Cardiff on the map.

Transverse Mercator Projection

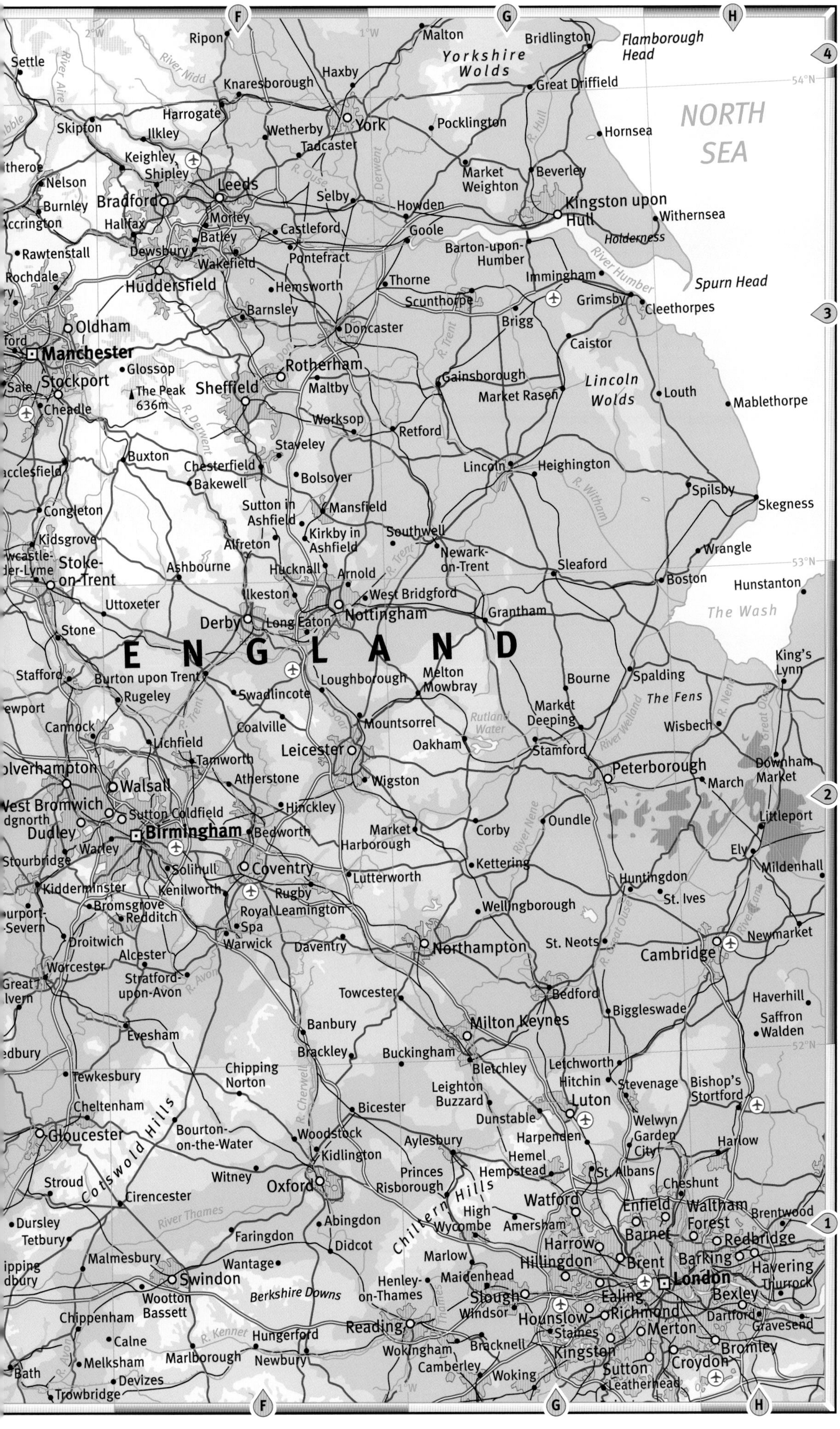

Locator

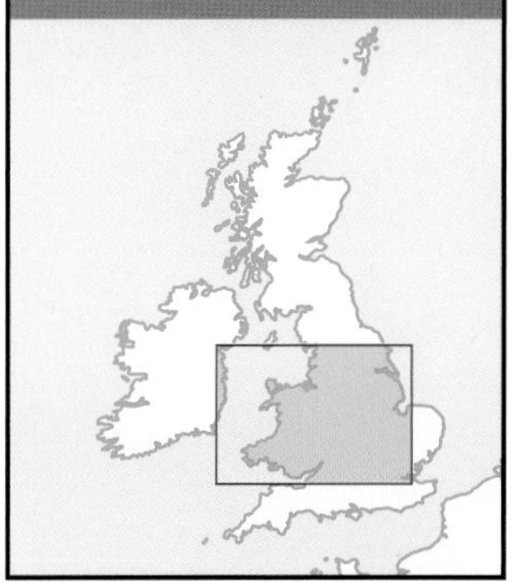

Key

- international boundary
- national boundary
- motorway
- main road
- railway
- main airport
- river
- canal
- lake

towns

- built-up area
- largest towns
- large towns
- other towns

land height

above sea level in metres

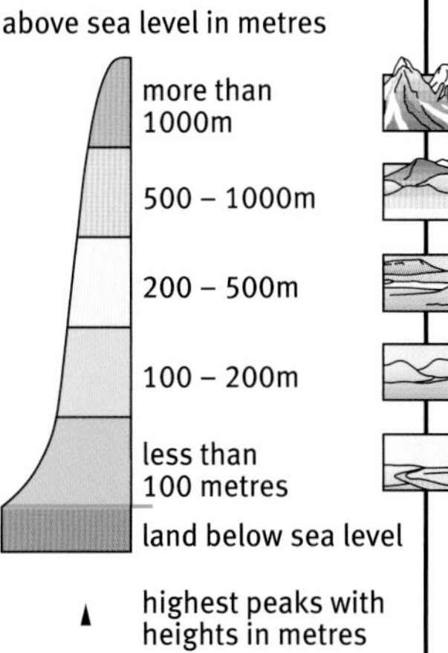
more than 1000m
500 – 1000m
200 – 500m
100 – 200m
less than 100 metres
land below sea level

highest peaks with heights in metres

Scale

One centimetre on the map represents 12.5 kilometres on the ground.

0 12.5 25 37.5km

Many towns and cities in England have grown together to make large built-up areas called **conurbations.**

South East England

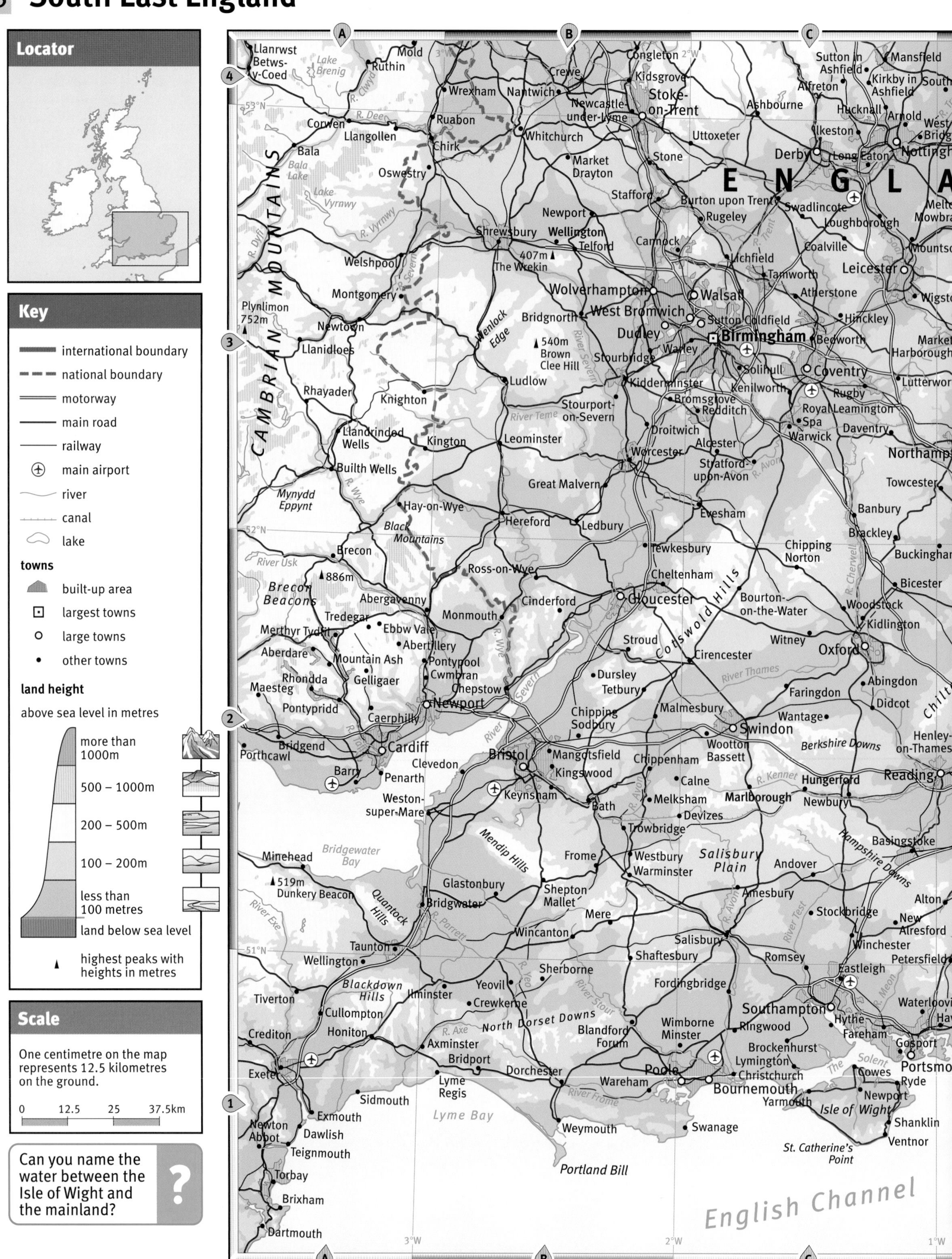
Locator
Key
international boundary
national boundary
motorway
main road
railway
main airport
river
canal
lake
towns
built-up area
largest towns
large towns
other towns
land height
above sea level in metres
more than 1000m
500 – 1000m
200 – 500m
100 – 200m
less than 100 metres
land below sea level
highest peaks with heights in metres
Scale
One centimetre on the map represents 12.5 kilometres on the ground.
0
12.5
25
37.5km
Can you name the water between the Isle of Wight and the mainland?
?
A
B
C
1
2
3
4
53°N
52°N
51°N
3°W
2°W
1°W
E N G L A
CAMBRIAN MOUNTAINS
Llanrwst
Betws-y-Coed
Lake Brenig
Mold
Ruthin
R. Clwyd
Wrexham
Nantwich
Crewe
Congleton
Kidsgrove
Stoke-on-Trent
Newcastle-under-Lyme
Ashbourne
Sutton in Ashfield
Mansfield
Alfreton
Kirkby in Ashfield
Hucknall
Arnold
West Bridgford
Nottingham
Ilkeston
Derby
Long Eaton
Corwen
R. Dee
Llangollen
Ruabon
Chirk
Whitchurch
Bala
Bala Lake
Oswestry
Market Drayton
Stone
Uttoxeter
Lake Vyrnwy
R. Vyrnwy
Stafford
Burton upon Trent
Swadlincote
Loughborough
Melton Mowbray
Newport
Rugeley
R. Dyfi
Shrewsbury
Wellington
Telford
Cannock
R. Trent
Coalville
R. Soar
Mountsorrel
407m
The Wrekin
Lichfield
Welshpool
R. Severn
Tamworth
Leicester
Montgomery
Wolverhampton
Walsall
Atherstone
Wigston
Plynlimon 752m
West Bromwich
Sutton Coldfield
Hinckley
Newtown
Wenlock Edge
Bridgnorth
Dudley
Birmingham
Bedworth
Market Harborough
Llanidloes
540m Brown Clee Hill
River Severn
Stourbridge
Warley
Solihull
Coventry
Rhayader
Ludlow
Kidderminster
Kenilworth
Rugby
Lutterworth
Knighton
Stourport-on-Severn
Bromsgrove
Redditch
Royal Leamington Spa
River Teme
Warwick
Daventry
Llandrindod Wells
Kington
Leominster
Droitwich
Alcester
Worcester
Stratford-upon-Avon
R. Avon
Northampton
Builth Wells
R. Wye
Great Malvern
Towcester
Mynydd Eppynt
Hay-on-Wye
Evesham
Banbury
Black Mountains
Hereford
Ledbury
Brackley
River Usk
Brecon
Tewkesbury
Chipping Norton
R. Cherwell
Buckingham
886m
Ross-on-Wye
Cheltenham
Bicester
Brecon Beacons
Abergavenny
Cinderford
Gloucester
Cotswold Hills
Bourton-on-the-Water
Woodstock
Tredegar
Monmouth
Kidlington
Merthyr Tydfil
Ebbw Vale
Abertillery
Stroud
Witney
Oxford
Aberdare
Mountain Ash
Pontypool
Cirencester
Cwmbran
Dursley
River Thames
Abingdon
Rhondda
Gelligaer
Chepstow
Tetbury
Faringdon
Maesteg
Didcot
Chiltern
Pontypridd
Newport
Malmesbury
Wantage
Caerphilly
Chipping Sodbury
Swindon
Henley-on-Thames
Bridgend
R. Taff
Cardiff
River Severn
Mangotsfield
Wootton Bassett
Berkshire Downs
Porthcawl
Bristol
Chippenham
Clevedon
Kingswood
Barry
R. Kennet
Hungerford
Reading
Penarth
Calne
Weston-super-Mare
Keynsham
Melksham
Marlborough
Newbury
Bath
R. Avon
Devizes
Trowbridge
Basingstoke
Mendip Hills
Minehead
Bridgewater Bay
Frome
Westbury
Salisbury Plain
Hampshire Downs
Andover
Warminster
519m Dunkery Beacon
Glastonbury
Shepton Mallet
Amesbury
Quantock Hills
Bridgwater
Alton
River Exe
R. Parrett
Mere
R. Avon
River Test
Stockbridge
New Alresford
Wincanton
Salisbury
Winchester
Taunton
Shaftesbury
Romsey
Petersfield
Wellington
Sherborne
R. Yeo
River Stour
Eastleigh
Blackdown Hills
Yeovil
Fordingbridge
R. Meon
Tiverton
Ilminster
Crewkerne
Southampton
Waterlooville
Havant
Cullompton
North Dorset Downs
Wimborne Minster
Ringwood
Hythe
R. Axe
Blandford Forum
Crediton
Honiton
Axminster
Fareham
Brockenhurst
Gosport
Bridport
Portsmouth
Lymington
The Solent
Exeter
Dorchester
Poole
Christchurch
Cowes
Lyme Regis
Wareham
Bournemouth
Ryde
River Frome
Sidmouth
Yarmouth
Newport
Exmouth
Lyme Bay
Isle of Wight
Newton Abbot
Weymouth
Swanage
Shanklin
Dawlish
Ventnor
Teignmouth
St. Catherine's Point
Torbay
Portland Bill
Brixham
English Channel
Dartmouth

Transverse Mercator Projection

D
E
F
G
4
3
2
1
1°E
0°
2°E
53°N
52°N
51°N
NORTH SEA
Spilsby
Skegness
Wrangle
Newark-on-Trent
Sleaford
Boston
Grantham
The Wash
Hunstanton
Wells-next-the-Sea
Cromer
Fakenham
North Walsham
Aylsham
R. Witham
Bourne
Spalding
King's Lynn
River Bure
River Wensum
The Fens
R. Nene
Market Deeping
Rutland Water
Wisbech
Norwich
Acle
Great Yarmouth
Stamford
River Welland
Great Ouse
Swaffham
East Dereham
Peterborough
Downham Market
March
Wymondham
Attleborough
Lowestoft
Corby
Oundle
River Nene
Bungay
Beccles
Littleport
Thetford
Kettering
Ely
Diss
Mildenhall
River Waveney
Huntingdon
St. Ives
Southwold
Wellingborough
R. Great Ouse
R. Cam
Newmarket
Bury St. Edmunds
Saxmundham
St. Neots
Cambridge
Stowmarket
Wickham Market
Aldeburgh
Bedford
Woodbridge
Haverhill
Milton Keynes
Biggleswade
Ipswich
Saffron Walden
Sudbury
Bletchley
Letchworth
River Stour
Felixstowe
Leighton Buzzard
Hitchin
Stevenage
Bishop's Stortford
River Colne
Harwich
Luton
Braintree
Colchester
Dunstable
Walton-on-the-Naze
Harpenden
Welwyn Garden City
Hemel Hempstead
Harlow
Witham
Clacton-on-Sea
St Albans
Chelmsford
Cheshunt
Watford
Enfield
Waltham Forest
Southminster
Amersham
Brentwood
Harrow
Barnet
Redbridge
Rayleigh
Hillingdon
Brent
Barking
Havering
Basildon
Slough
London
Southend-on-Sea
Ealing
Bexley
Thurrock
Hounslow
Richmond
Dartford
Gravesend
Sheerness
Staines
Merton
Herne Bay
Margate
North Foreland
Kingston
Bromley
Chatham
Gillingham
Whitstable
Ramsgate
Woking
Sutton
Croydon
Sittingbourne
Leatherhead
Canterbury
Farnborough
Reigate
Sevenoaks
R. Medway
Maidstone
North Downs
Aldershot
Guildford
Redhill
Tonbridge
Deal
Godalming
Dorking
East Grinstead
Ashford
North Downs
Royal Tunbridge Wells
Dover
Crawley
Folkestone
Haslemere
R. Arun
Hythe
Strait of Dover
Horsham
Crowborough
Midhurst
Billingshurst
New Romney
Haywards Heath
Uckfield
Rye
Dungeness
South Downs
Lewes
Hailsham
Hastings
Hove
Bexhill
Littlehampton
Brighton
Chichester
Worthing
Bognor Regis
Seaford
Eastbourne
Beachy Head
Selsey Bill
Nieuwpoort
Veurne
BELGIUM
Dunkerque
Calais
Ardres
Cassel
St-Omer
Boulogne-sur-Mer
Hazebrouck
Lillers
Béthune
Le Touquet-Paris-Plage
FRANCE

Eastern England is mostly low and flat. Some land is below sea level.

Brighton is one of Britain's oldest seaside resorts. Find it on the map.

Can you name the nearest French city to England?

South West England

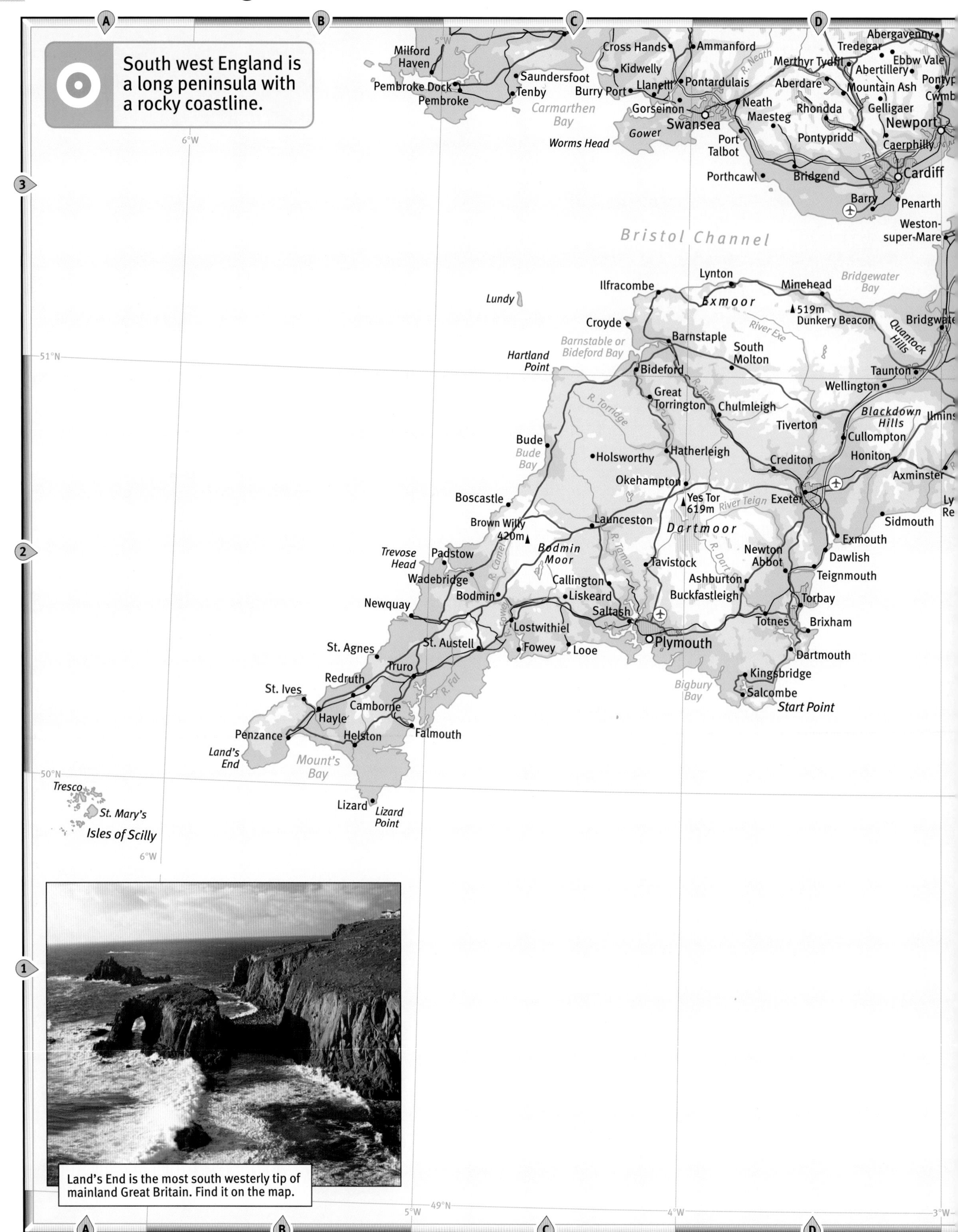
South west England is a long peninsula with a rocky coastline.
Milford Haven
Pembroke Dock
Pembroke
Saundersfoot
Tenby
Carmarthen Bay
Cross Hands
Ammanford
Kidwelly
Llanelli
Pontardulais
Burry Port
Gorseinon
Swansea
Gower
Worms Head
Port Talbot
Neath
R. Neath
Maesteg
Porthcawl
Bridgend
Merthyr Tydfil
Aberdare
Tredegar
Abergavenny
Ebbw Vale
Abertillery
Mountain Ash
Rhondda
Gelligaer
Pontypridd
Newport
Caerphilly
Cardiff
Barry
Penarth
Weston-super-Mare
Bristol Channel
Lundy
Ilfracombe
Lynton
Exmoor
Minehead
519m
Dunkery Beacon
Bridgewater Bay
Quantock Hills
Croyde
Barnstaple
Barnstable or Bideford Bay
River Exe
South Molton
Hartland Point
Bideford
Taunton
Wellington
Great Torrington
R. Taw
R. Torridge
Chulmleigh
Tiverton
Blackdown Hills
Cullompton
Honiton
Axminster
Bude
Bude Bay
Holsworthy
Hatherleigh
Crediton
Okehampton
Boscastle
Yes Tor 619m
River Teign
Exeter
Brown Willy 420m
Launceston
Dartmoor
Sidmouth
Exmouth
Trevose Head
Padstow
Bodmin Moor
R. Camel
R. Tamar
Tavistock
R. Dart
Newton Abbot
Dawlish
Teignmouth
Wadebridge
Callington
Ashburton
Bodmin
Liskeard
Buckfastleigh
Torbay
Newquay
Saltash
Totnes
Brixham
Lostwithiel
Plymouth
St. Agnes
St. Austell
Fowey
Looe
Dartmouth
Truro
Redruth
Kingsbridge
St. Ives
R. Fal
Camborne
Bigbury Bay
Salcombe
Hayle
Start Point
Penzance
Helston
Falmouth
Land's End
Mount's Bay
Tresco
St. Mary's
Isles of Scilly
Lizard
Lizard Point
6°W
5°W
4°W
3°W
51°N
50°N
49°N

Land's End is the most south westerly tip of mainland Great Britain. Find it on the map.

Transverse Mercator Projection

E
F
G
Cinderford
Monmouth
2°W
Witney
Kidlington
Aylesbury
Princes Risborough
Hemel Hempstead
St. Albans
Cheshunt
Stroud
Cirencester
Oxford
Chiltern Hills
High Wycombe
Amersham
Watford
Enfield
R. Wye
Dursley
Tetbury
River Thames
Abingdon
Barnet
Chepstow
River Severn
Faringdon
Didcot
Harrow
Brent
Chipping Sodbury
Malmesbury
Wantage
Marlow
Hillingdon
London
River
Swindon
Henley-on-Thames
Maidenhead
Ealing
Wootton Bassett
Berkshire Downs
Slough
Windsor
Hounslow
Richmond
Bristol
Mangotsfield
Chippenham
Reading
Staines
Merton
Clevedon
Kingswood
Calne
R. Kennet
Hungerford
Wokingham
Bracknell
Kingston
Keynsham
Melksham
Marlborough
Newbury
Sutton
Bath
R. Avon
Devizes
Camberley
Woking
Leatherhead
Trowbridge
Basingstoke
Hampshire Downs
Farnborough
Reigate
Mendip Hills
Westbury
Salisbury Plain
Aldershot
Guildford
Redhill
Frome
Warminster
Andover
Farnham
Dorking
Glastonbury
Shepton Mallet
Amesbury
Alton
Godalming
North Downs
ENGLAND
River Test
Stockbridge
New Alresford
Hindhead
R. Arun
Crawley
Wincanton
Mere
Salisbury
Winchester
Haslemere
Horsham
Shaftesbury
Romsey
Petersfield
Billingshurst
Eastleigh
Midhurst
Haywards Heath
Sherborne
R. Yeo
Fordingbridge
R. Meon
Yeovil
River Stour
Waterlooville
South Downs
Crewkerne
Southampton
Havant
Hove
North Dorset Downs
Wimborne Minster
Ringwood
Hythe
Littlehampton
Brighton
Axe
Blandford Forum
Fareham
Gosport
Chichester
Worthing
Brockenhurst
Solent
Portsmouth
Bognor Regis
Bridport
Dorchester
Lymington
The
Cowes
Poole
Christchurch
Ryde
Selsey Bill
Wareham
Bournemouth
Newport
River Frome
Yarmouth
Isle of Wight
Shanklin
Lyme Bay
Weymouth
Swanage
Ventnor
St. Catherine's Point
Portland Bill
English Channel
50°N
Alderney
Cap de la Hague
Auderville
Barfleur
Cherbourg
Valognes
Baie de la Seine
Guernsey
Herm
St. Peter Port
Sark
FRANCE
Carteret
Channel Islands
Carentan
Bayeux
St. John
Lessay
Jersey
St. Helier
Caen
St-Lô
Coutances
49°N
1°W
3
2
1
Locator
Key
international boundary
national boundary
motorway
main road
railway
main airport
river
canal
lake
towns
built-up area
largest towns
large towns
other towns
land height
above sea level in metres
more than 1000m
500 – 1000m
200 – 500m
100 – 200m
less than 100 metres
land below sea level
highest peaks with heights in metres
Scale
One centimetre on the map represents 12.5 kilometres on the ground.
0
12.5
25
37.5km
Are the Channel Islands nearer to England or to France?
?

United Kingdom People and cities

The most crowded part of the United Kingdom is between London and Manchester.

Key

Population density

- very crowded
- quite crowded
- quite empty

Cities and towns
numbers of people

- more than 1 000 000
- 400 000 – 1 000 000
- 100 000 – 400 000
- 25 000 – 100 000

Scale

One centimetre on the map represents 45 kilometres on the ground.

0 45 90 135km

How many people live in the UK?

England	51.5 million
Scotland	5.2 million
Wales	3.0 million
N. Ireland	1.8 million
UK total	**61.4 million**

Where people live

If there were 100 people in the United Kingdom, this is where they would live:

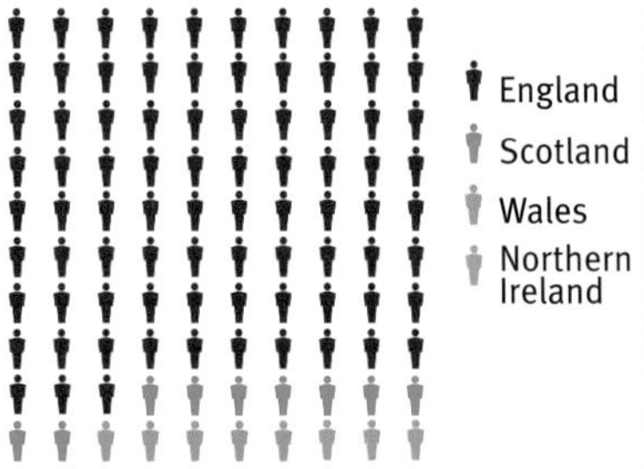

England
Scotland
Wales
Northern Ireland

Population pyramid

If there were 100 people in the United Kingdom, this is how old they would be:

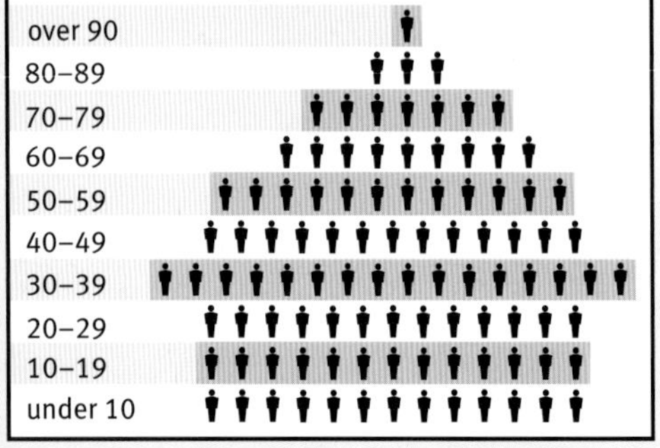

over 90
80–89
70–79
60–69
50–59
40–49
30–39
20–29
10–19
under 10

SCOTLAND
Glasgow
Edinburgh
NORTHERN IRELAND
ENGLAND
Leeds
Liverpool
Manchester
Sheffield
Birmingham
WALES
Bristol
London

Population density

The number of people that live in an area

very crowded

quite crowded

quite empty

Which parts of the UK have the fewest people?

Transverse Mercator Projection

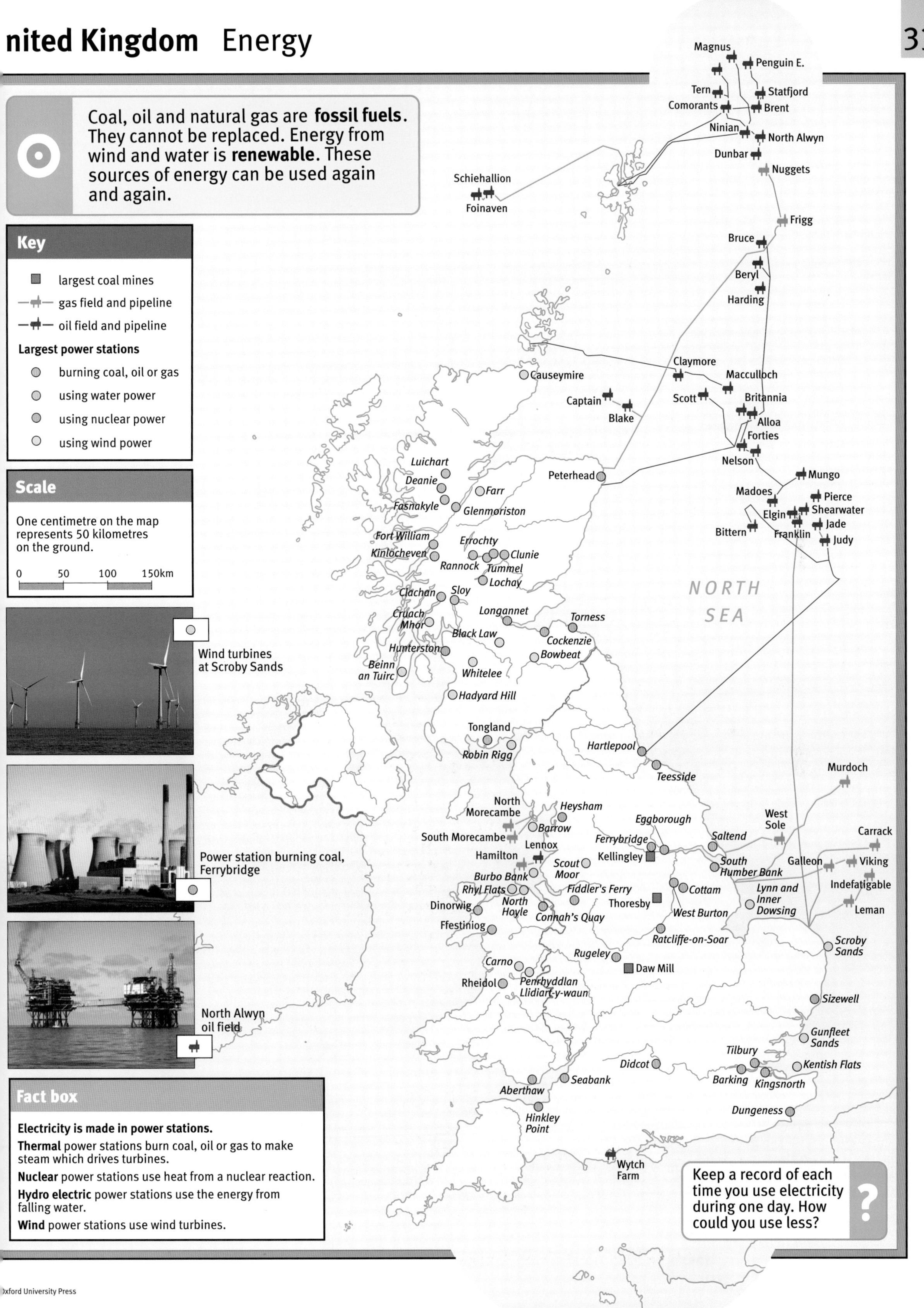
Coal, oil and natural gas are **fossil fuels**. They cannot be replaced. Energy from wind and water is **renewable**. These sources of energy can be used again and again.
Key
largest coal mines
gas field and pipeline
oil field and pipeline
Largest power stations
burning coal, oil or gas
using water power
using nuclear power
using wind power
Scale
One centimetre on the map represents 50 kilometres on the ground.
0 50 100 150km
Wind turbines at Scroby Sands
Power station burning coal, Ferrybridge
North Alwyn oil field
Fact box
Electricity is made in power stations.
Thermal power stations burn coal, oil or gas to make steam which drives turbines.
Nuclear power stations use heat from a nuclear reaction.
Hydro electric power stations use the energy from falling water.
Wind power stations use wind turbines.
Keep a record of each time you use electricity during one day. How could you use less?
?
NORTH SEA
Magnus
Penguin E.
Tern
Statfjord
Comorants
Brent
Ninian
North Alwyn
Dunbar
Nuggets
Schiehallion
Foinaven
Frigg
Bruce
Beryl
Harding
Claymore
Macculloch
Causeymire
Captain
Blake
Scott
Britannia
Alloa
Forties
Nelson
Mungo
Madoes
Pierce
Elgin
Shearwater
Jade
Bittern
Franklin
Judy
Peterhead
Luichart
Deanie
Farr
Fasnakyle
Glenmoriston
Fort William
Errochty
Kinlochevey
Clunie
Rannock
Tummel
Lochay
Clachan
Sloy
Cruach Mhor
Longannet
Torness
Black Law
Cockenzie
Hunterston
Bowbeat
Beinn an Tuirc
Whitelee
Hadyard Hill
Tongland
Robin Rigg
Hartlepool
Teesside
Murdoch
North Morecambe
Heysham
South Morecambe
Barrow
Lennox
Eggborough
West Sole
Saltend
Carrack
Ferrybridge
Hamilton
Kellingley
Scout Moor
South Humber Bank
Galleon
Viking
Burbo Bank
Rhyl Flats
Fiddler's Ferry
Cottam
Lynn and Inner Dowsing
Indefatigable
Dinorwig
North Hoyle
Thoresby
West Burton
Leman
Connah's Quay
Ffestiniog
Ratcliffe-on-Soar
Scroby Sands
Carno
Rugeley
Daw Mill
Rheidol
Penrhyddlan Llidiart-y-waun
Sizewell
Gunfleet Sands
Tilbury
Didcot
Kentish Flats
Seabank
Barking
Kingsnorth
Aberthaw
Dungeness
Hinkley Point
Wytch Farm

United Kingdom Pollution and recycling

Waste, noise and fumes can spoil the environment. Each person in the UK puts about half a tonne of waste in their dustbin each year. The government aims to recycle more of this waste.

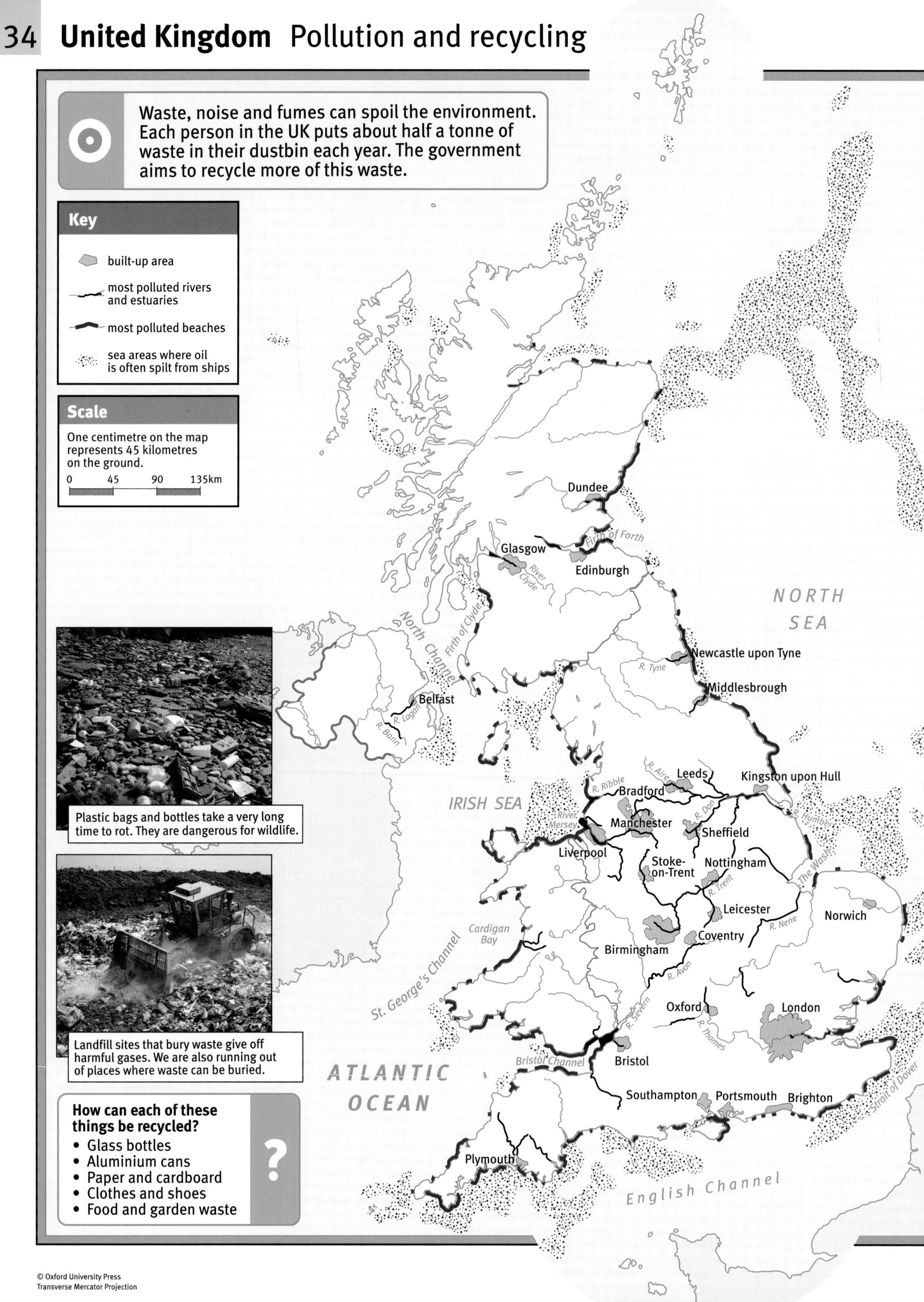
Key
built-up area
most polluted rivers and estuaries
most polluted beaches
sea areas where oil is often spilt from ships
Scale
One centimetre on the map represents 45 kilometres on the ground.
0
45
90
135km
NORTH SEA
IRISH SEA
ATLANTIC OCEAN
English Channel
North Channel
Firth of Clyde
Firth of Forth
St. George's Channel
Cardigan Bay
Bristol Channel
Strait of Dover
The Wash
Dundee
Glasgow
Edinburgh
River Clyde
Belfast
R. Lagan
R. Bann
Newcastle upon Tyne
R. Tyne
Middlesbrough
Leeds
R. Aire
R. Ribble
Bradford
Kingston upon Hull
R. Humber
River Mersey
Liverpool
Manchester
R. Don
Sheffield
Stoke-on-Trent
Nottingham
R. Trent
Leicester
Norwich
R. Nene
Coventry
Birmingham
R. Avon
R. Severn
Oxford
R. Thames
London
Bristol
Southampton
Portsmouth
Brighton
Plymouth

Plastic bags and bottles take a very long time to rot. They are dangerous for wildlife.

Landfill sites that bury waste give off harmful gases. We are also running out of places where waste can be buried.

How can each of these things be recycled?

- Glass bottles
- Aluminium cans
- Paper and cardboard
- Clothes and shoes
- Food and garden waste

?

Transverse Mercator Projection

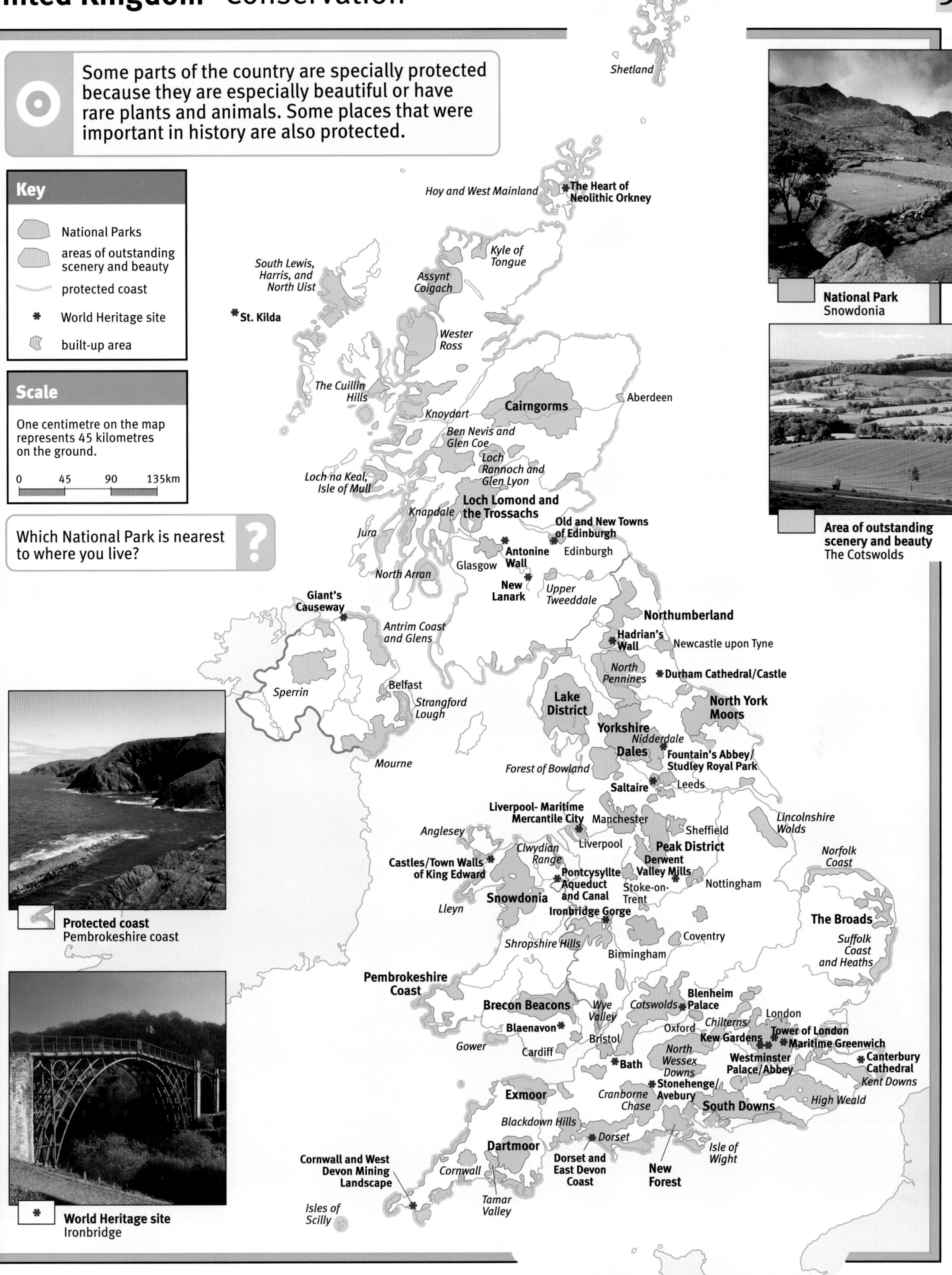
Some parts of the country are specially protected because they are especially beautiful or have rare plants and animals. Some places that were important in history are also protected.
Key
National Parks
areas of outstanding scenery and beauty
protected coast
World Heritage site
built-up area
Scale
One centimetre on the map represents 45 kilometres on the ground.
0 45 90 135km
Which National Park is nearest to where you live?
Shetland
Hoy and West Mainland
The Heart of Neolithic Orkney
Kyle of Tongue
South Lewis, Harris, and North Uist
Assynt Coigach
St. Kilda
Wester Ross
The Cuillin Hills
Knoydart
Cairngorms
Aberdeen
Ben Nevis and Glen Coe
Loch Rannoch and Glen Lyon
Loch na Keal, Isle of Mull
Loch Lomond and the Trossachs
Knapdale
Jura
Old and New Towns of Edinburgh
Edinburgh
Antonine Wall
Glasgow
North Arran
New Lanark
Upper Tweeddale
Giant's Causeway
Antrim Coast and Glens
Northumberland
Hadrian's Wall
Newcastle upon Tyne
North Pennines
Durham Cathedral/Castle
Sperrin
Belfast
Strangford Lough
Lake District
North York Moors
Yorkshire Dales
Nidderdale
Fountain's Abbey/ Studley Royal Park
Mourne
Forest of Bowland
Saltaire
Leeds
Liverpool- Maritime Mercantile City
Manchester
Sheffield
Lincolnshire Wolds
Anglesey
Clwydian Range
Liverpool
Peak District
Norfolk Coast
Castles/Town Walls of King Edward
Derwent Valley Mills
Pontcysyllte Aqueduct and Canal
Nottingham
Stoke-on-Trent
Snowdonia
Lleyn
Ironbridge Gorge
The Broads
Coventry
Shropshire Hills
Birmingham
Suffolk Coast and Heaths
Pembrokeshire Coast
Brecon Beacons
Wye Valley
Cotswolds
Blenheim Palace
London
Chilterns
Blaenavon
Oxford
Kew Gardens
Tower of London
Maritime Greenwich
Gower
Cardiff
Bristol
Westminster Palace/Abbey
Canterbury Cathedral
Bath
North Wessex Downs
Kent Downs
Stonehenge/ Avebury
Exmoor
Cranborne Chase
South Downs
High Weald
Blackdown Hills
Dorset
Dartmoor
Isle of Wight
Cornwall and West Devon Mining Landscape
Cornwall
Dorset and East Devon Coast
New Forest
Tamar Valley
Isles of Scilly

National Park
Snowdonia

Area of outstanding scenery and beauty
The Cotswolds

Protected coast
Pembrokeshire coast

World Heritage site
Ironbridge

Transverse Mercator Projection

United Kingdom Connections

Roads and railways connect places within the UK. Ports, airports and the Channel Tunnel link the UK to the rest of Europe and beyond.

Sullom Voe

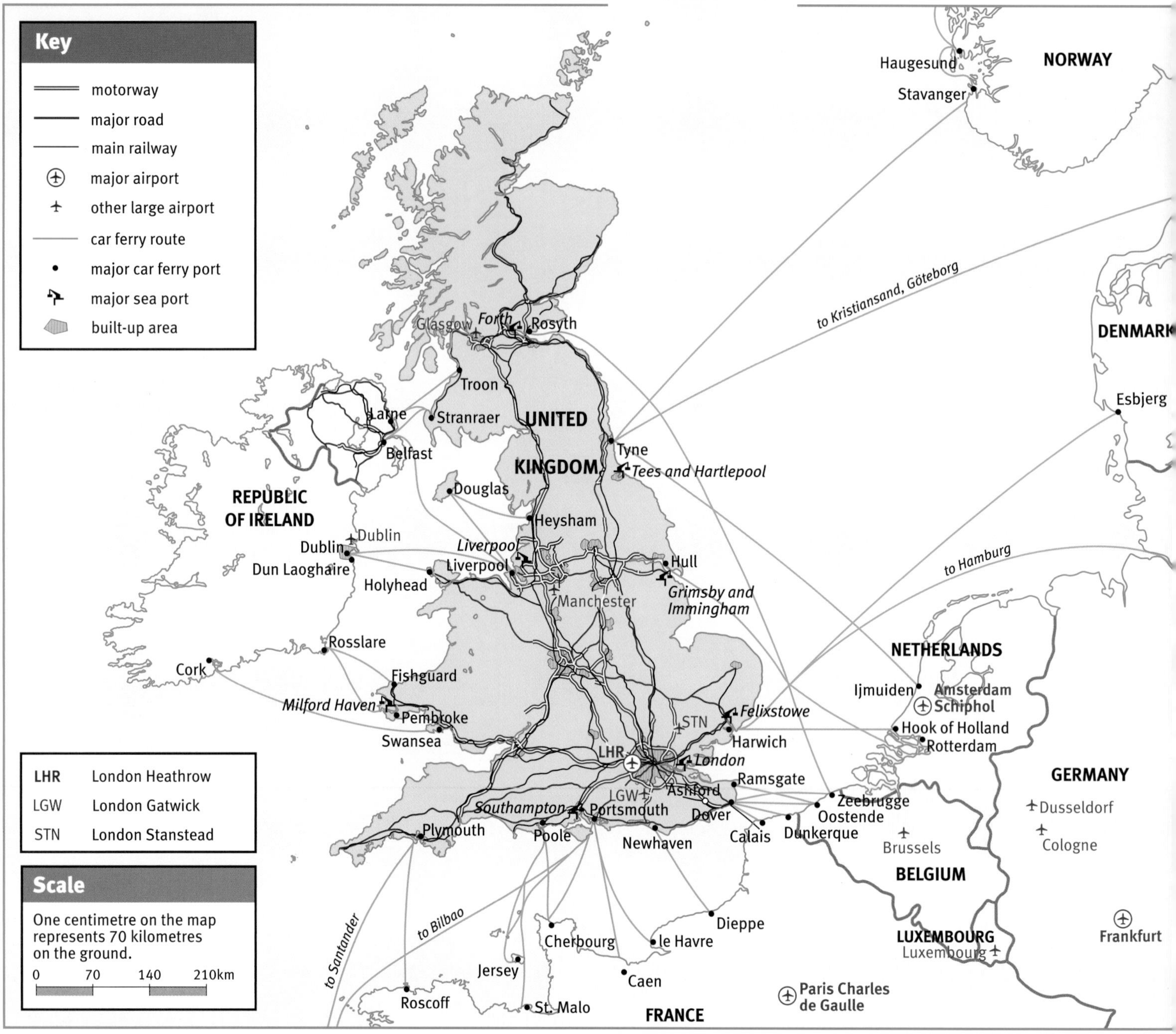

Key

- motorway
- major road
- main railway
- major airport
- other large airport
- car ferry route
- major car ferry port
- major sea port
- built-up area

LHR	London Heathrow
LGW	London Gatwick
STN	London Stanstead

Scale

One centimetre on the map represents 70 kilometres on the ground.

0 70 140 210km

Haugesund
Stavanger
NORWAY
to Kristiansand, Göteborg
DENMARK
Esbjerg
Glasgow
Forth
Rosyth
Troon
Larne
Stranraer
UNITED KINGDOM
Belfast
Tyne
Tees and Hartlepool
REPUBLIC OF IRELAND
Douglas
Heysham
Dublin
Dublin
Dun Laoghaire
Liverpool
Liverpool
Holyhead
Hull
Manchester
Grimsby and Immingham
to Hamburg
Rosslare
Cork
Fishguard
Milford Haven
Pembroke
Swansea
NETHERLANDS
Ijmuiden
Amsterdam Schiphol
Felixstowe
STN
Harwich
Hook of Holland
Rotterdam
LHR
London
Ramsgate
GERMANY
LGW
Ashford
Zeebrugge
Southampton
Portsmouth
Dover
Oostende
Dusseldorf
Plymouth
Poole
Newhaven
Calais
Dunkerque
Brussels
Cologne
BELGIUM
to Santander
to Bilbao
Dieppe
Cherbourg
le Havre
LUXEMBOURG
Luxembourg
Frankfurt
Jersey
Caen
Roscoff
St. Malo
FRANCE
Paris Charles de Gaulle

Major car ferry port, Dover.

Major airport, London Heathrow.

Channel Tunnel terminal, Ashford.

If you were going to travel to France, which way would you go?

Transverse Mercator Projection

United Kingdom Holidays and tourism

Holidays are time off work or school. **Tourism** is travelling to other places for a holiday.

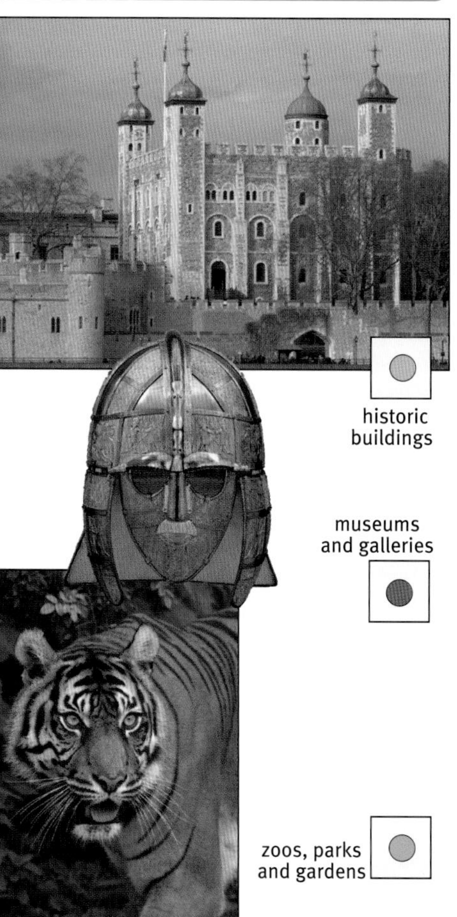

historic buildings

museums and galleries

zoos, parks and gardens

theme parks and piers

Top UK tourist attractions

Key

Symbol **colour** shows the type of tourist attraction

- historic buildings
- museums and galleries
- zoos, parks and gardens
- theme parks and piers

Symbol **size** shows how many people visit each year

- over 2 million visitors
- 1–2 million visitors
- under 1 million visitors
- built-up area

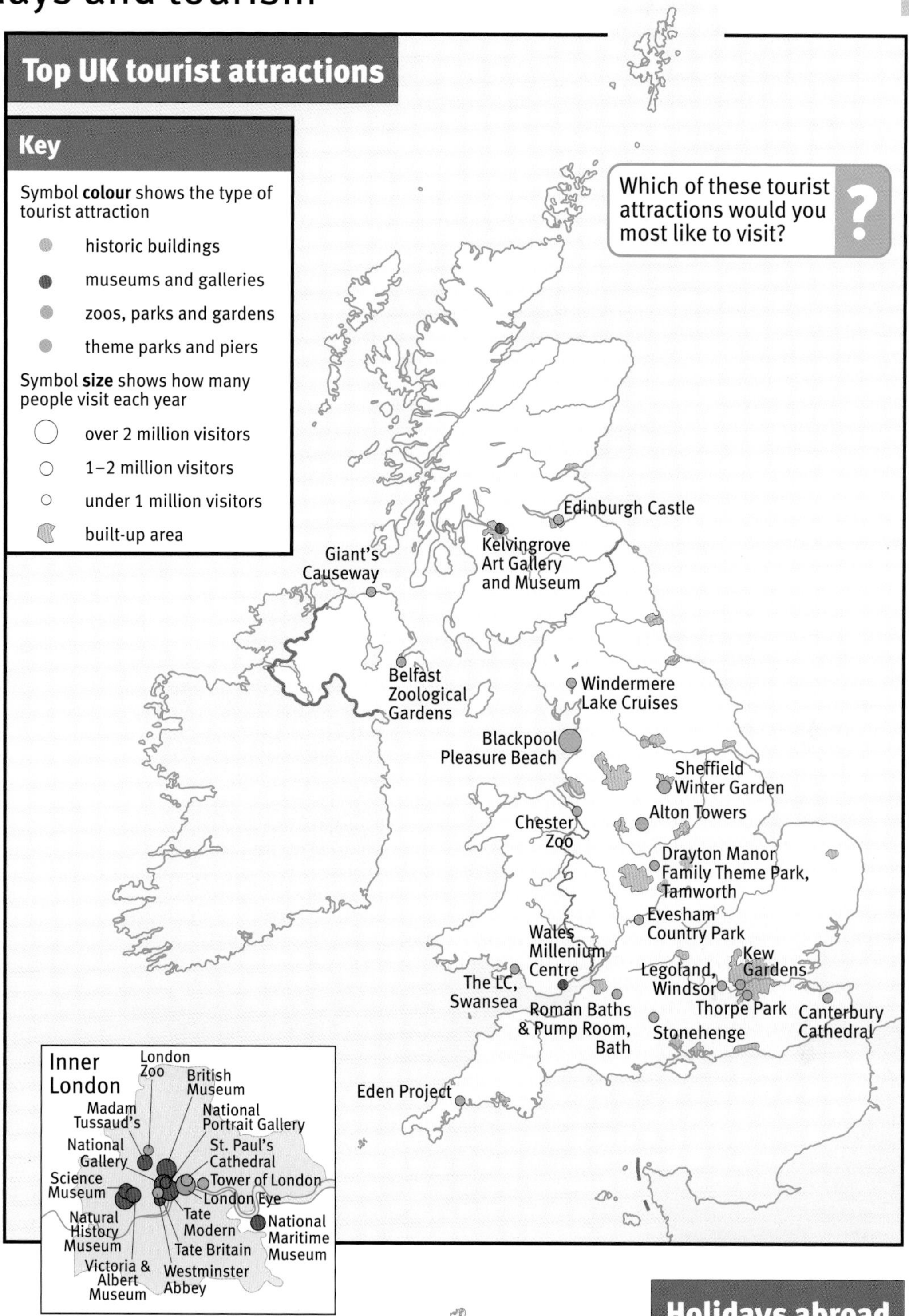

Which of these tourist attractions would you most like to visit?

Edinburgh Castle

Kelvingrove Art Gallery and Museum

Giant's Causeway

Belfast Zoological Gardens

Windermere Lake Cruises

Blackpool Pleasure Beach

Sheffield Winter Garden

Alton Towers

Chester Zoo

Drayton Manor Family Theme Park, Tamworth

Evesham Country Park

Wales Millenium Centre

The LC, Swansea

Legoland, Windsor

Kew Gardens

Roman Baths & Pump Room, Bath

Thorpe Park

Stonehenge

Canterbury Cathedral

Eden Project

Inner London

London Zoo

British Museum

Madam Tussaud's

National Portrait Gallery

National Gallery

St. Paul's Cathedral

Science Museum

Tower of London

London Eye

Natural History Museum

Tate Modern

National Maritime Museum

Tate Britain

Victoria & Albert Museum

Westminster Abbey

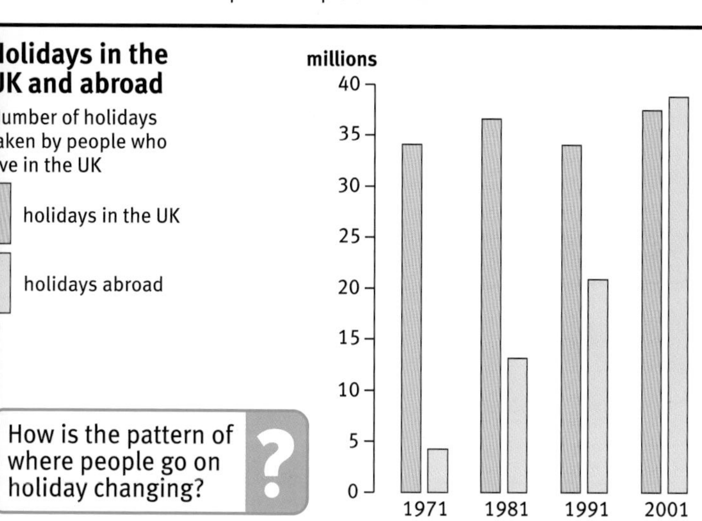

Holidays in the UK and abroad
Number of holidays taken by people who live in the UK
holidays in the UK
holidays abroad
millions
40
35
30
25
20
15
10
5
0
1971
1981
1991
2001

How is the pattern of where people go on holiday changing?

Holidays abroad

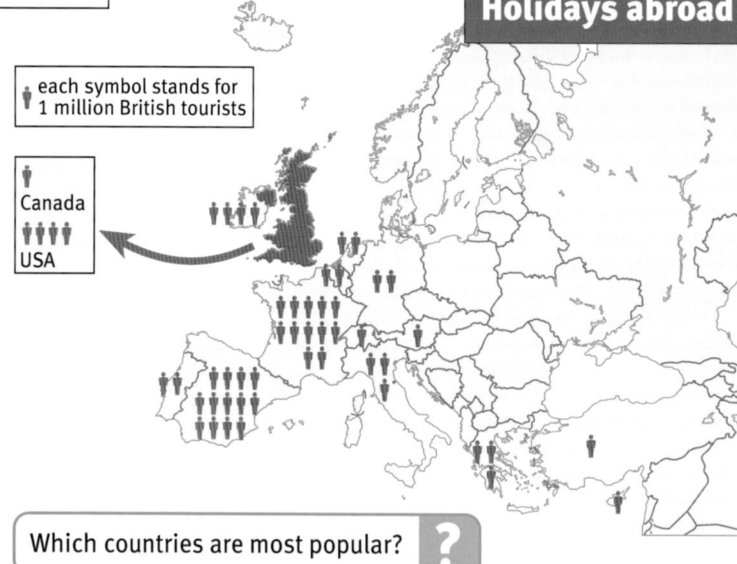

each symbol stands for 1 million British tourists
Canada
USA

Which countries are most popular?

Europe is a continent of peninsulas and islands. The Ural Mountains form its eastern boundary.
A
B
C
D
E
F
3
2
1
20°W
0°
20°E
40°E
60°E
60°N
40°N
Prime Meridian
GREENLAND SEA
Iceland
1491m Mount Hekla
N
Faroe Islands
Shetland Islands
Orkney Islands
ATLANTIC OCEAN
Ireland
Great Britain
NORTH SEA
Lofoten Islands
Scandinavia
Lappland
Kola Peninsula
WHITE SEA
Gulf of Bothnia
Lake Vänern
Lake Vättern
Gotland
BALTIC SEA
Jylland
Bornholm
Friesian Islands
R. Thames
English Channel
River Elbe
R. Rhine
River Oder
R. Vistula
North European Plain
Lake Onega
Lake Ladoga
Lake Peipus
Rybinsk Reservoir
River North Dvina
R. Pechora
River Ob
URAL MOUNTAINS
Central Russian Uplands
River Dniepr
River Volga
River Don
River Donets
R. Dniester
CARPATHIANS
Hungarian Basin
2548m
SEA OF AZOV
CASPIAN SEA
CAUCASUS
5642m Mt. Elbrus
BLACK SEA
River Danube
River Seine
River Loire
Bay of Biscay
Cape Finisterre
Cantabrian Mts.
Jura
4807m Mont Blanc
ALPS
Massif Central
River Rhône
River Po
Pyrénées
River Ebro
River Duero
R. Tagus
Cape St. Vincent
Balearic Islands
Ibiza
Mallorca
Menorca
Corsica
Sardinia
APPENNINES
Dinaric Alps
ADRIATIC SEA
Pindus Mountains
2917m Mt. Olympus
AEGEAN SEA
TYRRHENIAN SEA
IONIAN SEA
Mt. Etna 3323m
Sicily
Malta
Peloponnese
Crete
Rhodes
Cyprus
MEDITERRANEAN SEA
Anatolian Plateau
Taurus Mountains
5123m Mt. Ararat
Lake Van
Key
land height in metres above sea level
more than 2000m
1000 – 2000m
500 – 1000m
200 – 500m
less than 200 metres
land below sea level
highest peaks with heights in metres
lake
river
Fact box
area: 10 214 392km²
highest point: Mt. Elbrus 5 642m
lowest point: Caspian Sea 28m below sea level
longest river: River Volga 3 688km
Scale
One centimetre on the map represents 240 kilometres on the ground.
0 240 480 720km
Can you name the water that separates Great Britain from France?
?

Conical Orthomorphic Projection

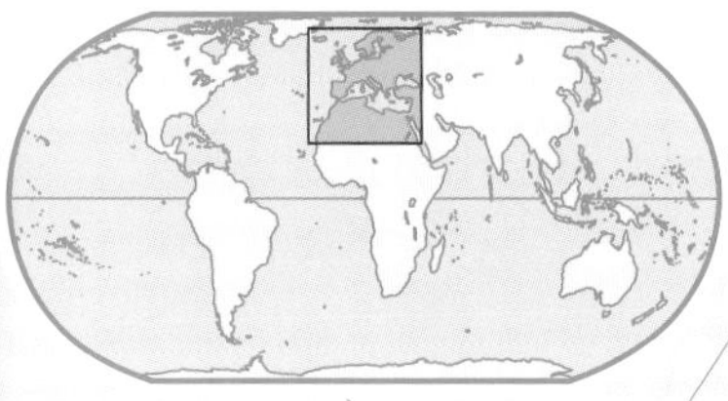

Europeans have settled all over the world and European languages can be heard in every other continent.

Key

- colours show countries
- ITALY — country names are labelled like this
- ■ capital cities
- ● other important cities

Fact box

population:	655 884 785 people *
largest country:	Ukraine 603 698km^2
country with most people:	Germany 82 698 000
largest city:	Istanbul, Turkey 9 946 000

* does not include Russian Federation

Many languages are spoken in Europe How many can you name?

Northern Europe

Low, flat land and shallow seas stretch all the way from the UK to Moscow and beyond.

A
B
C
D
E
1
2
3
30°W
20°W
10°W
0°
10°E
70°N
60°N
50°N
Prime Meridian
Arctic Circle
Ísafjördur
Reykjavik
ICELAND
Akureyri
Mount Hekla
1491
Höfn
NORWEGIAN SEA
Vesteralen Is.
Lofoten Is.
Bodo
NORWAY
SWEDEN
Scandinavia
Trondheim
Galdhopiggen
2470m
R. Glama
R. Indals
Bergen
Oslo
Stavanger
Lake Vänern
Lake Vättern
Stockhol
Uppsa
Jönköping
Göteborg
Faroe Islands (Den.)
Shetland Islands
Orkney Islands
Outer Hebrides
ATLANTIC OCEAN
Inverness
1344m
Ben Nevis
Aberdeen
Dundee
Glasgow
Edinburgh
Belfast
Galway
REPUBLIC OF IRELAND
Dublin
Cork
Newcastle upon Tyne
UNITED KINGDOM
Manchester
Liverpool
Leeds
Birmingham
Cardiff
Bristol
Norwich
London
Plymouth
Land's End
Isles of Scilly
Southampton
R. Thames
Strait of Dover
English Channel
Channel Islands
NORTH SEA
Skagerrak
Kattegat
Ålborg
DENMARK
Århus
Copenhagen
Malmö
Odense
Bornholm
Kiel
Rostock
Frisian Is.
Hamburg
NETHERLANDS
Amsterdam
The Hague
Rotterdam
Bremen
R. Elbe
Szczecin
Berlin
Hannover
Pozna
R. Oder
Essen
Antwerp
Calais
BELGIUM
Lille
Brussels
Düsseldorf
Cologne
Bonn
Leipzig
Wroclaw
Dresden
GERMANY
Frankfurt-am-Main
LUXEMBOURG
Luxembourg
R. Rhine
Prague
CZECH RE
Brno
Nuremberg
Stuttgart
River Danube
Munich
Salzburg
Linz
Bratisl
Vienna
AUSTRIA
Innsbruck
LIECHTENSTEIN
Zürich
Basel
SWITZERLAND
Bern
Strasbourg
Nancy
Reims
Brest
le Havre
Rouen
Paris
Rennes
le Mans
Orléans
Tours
Nantes
River Loire
River Seine
River Saône
Dijon
FRANCE
Bay of Biscay
Öl
Conical Orthomorphic Projection

Norway's fiords are long narrow fingers of sea between steep mountains.

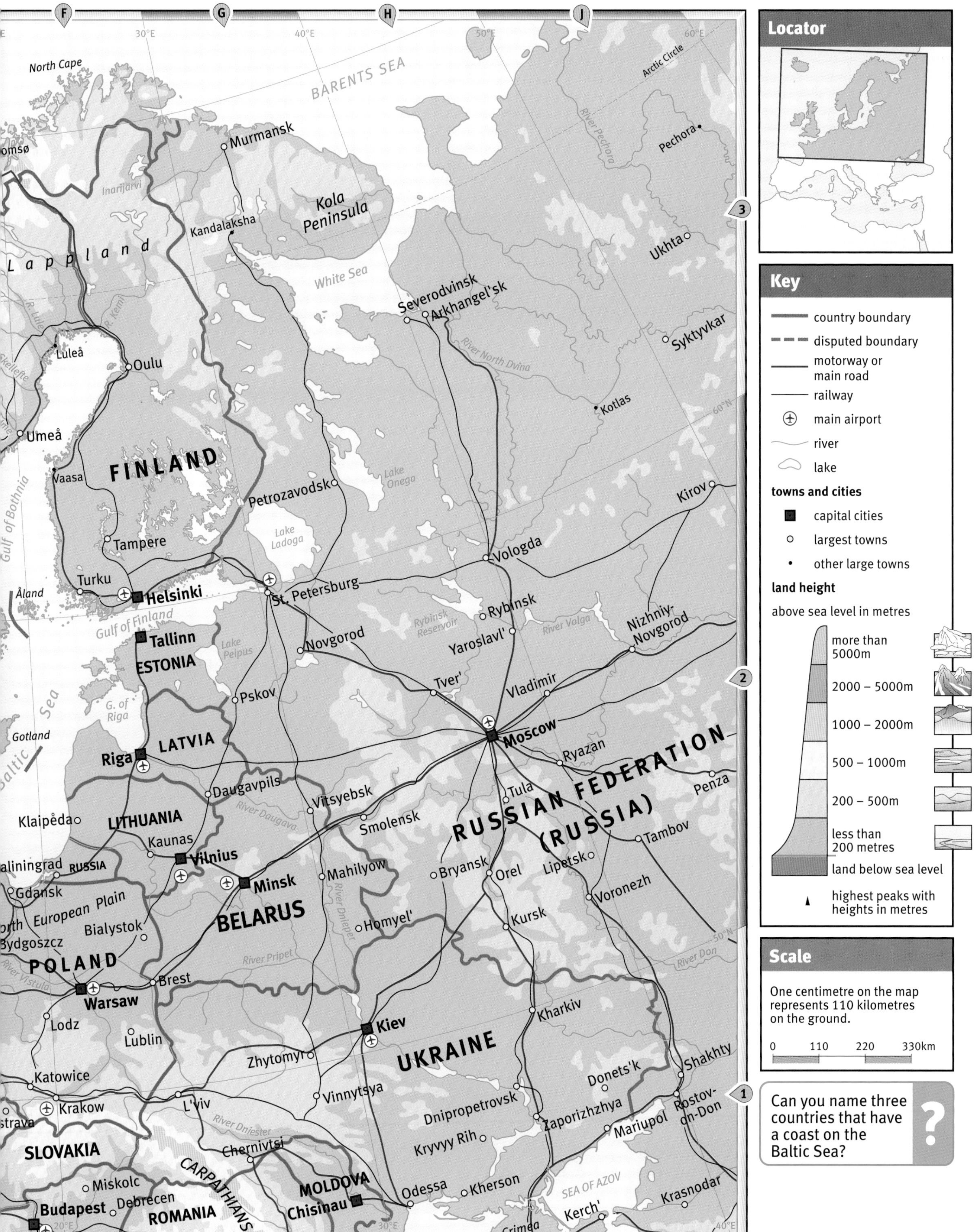
North Cape
BARENTS SEA
Arctic Circle
Murmansk
Inarijärvi
Kola Peninsula
Kandalaksha
Lappland
White Sea
Severodvinsk
Arkhangel'sk
River North Dvina
River Pechora
Pechora
Ukhta
Syktyvkar
Kotlas
Luleå
Oulu
Umeå
Vaasa
FINLAND
Gulf of Bothnia
Petrozavodsk
Lake Onega
Lake Ladoga
Tampere
Turku
Åland
Helsinki
Gulf of Finland
St. Petersburg
Vologda
Kirov
Rybinsk Reservoir
Rybinsk
Yaroslavl'
River Volga
Nizhniy-Novgorod
Novgorod
Tallinn
ESTONIA
Lake Peipus
G. of Riga
Pskov
Tver'
Vladimir
Moscow
Ryazan
Gotland
Riga
LATVIA
RUSSIAN FEDERATION (RUSSIA)
Penza
Daugavpils
River Daugava
Vitsyebsk
Smolensk
Tula
Tambov
Klaipėda
LITHUANIA
Kaunas
Vilnius
Kaliningrad
RUSSIA
Minsk
Mahilyow
Bryansk
Orel
Lipetsk
Voronezh
Gdansk
European Plain
Bialystok
Bydgoszcz
BELARUS
River Dnieper
Homyel'
Kursk
POLAND
River Vistula
River Pripet
River Don
Brest
Warsaw
Lodz
Lublin
Kiev
Kharkiv
UKRAINE
Zhytomyr
Shakhty
Katowice
Donets'k
Krakow
L'viv
Vinnytsya
Dnipropetrovsk
Zaporizhzhya
Mariupol
Rostov-on-Don
River Dniester
SLOVAKIA
Chernivtsi
Kryvyy Rih
CARPATHIANS
Miskolc
Debrecen
MOLDOVA
Chisinau
Odessa
Kherson
SEA OF AZOV
Krasnodar
Budapest
ROMANIA
Kerch'
Crimea
30°E
40°E
50°E
60°E
60°N
50°N
20°E
F
G
H
J
1
2
3

Locator

Key

country boundary
disputed boundary
motorway or main road
railway
main airport
river
lake

towns and cities

capital cities
largest towns
other large towns

land height

above sea level in metres

more than 5000m
2000 – 5000m
1000 – 2000m
500 – 1000m
200 – 500m
less than 200 metres
land below sea level
highest peaks with heights in metres

Scale

One centimetre on the map represents 110 kilometres on the ground.

0 110 220 330km

Can you name three countries that have a coast on the Baltic Sea?

A
B
C
D
3
2
UNITED KINGDOM
London
Norwich
Cardiff
Bristol
Plymouth
Southampton
Land's End
Isles of Scilly
English Channel
Strait of Dover
Channel Islands
R. Thames
50°N
10°W
10°E
Frisian Is.
NETHERLANDS
Amsterdam
The Hague
Rotterdam
Antwerp
BELGIUM
Brussels
Calais
Lille
Essen
Düsseldorf
Cologne
Bonn
LUXEMBOURG
Luxembourg
GERMANY
Kiel
Rostock
Hamburg
Bremen
R. Elbe
Hannover
Berlin
Szczecin
Poznań
R. Oder
Leipzig
Dresden
Wroclaw
Frankfurt-am-Main
R. Rhine
Nuremberg
Stuttgart
River Danube
Munich
Prague
CZECH REP.
Brno
Linz
Salzburg
Bratislava
Vienna
AUSTRIA
Innsbruck
Graz
LIECHTENSTEIN
Basel
Zürich
Bern
SWITZERLAND
Lake Geneva
Geneva
4807m
Mont Blanc
ALPS
Ljubljana
SLOVENIA
Zagreb
CROATIA
Dinaric Alps
Split
FRANCE
Brest
le Havre
Rouen
Reims
Paris
Rennes
le Mans
Nancy
Strasbourg
Orléans
Tours
Nantes
River Loire
R. Seine
Dijon
River Saône
Bay of Biscay
Limoges
Clermont-Ferrand
Lyons
St-Étienne
MASSIF CENTRAL
Grenoble
River Rhône
R. Dordogne
Bordeaux
R. Garonne
Toulouse
Nîmes
Avignon
Marseilles
Nice
MONACO
PYRÉNÉES
ANDORRA
SPAIN
A Coruña
Cape Finisterre
Gijón
Oviedo
Santander
Bilbao
San Sebastián
Vigo
Cantabrian Mts.
León
Valladolid
River Douro
River Duero
Oporto
River Ebro
Zaragoza
PORTUGAL
Coimbra
Madrid
Barcelona
Lisbon
River Tagus
River Guadiana
Valencia
Sierra Morena
Seville
River Guadalquivir
Faro
Cape St. Vincent
Jerez de la Frontera
Cádiz
Murcia
Alicante
Sierra Nevada
Cartagena
Málaga
Gibraltar (UK)
Balearic Islands
Menorca
Mallorca
Palma
Ibiza
ITALY
Milan
Turin
River Po
Venice
Verona
Trieste
Módena
Genoa
Bologna
SAN MARINO
Florence
Elba
APPENNINES
ADRIATIC SEA
Corsica (France)
Ajaccio
Rome
Naples
Vesuvius 1277m
Salerno
Bari
Taranto
Sardinia (Italy)
Sassari
Cagliari
TYRRHENIAN SEA
Palermo
Messina
Reggio Calabria
Sicily
Mt Etna 3323m
Catania
MALTA
Valletta
MEDITERRANEAN
Tangier
Ceuta (Sp.)
Tétouan
Melilla (Sp.)
Oran
Algiers
Blida
Bejaïa
Skikda
Annaba
Bizerte
Tunis
Constantine
Sétif
Ech Cheliff
Sidi-Bel-Abbès
Oudja
Fès
Meknès
MOROCCO
ATLAS MOUNTAINS
Bou Saâda
Djelfa
El Bayadh
Bouârfa
Aïn Sefra
Béchar
Prime Meridian
0°
Tébessa
Biskra
TUNISIA
Sousse
Sfax
Gafsa
Tozeur
Gabès
Touggourt
Hassi Messaoud
ALGERIA
El Golea
30°N
Tripoli
Misratah
Sirt
LIBYA

The countries of southern Europe share a coastline on the Mediterranean Sea.

Hot, dry summers make the Mediterranean coast a popular choice for holidays.

Conical Orthomorphic Projection

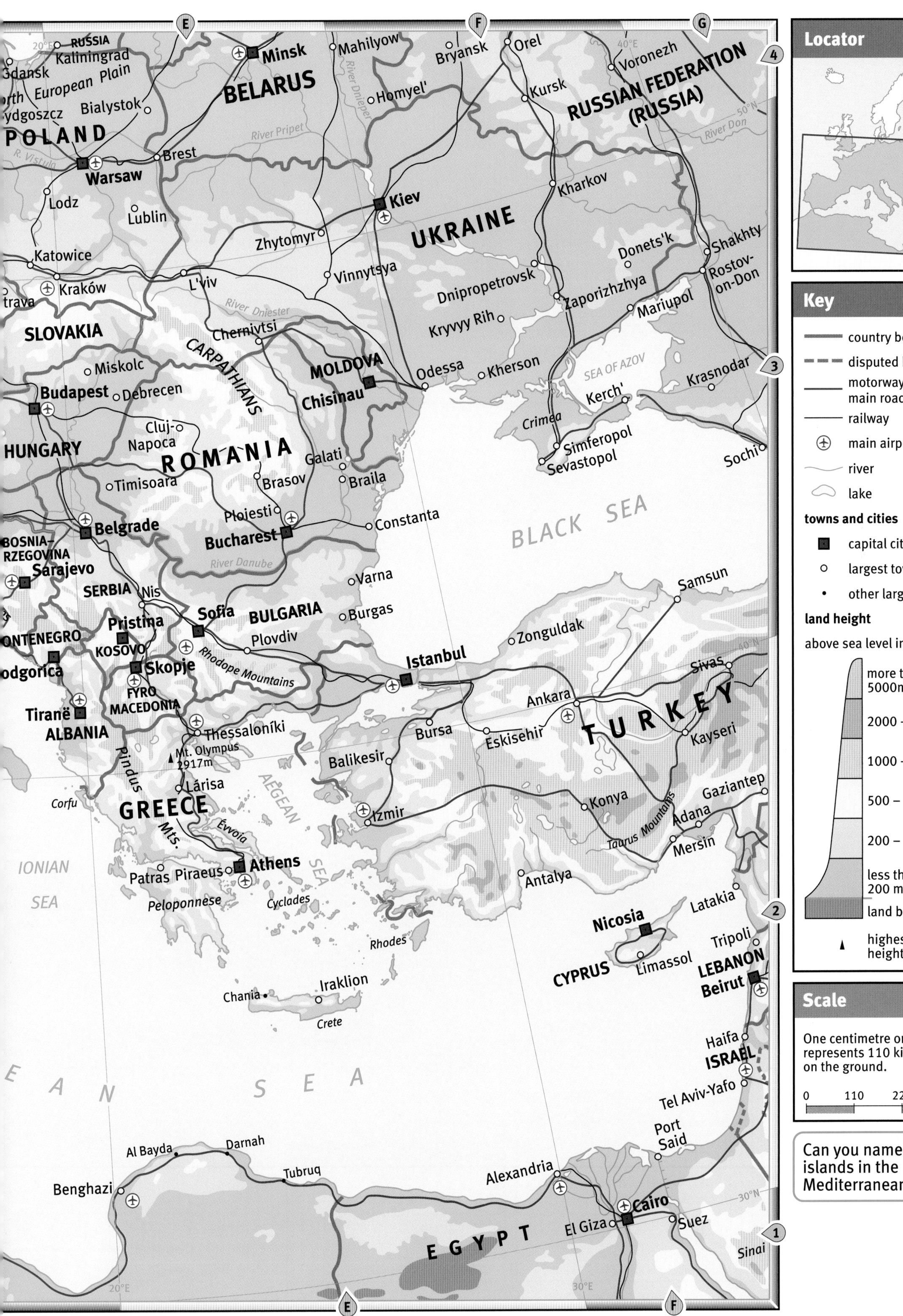

E
F
G
4
3
2
1
RUSSIA
Kaliningrad
Gdansk
North European Plain
Bydgoszcz
Bialystok
POLAND
R. Vistula
Warsaw
Brest
Lodz
Lublin
Katowice
Kraków
Ostrava
SLOVAKIA
Minsk
BELARUS
Mahilyow
River Dnieper
Homyel'
River Pripet
Bryansk
Orel
Kursk
Voronezh
RUSSIAN FEDERATION (RUSSIA)
River Don
Kiev
Kharkov
UKRAINE
Zhytomyr
Vinnytsya
L'viv
River Dniester
Chernivtsi
Dnipropetrovsk
Zaporizhzhya
Donets'k
Shakhty
Rostov-on-Don
Mariupol
Kryvyy Rih
Odessa
Kherson
SEA OF AZOV
Krasnodar
Kerch'
Crimea
Simferopol
Sevastopol
Sochi
MOLDOVA
Chisinau
CARPATHIANS
Miskolc
Budapest
Debrecen
HUNGARY
Cluj-Napoca
ROMANIA
Galati
Braila
Brasov
Timisoara
Ploiesti
Bucharest
Constanta
River Danube
Belgrade
BOSNIA-HERZEGOVINA
Sarajevo
SERBIA
Nis
Sofia
BULGARIA
Varna
Burgas
Plovdiv
Pristina
KOSOVO
MONTENEGRO
Podgorica
Skopje
FYRO MACEDONIA
Rhodope Mountains
Tiranë
ALBANIA
BLACK SEA
Samsun
Zonguldak
Istanbul
Sivas
Ankara
TURKEY
Bursa
Eskisehir
Kayseri
Balikesir
Thessaloníki
Mt. Olympus 2917m
Pindus Mts.
Lárisa
Corfu
GREECE
AEGEAN SEA
Évvoia
Izmir
Konya
Gaziantep
Adana
Taurus Mountains
Mersin
IONIAN SEA
Patras
Piraeus
Athens
Antalya
Peloponnese
Cyclades
Rhodes
Latakia
Nicosia
CYPRUS
Limassol
Tripoli
LEBANON
Beirut
Chania
Iraklion
Crete
Haifa
ISRAEL
Tel Aviv-Yafo
MEDITERRANEAN SEA
Port Said
Al Bayda
Darnah
Tubruq
Benghazi
Alexandria
Cairo
El Giza
Suez
EGYPT
Sinai
20°E
30°E
40°E
50°N
40°N
30°N

Locator

Key

- country boundary
- disputed boundary
- motorway or main road
- railway
- main airport
- river
- lake

towns and cities

- capital cities
- largest towns
- other large towns

land height

above sea level in metres

- more than 5000m
- 2000 – 5000m
- 1000 – 2000m
- 500 – 1000m
- 200 – 500m
- less than 200 metres
- land below sea level
- highest peaks with heights in metres

Scale

One centimetre on the map represents 110 kilometres on the ground.

0 110 220 330km

Can you name six islands in the Mediterranean Sea? ?

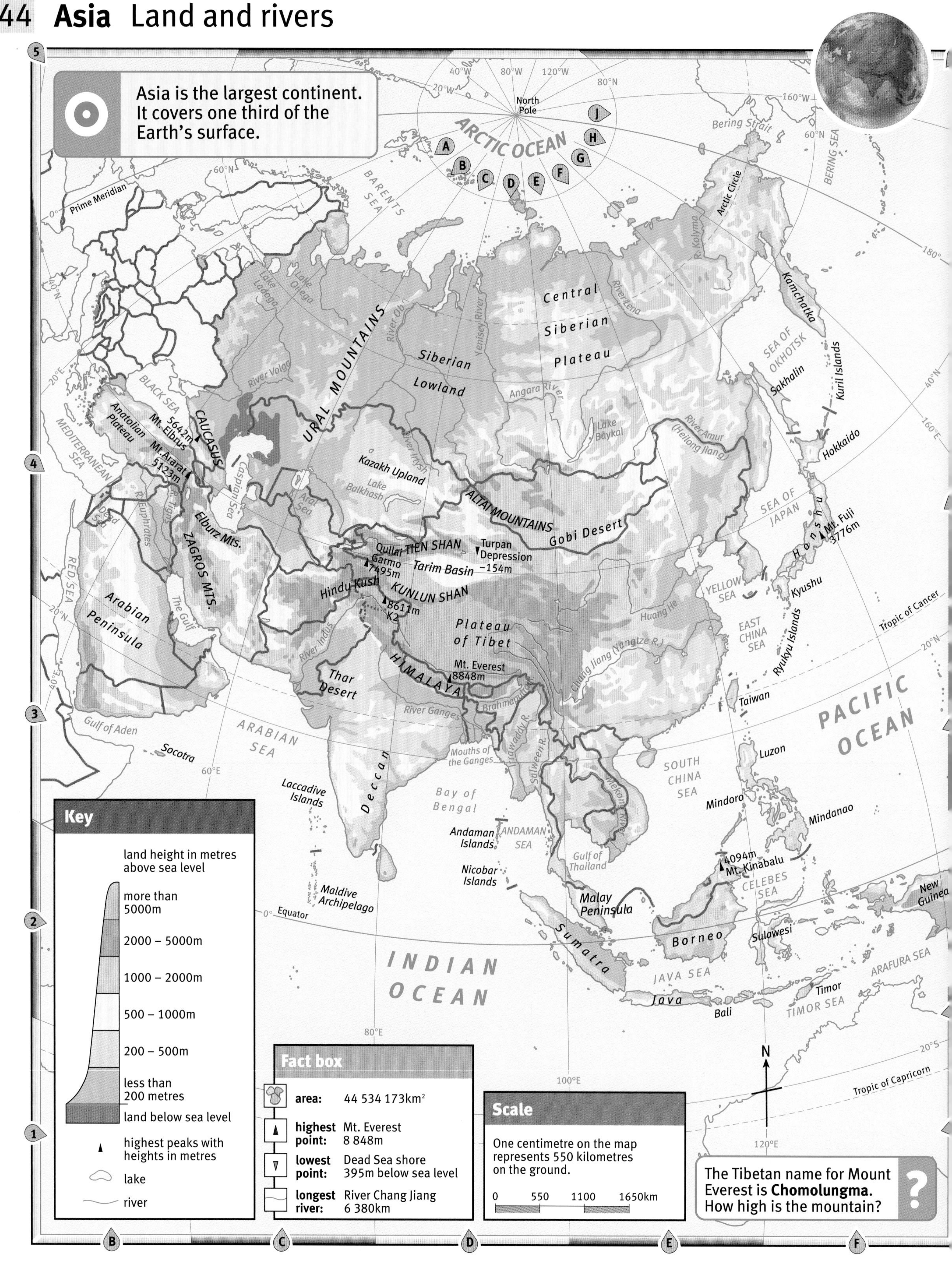
Asia is the largest continent. It covers one third of the Earth's surface.
North Pole
ARCTIC OCEAN
A
B
C
D
E
F
G
H
J
40°W
80°W
120°W
20°W
80°N
60°N
160°W
Bering Strait
BERING SEA
Arctic Circle
BARENTS SEA
Prime Meridian
0°
40°N
20°E
40°E
180°
160°E
R. Kolyma
Kamchatka
River Lena
Central Siberian Plateau
Yenisey River
River Ob
Lake Onega
Lake Ladoga
URAL MOUNTAINS
Siberian Lowland
River Volga
BLACK SEA
Angara River
Lake Baykal
SEA OF OKHOTSK
Sakhalin
Kuril Islands
River Amur (Heilong Jiang)
Hokkaido
MEDITERRANEAN SEA
Anatolian Plateau
5642m Mt. Elbrus
CAUCASUS
Mt. Ararat 5123m
Caspian Sea
River Irtysh
Kazakh Upland
Lake Balkhash
Aral Sea
ALTAI MOUNTAINS
Gobi Desert
SEA OF JAPAN
Honshu
Mt. Fuji 3776m
Dead Sea
R. Euphrates
R. Tigris
Elburz Mts.
ZAGROS MTS.
Qullai Garmo 7495m
TIEN SHAN
Turpan Depression −154m
Tarim Basin
RED SEA
Arabian Peninsula
The Gulf
Hindu Kush
KUNLUN SHAN
8611m K2
YELLOW SEA
Kyushu
20°N
River Indus
Plateau of Tibet
Huang He
EAST CHINA SEA
Ryukyu Islands
Tropic of Cancer
Chang Jiang (Yangtze R.)
HIMALAYA
Mt. Everest 8848m
Thar Desert
Taiwan
Brahmaputra
River Ganges
PACIFIC OCEAN
Gulf of Aden
ARABIAN SEA
Socotra
60°E
Irrawaddy R.
Salween R.
Mouths of the Ganges
Mekong River
SOUTH CHINA SEA
Luzon
Laccadive Islands
Deccan
Bay of Bengal
Mindoro
Andaman Islands
ANDAMAN SEA
Mindanao
Gulf of Thailand
4094m Mt. Kinabalu
Nicobar Islands
CELEBES SEA
Maldive Archipelago
Malay Peninsula
New Guinea
0° Equator
Sumatra
Borneo
Sulawesi
INDIAN OCEAN
JAVA SEA
ARAFURA SEA
Java
Bali
Timor
TIMOR SEA
80°E
100°E
120°E
20°S
Tropic of Capricorn
N
Key
land height in metres above sea level
more than 5000m
2000 – 5000m
1000 – 2000m
500 – 1000m
200 – 500m
less than 200 metres
land below sea level
highest peaks with heights in metres
lake
river
Fact box
area: 44 534 173km²
highest point: Mt. Everest 8 848m
lowest point: Dead Sea shore 395m below sea level
longest river: River Chang Jiang 6 380km
Scale
One centimetre on the map represents 550 kilometres on the ground.
0 550 1100 1650km
The Tibetan name for Mount Everest is Chomolungma. How high is the mountain?
?
1
2
3
4
5
B
C
D
E
F

Zenithal Equal Area Projection

Of all the continents, Asia has the greatest variety of landscapes and cultures.

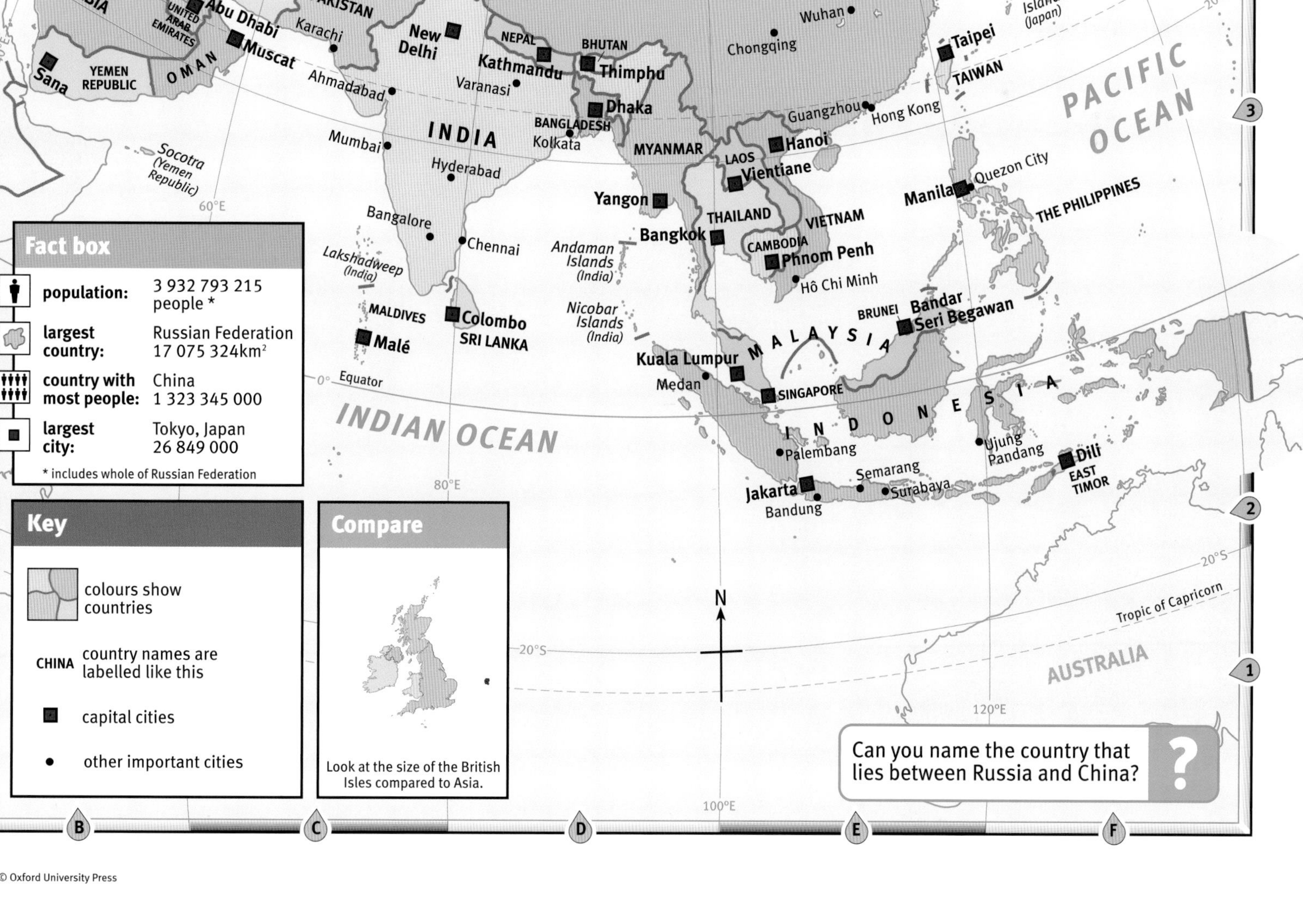
RUSSIAN FEDERATION
(RUSSIA)
ARCTIC OCEAN
North Pole
Prime Meridian
Arctic Circle
KAZAKHSTAN
MONGOLIA
CHINA
INDIA
PACIFIC OCEAN
INDIAN OCEAN
INDONESIA
MALAYSIA
AUSTRALIA
Tropic of Cancer
Tropic of Capricorn
Equator
Moscow
St. Petersburg
Nizhniy-Novgorod
Perm
Chelyabinsk
Omsk
Novosibirsk
Volgograd
Astana
Ulan Bator
Beijing
Tianjin
Harbin
Shenyang
Pyongyang
Seoul
Pusan
Tokyo
Osaka
Fukuoka
Sapporo
Lanzhou
Xi'an
Shanghai
Wuhan
Chongqing
Taipei
Guangzhou
Hong Kong
Hanoi
Vientiane
Yangon
Bangkok
Phnom Penh
Hô Chi Minh
Manila
Quezon City
Bandar Seri Begawan
Kuala Lumpur
Medan
SINGAPORE
Palembang
Jakarta
Bandung
Semarang
Surabaya
Ujung Pandang
Dili
EAST TIMOR
New Delhi
Kathmandu
Thimphu
Dhaka
Kolkata
Varanasi
Mumbai
Hyderabad
Bangalore
Chennai
Colombo
SRI LANKA
Malé
MALDIVES
Islamabad
Lahore
Karachi
Ahmadabad
Kabul
Tashkent
Bishkek
Almaty
Dushanbe
Ashgabat
Tehran
Mashhad
Esfahan
Shiraz
Tabriz
Baku
Yerevan
T'bilisi
Ankara
Istanbul
Adana
Aleppo
Damascus
Beirut
Jerusalem
Amman
Baghdad
Kuwait
Manama
Riyadh
Doha
Abu Dhabi
Muscat
Sana
Jedda
Ürümqi
Lakshadweep (India)
Andaman Islands (India)
Nicobar Islands (India)
Socotra (Yemen Republic)
Kuril Islands (Russia)
Ryukyu Islands (Japan)
KALININGRAD (Russia)
Jammu & Kashmir
Fact box
population: 3 932 793 215 people *
largest country: Russian Federation 17 075 324km²
country with most people: China 1 323 345 000
largest city: Tokyo, Japan 26 849 000
* includes whole of Russian Federation
Key
colours show countries
CHINA country names are labelled like this
capital cities
other important cities
Compare
Look at the size of the British Isles compared to Asia.

Can you name the country that lies between Russia and China?

India, Pakistan and Bangladesh

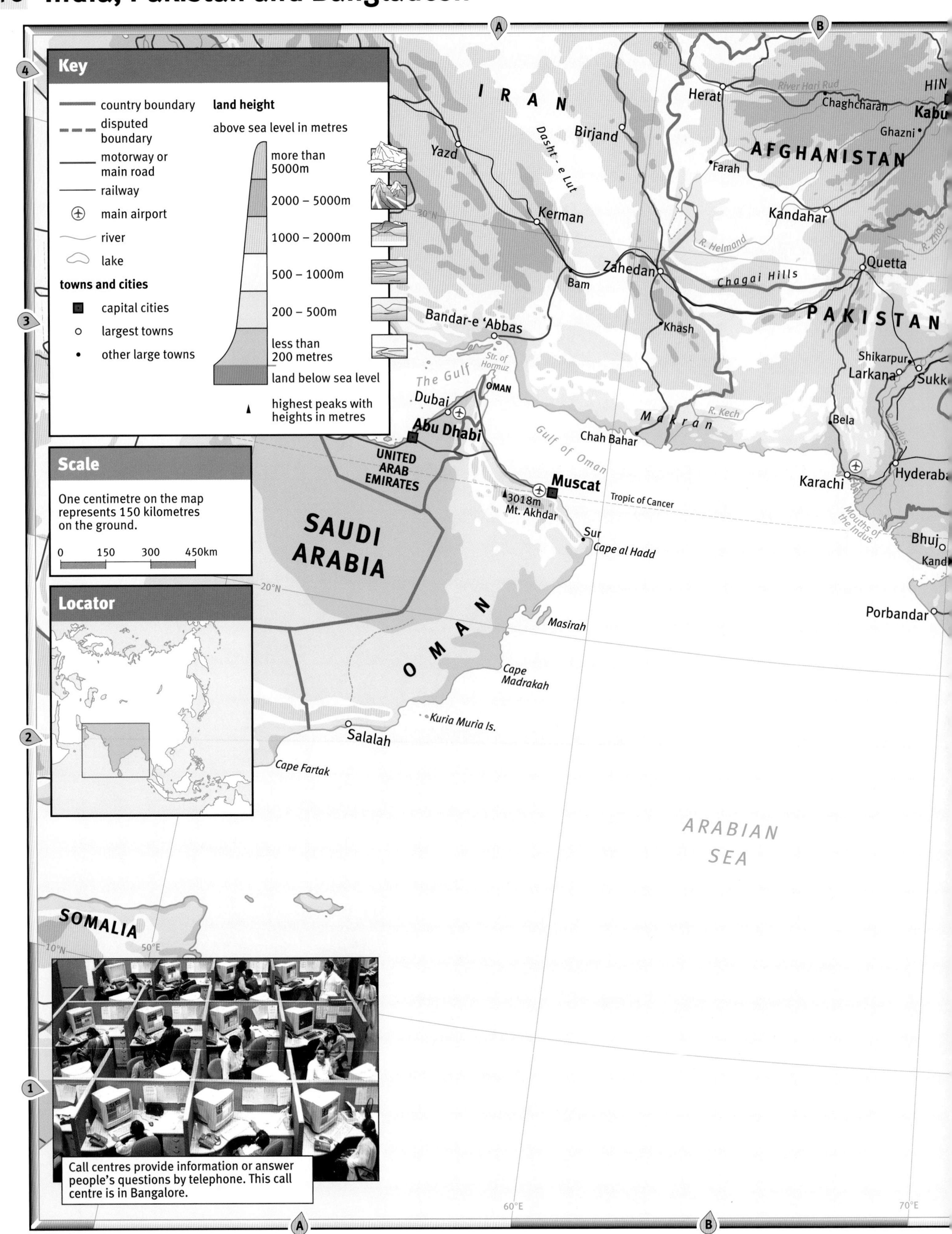

A
B
4
3
2
1
Key
country boundary
disputed boundary
motorway or main road
railway
main airport
river
lake
towns and cities
capital cities
largest towns
other large towns
land height
above sea level in metres
more than 5000m
2000 – 5000m
1000 – 2000m
500 – 1000m
200 – 500m
less than 200 metres
land below sea level
highest peaks with heights in metres
Scale
One centimetre on the map represents 150 kilometres on the ground.
0
150
300
450km
Locator
IRAN
Dasht - e Lut
Yazd
Birjand
Kerman
Bam
Zahedan
Khash
Bandar-e 'Abbas
Str. of Hormuz
The Gulf
OMAN
Dubai
Abu Dhabi
UNITED ARAB EMIRATES
SAUDI ARABIA
Muscat
3018m
Mt. Akhdar
Tropic of Cancer
Sur
Cape al Hadd
Gulf of Oman
Chah Bahar
Makran
R. Kech
Masirah
OMAN
Cape Madrakah
Kuria Muria Is.
Salalah
Cape Fartak
SOMALIA
ARABIAN SEA
Herat
River Hari Rud
Chaghcharan
Kabul
Ghazni
AFGHANISTAN
Farah
Kandahar
R. Helmand
Chagai Hills
Quetta
R. Zhob
PAKISTAN
Shikarpur
Larkana
Sukkur
Bela
R. Indus
Karachi
Hyderabad
Mouths of the Indus
Bhuj
Kandla
Porbandar
60°E
70°E
50°E
30°N
20°N
10°N

Call centres provide information or answer people's questions by telephone. This call centre is in Bangalore.

Conical Orthomorphic Projection

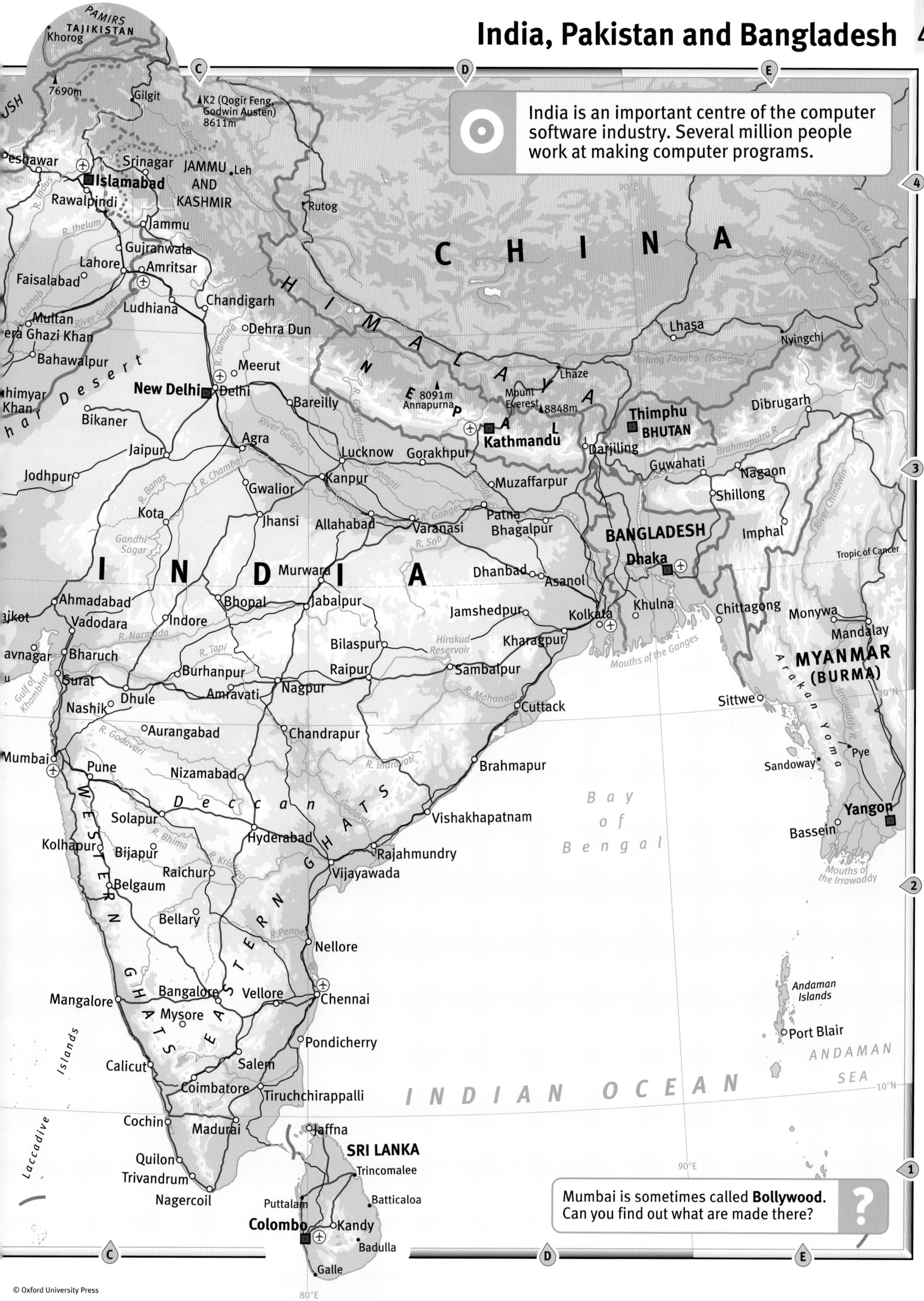

India is an important centre of the computer software industry. Several million people work at making computer programs.

PAMIRS
TAJIKISTAN
Khorog
7690m
Gilgit
K2 (Qogir Feng, Godwin Austen) 8611m
Peshawar
Srinagar
Islamabad
JAMMU AND KASHMIR
Leh
Rawalpindi
Rutog
Jammu
CHINA
Gujranwala
Lahore
Amritsar
Faisalabad
Chandigarh
Ludhiana
Multan
Dera Ghazi Khan
Dehra Dun
Lhasa
Nyingchi
Bahawalpur
HIMALAYA
Meerut
NEPAL
Lhaze
New Delhi
Delhi
8091m Annapurna
Mount Everest 8848m
Thimphu
BHUTAN
Dibrugarh
Bikaner
Bareilly
Kathmandu
Darjiling
Agra
Jaipur
Lucknow
Gorakhpur
Guwahati
Nagaon
Jodhpur
Kanpur
Muzaffarpur
Shillong
Gwalior
Kota
Jhansi
Allahabad
Varanasi
Patna
Bhagalpur
BANGLADESH
Imphal
Tropic of Cancer
INDIA
Murwara
Dhanbad
Asanol
Dhaka
Ahmadabad
Bhopal
Jabalpur
Jamshedpur
Kolkata
Khulna
Chittagong
Monywa
Mandalay
Vadodara
Indore
Bilaspur
Kharagpur
Bharuch
Hirakud Reservoir
Mouths of the Ganges
MYANMAR (BURMA)
Surat
Burhanpur
Raipur
Sambalpur
Amravati
Nagpur
Dhule
Nashik
Cuttack
Sittwe
Aurangabad
Chandrapur
Mumbai
Pune
Nizamabad
Brahmapur
Sandoway
Pye
Deccan
Bay of Bengal
Solapur
Vishakhapatnam
Yangon
Hyderabad
Bassein
Kolhapur
Bijapur
Rajahmundry
Raichur
Vijayawada
Mouths of the Irrawaddy
Belgaum
Bellary
WESTERN GHATS
EASTERN GHATS
Nellore
Andaman Islands
Bangalore
Vellore
Chennai
Mangalore
Mysore
Pondicherry
Port Blair
Calicut
Salem
ANDAMAN SEA
Coimbatore
Tiruchchirappalli
INDIAN OCEAN
Cochin
Madurai
Jaffna
SRI LANKA
Laccadive Islands
Quilon
Trincomalee
Trivandrum
Nagercoil
Puttalam
Batticaloa
Colombo
Kandy
Badulla
Galle

Mumbai is sometimes called **Bollywood**. Can you find out what are made there?

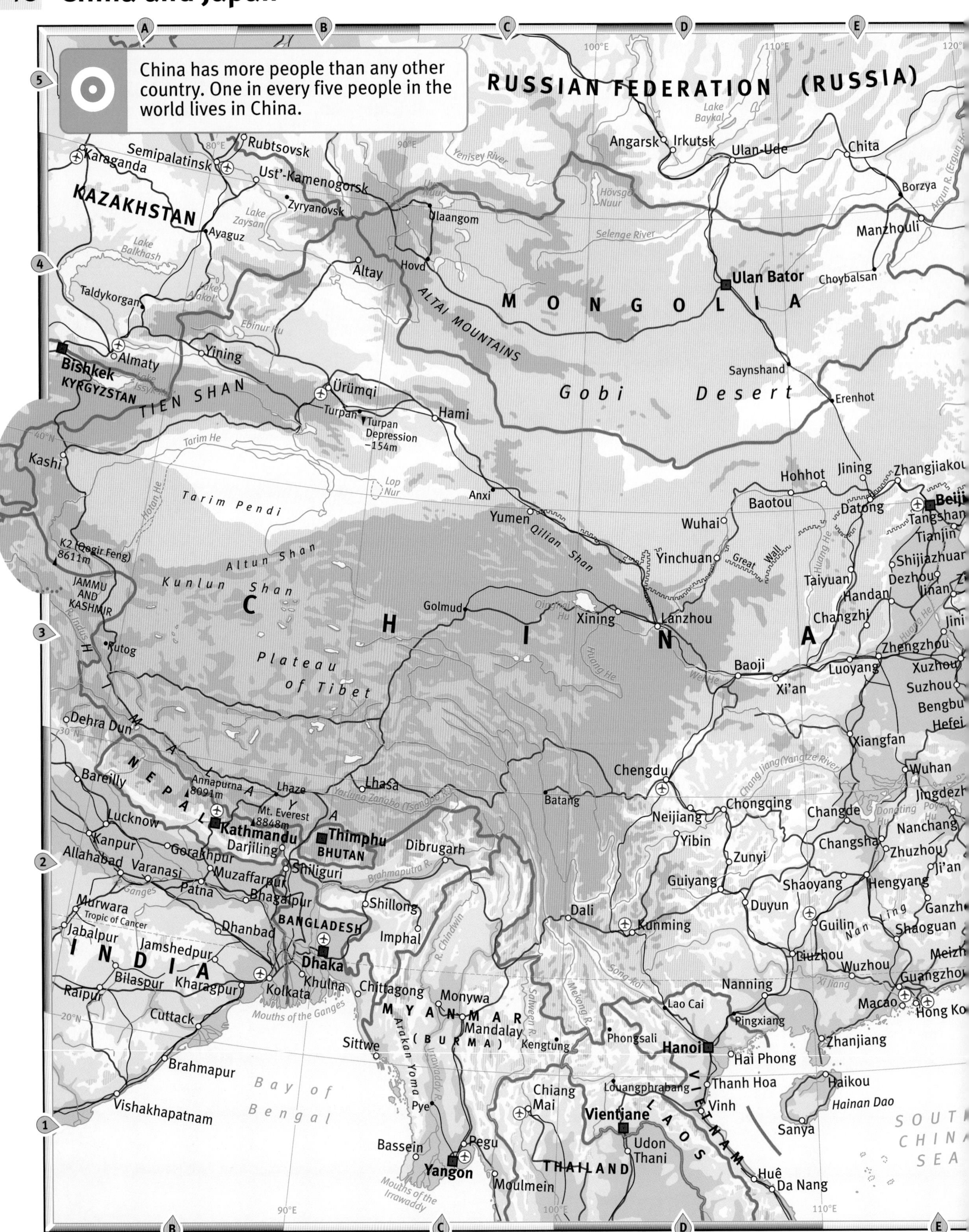

China has more people than any other country. One in every five people in the world lives in China.
RUSSIAN FEDERATION (RUSSIA)
KAZAKHSTAN
MONGOLIA
KYRGYZSTAN
CHINA
NEPAL
BHUTAN
BANGLADESH
INDIA
MYANMAR (BURMA)
THAILAND
LAOS
VIETNAM
JAMMU AND KASHMIR
TIEN SHAN
ALTAI MOUNTAINS
HIMALAYA
Gobi Desert
Tarim Pendi
Plateau of Tibet
Kunlun Shan
Altun Shan
Qilian Shan
Great Wall
Lake Baykal
Lake Balkhash
Lake Zaysan
Lake Alakol'
Lake Issyk-Kul
Ebinur Hu
Hövsgöl Nuur
Uvs Nuur
Lop Nur
Qinghai Hu
Dongting Hu
Poyang Hu
Yenisey River
Selenge River
Argun R. (Ergun He)
Tarim He
Hotan He
Huang He
Wei He
Chang Jiang (Yangtze River)
Yarlung Zangbo (Tsangpo) R.
Brahmaputra R.
Ganges
R. Indus
R. Chindwin
Irrawaddy R.
Salween R.
Mekong R.
Song Koi
Xi Jiang
Nan Ling
Arakan Yoma
Bay of Bengal
SOUTH CHINA SEA
Mouths of the Ganges
Mouths of the Irrawaddy
Hainan Dao
Tropic of Cancer
K2 (Qogir Feng) 8611m
Annapurna 8091m
Mt. Everest 8848m
Turpan Depression −154m
Angarsk
Irkutsk
Ulan-Ude
Chita
Borzya
Manzhouli
Choybalsan
Ulan Bator
Saynshand
Erenhot
Rubtsovsk
Semipalatinsk
Karaganda
Ust'-Kamenogorsk
Zyryanovsk
Ulaangom
Ayaguz
Hovd
Altay
Taldykorgan
Almaty
Bishkek
Yining
Ürümqi
Turpan
Hami
Kashi
Anxi
Yumen
Hohhot
Jining
Zhangjiakou
Baotou
Datong
Beijing
Tangshan
Tianjin
Wuhai
Yinchuan
Shijiazhuang
Dezhou
Jinan
Taiyuan
Handan
Golmud
Xining
Lanzhou
Changzhi
Rutog
Baoji
Luoyang
Zhengzhou
Xuzhou
Xi'an
Suzhou
Bengbu
Hefei
Dehra Dun
Xiangfan
Chengdu
Wuhan
Jingdezhen
Bareilly
Lhaze
Lhasa
Batang
Chongqing
Neijiang
Changde
Nanchang
Lucknow
Kathmandu
Thimphu
Yibin
Changsha
Zhuzhou
Kanpur
Gorakhpur
Darjiling
Dibrugarh
Zunyi
Ji'an
Allahabad
Varanasi
Muzaffarpur
Shiliguri
Guiyang
Shaoyang
Hengyang
Patna
Bhagalpur
Duyun
Ganzhou
Murwara
Shillong
Dali
Kunming
Guilin
Shaoguan
Jabalpur
Dhanbad
Imphal
Jamshedpur
Dhaka
Liuzhou
Meizhou
Wuzhou
Khulna
Guangzhou
Bilaspur
Kharagpur
Kolkata
Chittagong
Monywa
Nanning
Raipur
Lao Cai
Macao
Hong Kong
Cuttack
Mandalay
Pingxiang
Sittwe
Kengtung
Phongsali
Hanoi
Zhanjiang
Hai Phong
Brahmapur
Louangphrabang
Thanh Hoa
Haikou
Chiang Mai
Vishakhapatnam
Pye
Vinh
Vientiane
Sanya
Udon Thani
Pegu
Bassein
Yangon
Moulmein
Huê
Da Nang

Conical Orthomorphic Projection

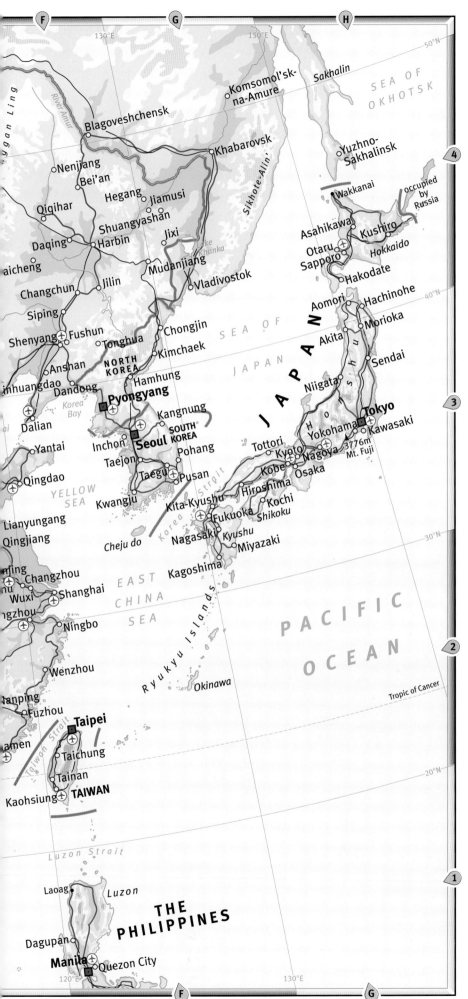

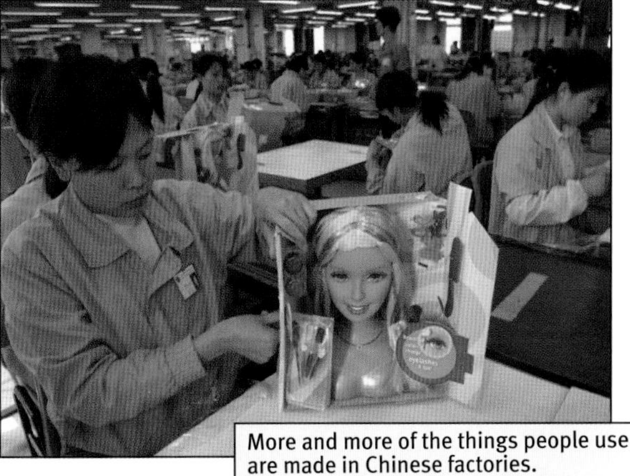

More and more of the things people use are made in Chinese factories.

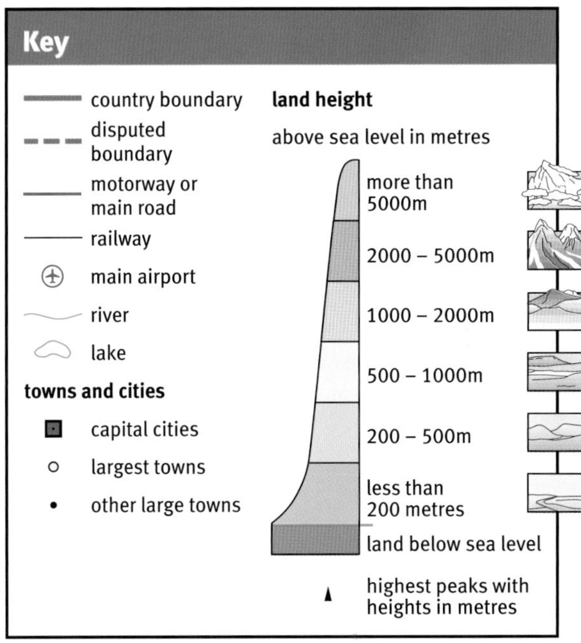
Key
country boundary
disputed boundary
motorway or main road
railway
main airport
river
lake
towns and cities
capital cities
largest towns
other large towns
land height
above sea level in metres
more than 5000m
2000 – 5000m
1000 – 2000m
500 – 1000m
200 – 500m
less than 200 metres
land below sea level
highest peaks with heights in metres

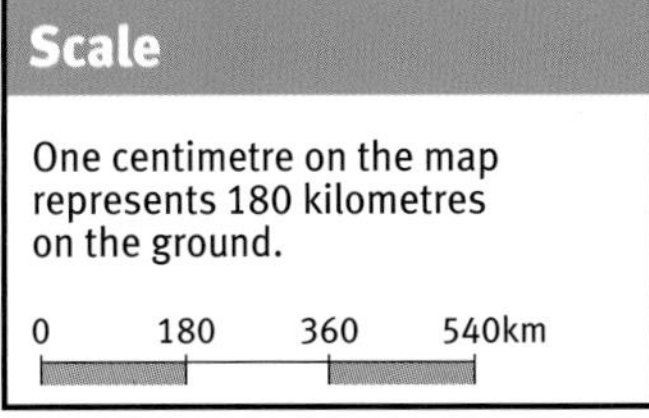
Scale
One centimetre on the map represents 180 kilometres on the ground.
0
180
360
540km

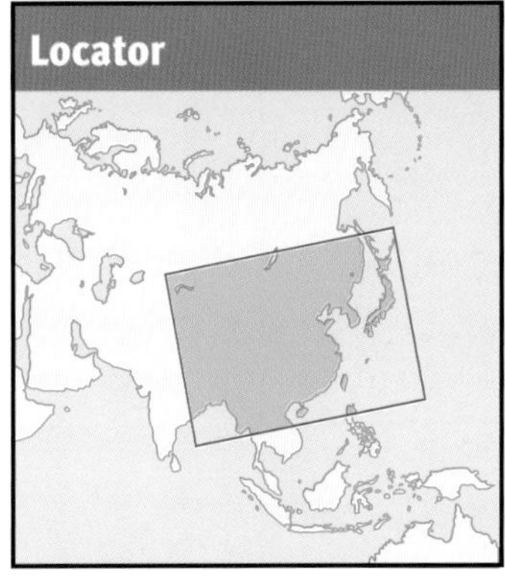
Locator

Japan is a country of islands. Can you name the largest island?

© Oxford University Press

Africa Land and rivers

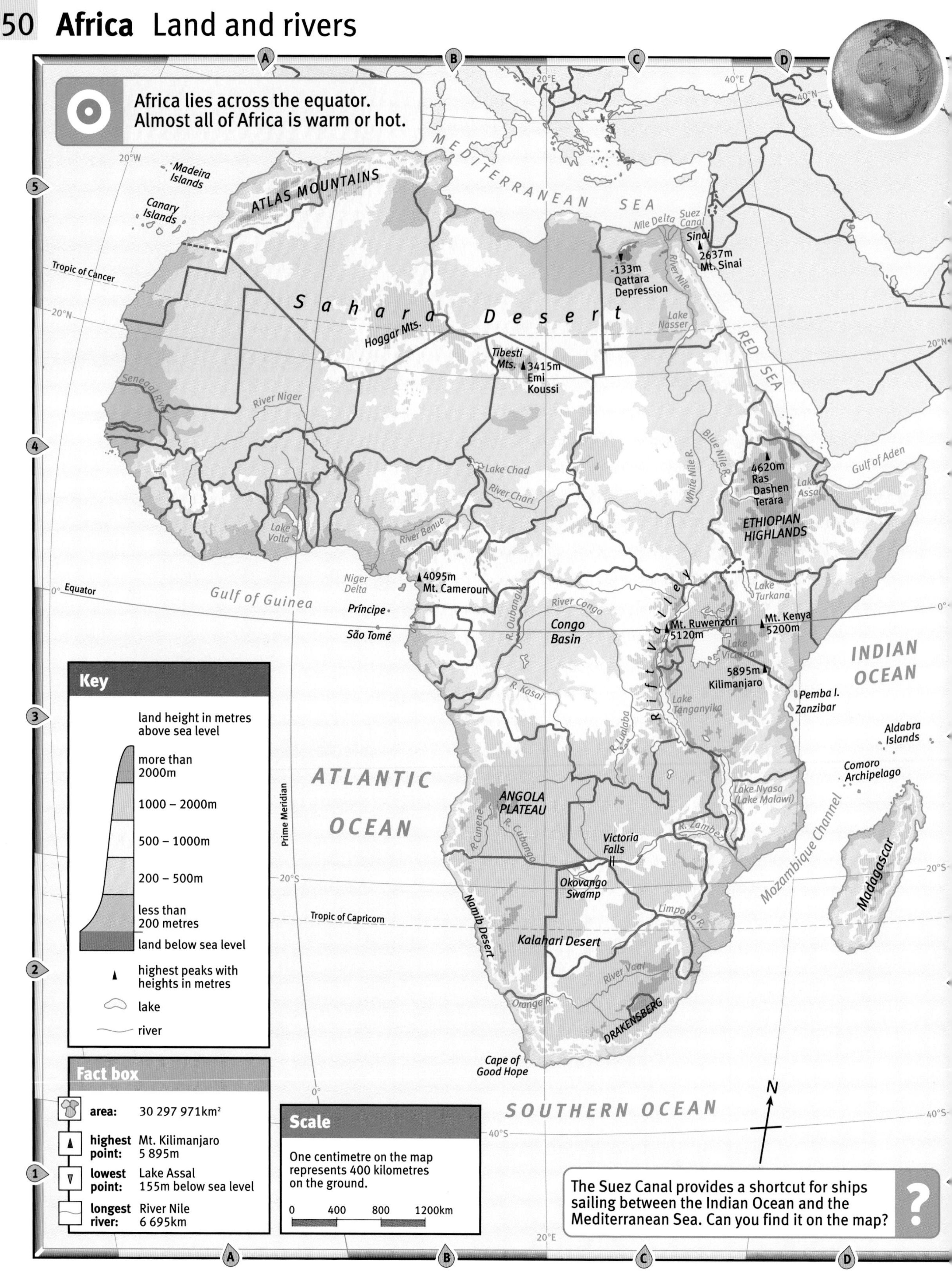
Africa lies across the equator.
Almost all of Africa is warm or hot.
MEDITERRANEAN SEA
Madeira Islands
Canary Islands
ATLAS MOUNTAINS
Tropic of Cancer
Sahara Desert
Hoggar Mts.
Nile Delta
Suez Canal
Sinai
2637m Mt. Sinai
-133m Qattara Depression
River Nile
Lake Nasser
RED SEA
Tibesti Mts.
3415m Emi Koussi
Senegal R.
River Niger
Blue Nile R.
White Nile R.
4620m Ras Dashen Terara
Lake Assal
Gulf of Aden
ETHIOPIAN HIGHLANDS
Lake Chad
River Chari
River Benue
Lake Volta
Niger Delta
4095m Mt. Cameroun
Equator
Gulf of Guinea
Príncipe
São Tomé
R. Oubangui
River Congo
Congo Basin
Rift Valley
Mt. Ruwenzori 5120m
Lake Turkana
Mt. Kenya 5200m
Lake Victoria
5895m Kilimanjaro
INDIAN OCEAN
Pemba I.
Zanzibar
Aldabra Islands
Comoro Archipelago
R. Kasai
R. Lualaba
Lake Tanganyika
ATLANTIC OCEAN
Prime Meridian
ANGOLA PLATEAU
R. Cunene
R. Cubango
Victoria Falls
R. Zambezi
Lake Nyasa (Lake Malawi)
Mozambique Channel
Madagascar
Okovango Swamp
Tropic of Capricorn
Namib Desert
Limpopo R.
Kalahari Desert
River Vaal
Orange R.
DRAKENSBERG
Cape of Good Hope
SOUTHERN OCEAN
N
20°W
20°E
40°E
40°N
20°N
0°
20°S
40°S
A
B
C
D
1
2
3
4
5

Key

land height in metres above sea level

- more than 2000m
- 1000 – 2000m
- 500 – 1000m
- 200 – 500m
- less than 200 metres
- land below sea level
- ▲ highest peaks with heights in metres
- lake
- river

Fact box

area:	30 297 971km²
highest point:	Mt. Kilimanjaro 5 895m
lowest point:	Lake Assal 155m below sea level
longest river:	River Nile 6 695km

Scale

One centimetre on the map represents 400 kilometres on the ground.

0 400 800 1200km

The Suez Canal provides a shortcut for ships sailing between the Indian Ocean and the Mediterranean Sea. Can you find it on the map?

Zenithal Equal Area Projection

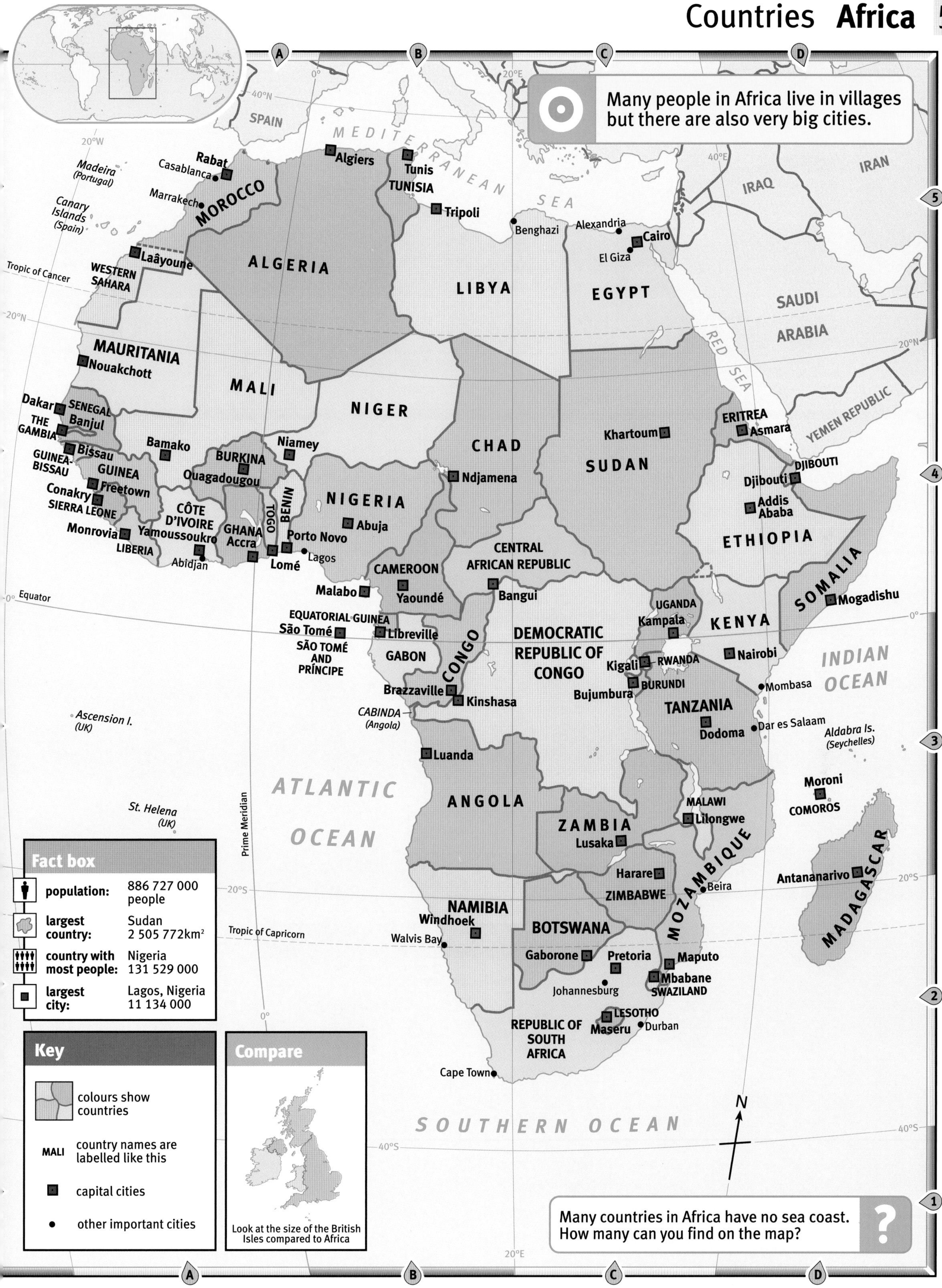

Many people in Africa live in villages but there are also very big cities.

Fact box

population:	886 727 000 people
largest country:	Sudan 2 505 772km²
country with most people:	Nigeria 131 529 000
largest city:	Lagos, Nigeria 11 134 000

Key

colours show countries

MALI country names are labelled like this

capital cities

other important cities

Compare

Look at the size of the British Isles compared to Africa

Many countries in Africa have no sea coast. How many can you find on the map?

Egypt

Most of Egypt is desert, except for a long strip of cultivated land along the River Nile.

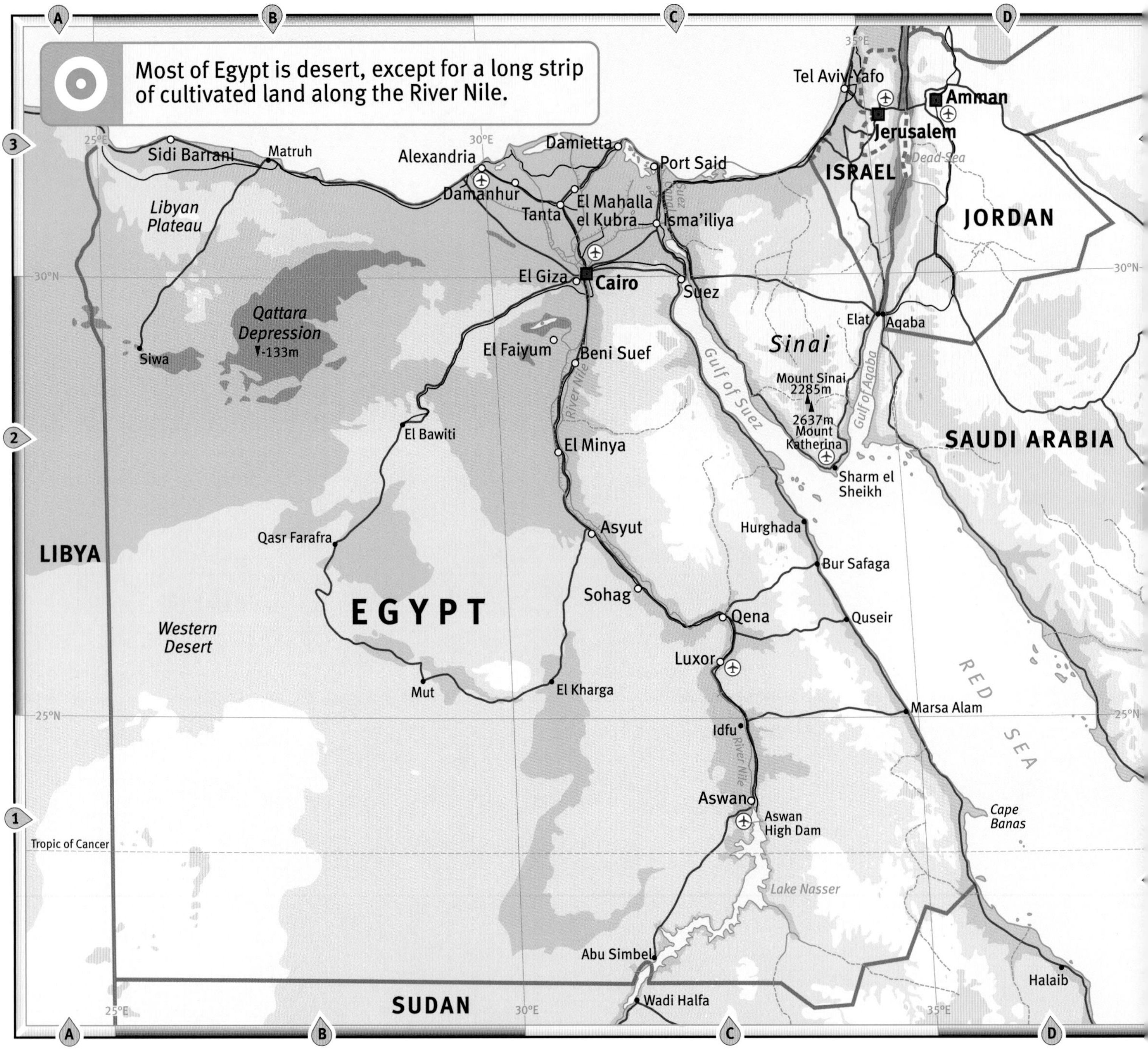

A B C D
3 2 1

25°E 30°E 35°E 30°N 25°N

Tel Aviv-Yafo
Amman
Jerusalem
Dead Sea
ISRAEL
JORDAN
Sidi Barrani
Matruh
Alexandria
Damietta
Port Said
Damanhur
Tanta
El Mahalla el Kubra
Isma'iliya
Suez Canal
Libyan Plateau
El Giza
Cairo
Suez
Elat
Aqaba
Qattara Depression
-133m
Siwa
El Faiyum
Beni Suef
Sinai
Gulf of Suez
Gulf of Aqaba
Mount Sinai 2285m
2637m Mount Katherina
River Nile
El Bawiti
El Minya
SAUDI ARABIA
Sharm el Sheikh
Hurghada
Asyut
Qasr Farafra
LIBYA
Bur Safaga
Sohag
EGYPT
Qena
Quseir
Western Desert
Luxor
RED SEA
Mut
El Kharga
Marsa Alam
Idfu
Aswan
Aswan High Dam
Cape Banas
Tropic of Cancer
Lake Nasser
Abu Simbel
Halaib
SUDAN
Wadi Halfa

The Pyramids at El Giza, near Cairo, are where the ancient Egyptians buried their dead kings 5000 years ago.

The Aswan High Dam holds back the water of Lake Nasser and prevents the River Nile from flooding. Can you find the dam on the map?

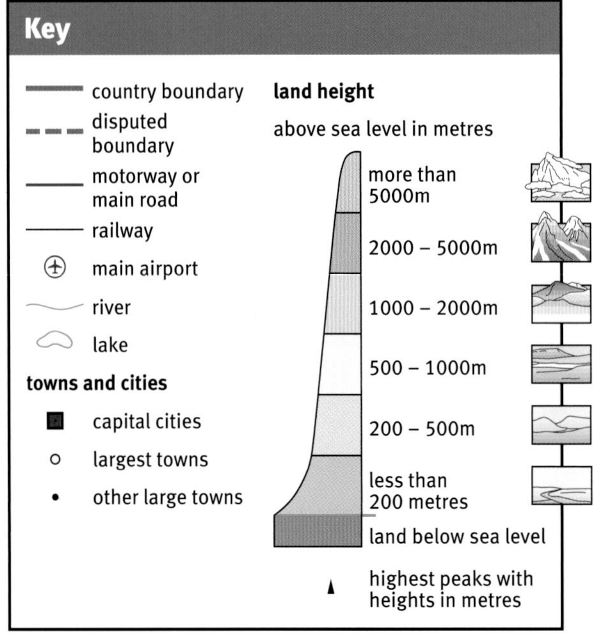
Key
country boundary
disputed boundary
motorway or main road
railway
main airport
river
lake
towns and cities
capital cities
largest towns
other large towns
land height
above sea level in metres
more than 5000m
2000 – 5000m
1000 – 2000m
500 – 1000m
200 – 500m
less than 200 metres
land below sea level
highest peaks with heights in metres

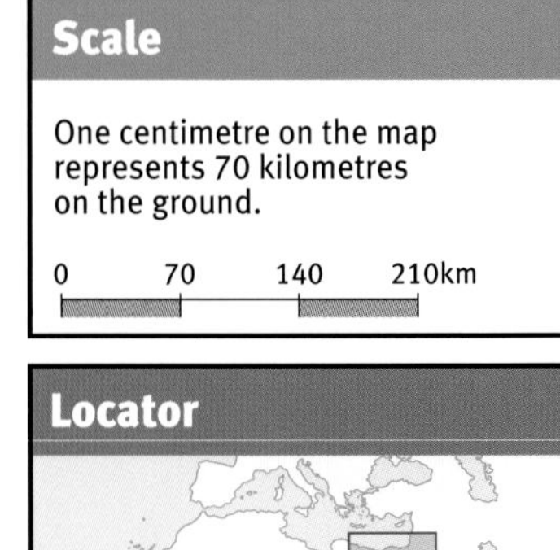
Scale
One centimetre on the map represents 70 kilometres on the ground.
0
70
140
210km

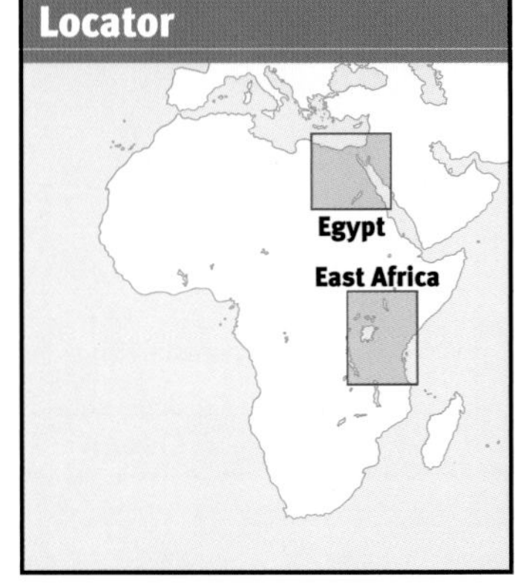
Locator
Egypt
East Africa

 Zenithal Equal Area Projection

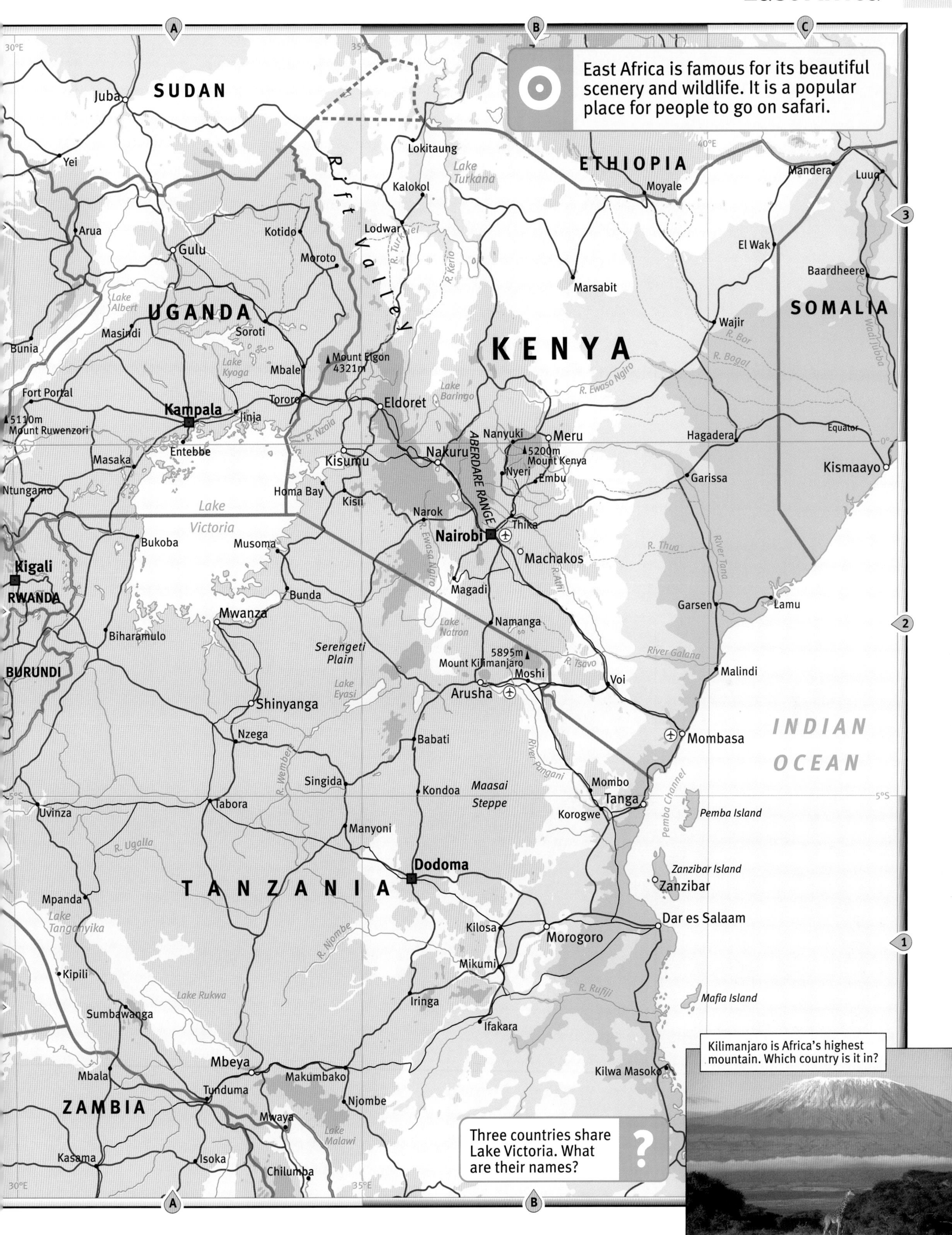
East Africa is famous for its beautiful scenery and wildlife. It is a popular place for people to go on safari.
Kilimanjaro is Africa's highest mountain. Which country is it in?
Three countries share Lake Victoria. What are their names?
?
A
B
C
1
2
3
30°E
35°E
40°E
Equator
0°
5°S
SUDAN
ETHIOPIA
SOMALIA
KENYA
UGANDA
RWANDA
BURUNDI
TANZANIA
ZAMBIA
INDIAN OCEAN
Juba
Yei
Arua
Gulu
Kotido
Moroto
Lokitaung
Kalokol
Lodwar
Lake Turkana
R. Turkwel
R. Kerio
Rift Valley
Moyale
Mandera
Luuq
El Wak
Baardheere
Marsabit
Wajir
R. Bor
R. Bogal
Wadi Jubba
Lake Albert
Masindi
Soroti
Lake Kyoga
Mbale
Mount Elgon 4321m
Bunia
Fort Portal
5110m Mount Ruwenzori
Kampala
Jinja
Entebbe
Tororo
Eldoret
Lake Baringo
R. Ewaso Ngiro
R. Nzoia
Masaka
Ntungamo
Kisumu
Nakuru
Nanyuki
Meru
5200m Mount Kenya
Nyeri
Embu
ABERDARE RANGE
Hagadera
Garissa
Kismaayo
Homa Bay
Kisii
Narok
Thika
Nairobi
Machakos
R. Thua
River Tana
Lake Victoria
Bukoba
Musoma
Kigali
Bunda
Magadi
Ewaso Ngiro
R. Athi
Garsen
Lamu
Mwanza
Biharamulo
Lake Natron
Namanga
Serengeti Plain
5895m Mount Kilimanjaro
Moshi
R. Tsavo
River Galana
Malindi
Voi
Lake Eyasi
Arusha
Shinyanga
Mombasa
Nzega
Babati
River Pangani
R. Wembere
Singida
Kondoa
Maasai Steppe
Mombo
Tanga
Korogwe
Pemba Channel
Pemba Island
Uvinza
Tabora
Manyoni
R. Ugalla
Dodoma
Zanzibar Island
Zanzibar
Mpanda
Lake Tanganyika
Dar es Salaam
Kilosa
Morogoro
R. Njombe
Mikumi
Kipili
R. Rufiji
Mafia Island
Lake Rukwa
Iringa
Sumbawanga
Ifakara
Mbeya
Kilwa Masoko
Mbala
Makumbako
Tunduma
Njombe
Mwaya
Lake Malawi
Kasama
Isoka
Chilumba

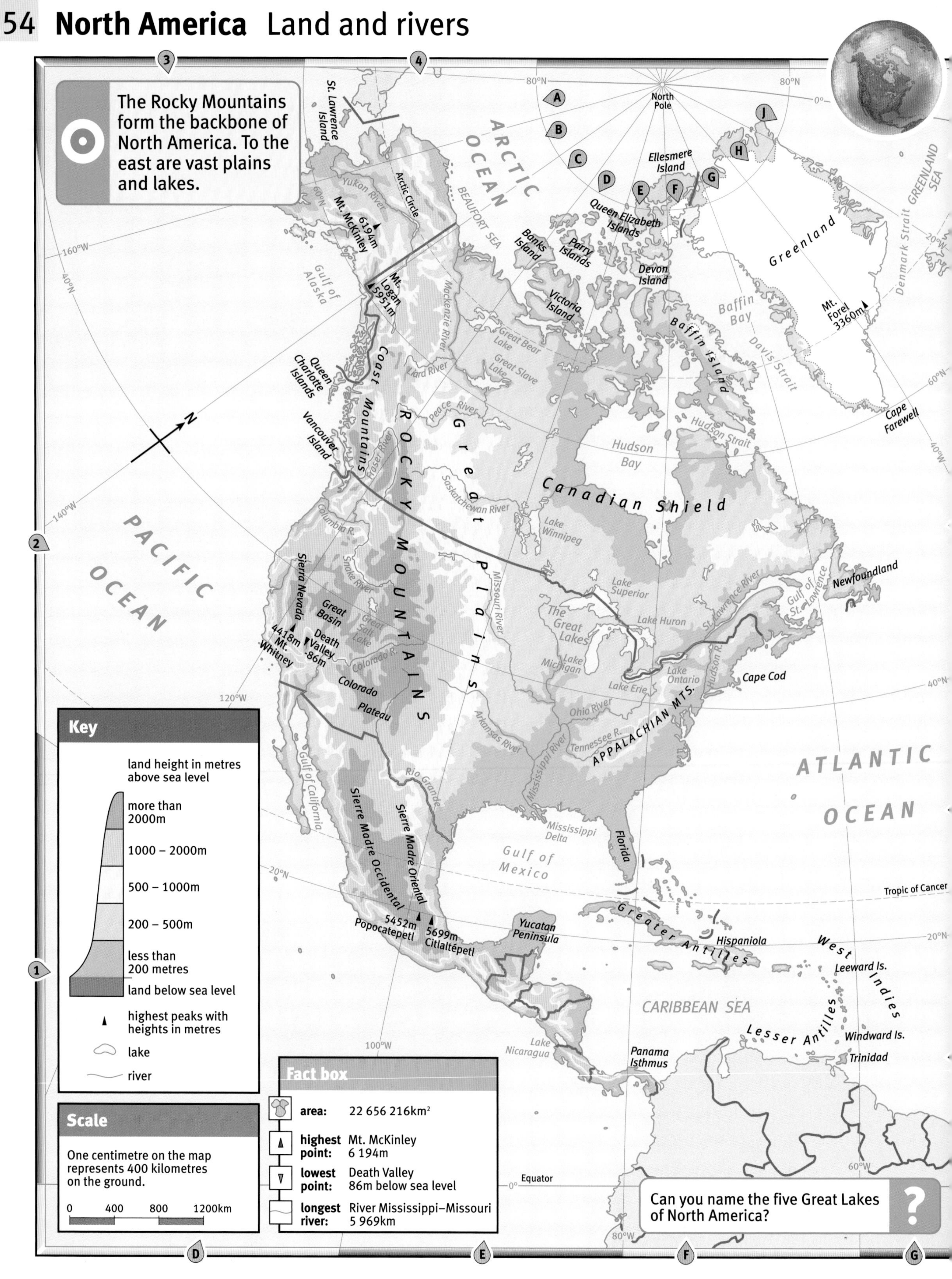
The Rocky Mountains form the backbone of North America. To the east are vast plains and lakes.
ARCTIC OCEAN
BEAUFORT SEA
North Pole
80°N
St. Lawrence Island
Yukon River
Arctic Circle
Mt. McKinley 6194m
Gulf of Alaska
Mt. Logan 5951m
Mackenzie River
Ellesmere Island
Queen Elizabeth Islands
Banks Island
Parry Islands
Devon Island
Victoria Island
Greenland
Mt. Forel 3360m
GREENLAND SEA
Denmark Strait
Baffin Bay
Davis Strait
Baffin Island
Great Bear Lake
Great Slave Lake
Liard River
Queen Charlotte Islands
Coast Mountains
Peace River
Cape Farewell
Hudson Strait
Hudson Bay
Vancouver Island
Fraser River
ROCKY MOUNTAINS
Great Plains
Canadian Shield
Saskatchewan River
Lake Winnipeg
PACIFIC OCEAN
Columbia R.
Sierra Nevada
Snake River
Missouri River
Lake Superior
St. Lawrence River
Gulf of St. Lawrence
Newfoundland
Great Basin
Great Salt Lake
The Great Lakes
Lake Huron
Lake Michigan
4418m Mt. Whitney
Death Valley -86m
Colorado R.
Lake Ontario
Hudson R.
Cape Cod
Colorado Plateau
Lake Erie
Ohio River
APPALACHIAN MTS.
Arkansas River
Tennessee R.
Mississippi River
ATLANTIC OCEAN
Gulf of California
Rio Grande
Sierre Madre Occidental
Sierre Madre Oriental
Mississippi Delta
Florida
Gulf of Mexico
Tropic of Cancer
5452m Popocatepetl
5699m Citlaltépetl
Yucatan Peninsula
Greater Antilles
Hispaniola
West Indies
Leeward Is.
CARIBBEAN SEA
Lesser Antilles
Windward Is.
Trinidad
Lake Nicaragua
Panama Isthmus
Equator
160°W
140°W
120°W
100°W
80°W
60°W
60°N
40°N
20°N
0°
20°W
40°W
A B C D E F G H J
1 2 3 4
D E F G
Key
land height in metres above sea level
more than 2000m
1000 – 2000m
500 – 1000m
200 – 500m
less than 200 metres
land below sea level
highest peaks with heights in metres
lake
river
Scale
One centimetre on the map represents 400 kilometres on the ground.
0 400 800 1200km
Fact box
area: 22 656 216km²
highest point: Mt. McKinley 6 194m
lowest point: Death Valley 86m below sea level
longest river: River Mississippi–Missouri 5 969km
Can you name the five Great Lakes of North America?
?

Oblique Mercator Projection

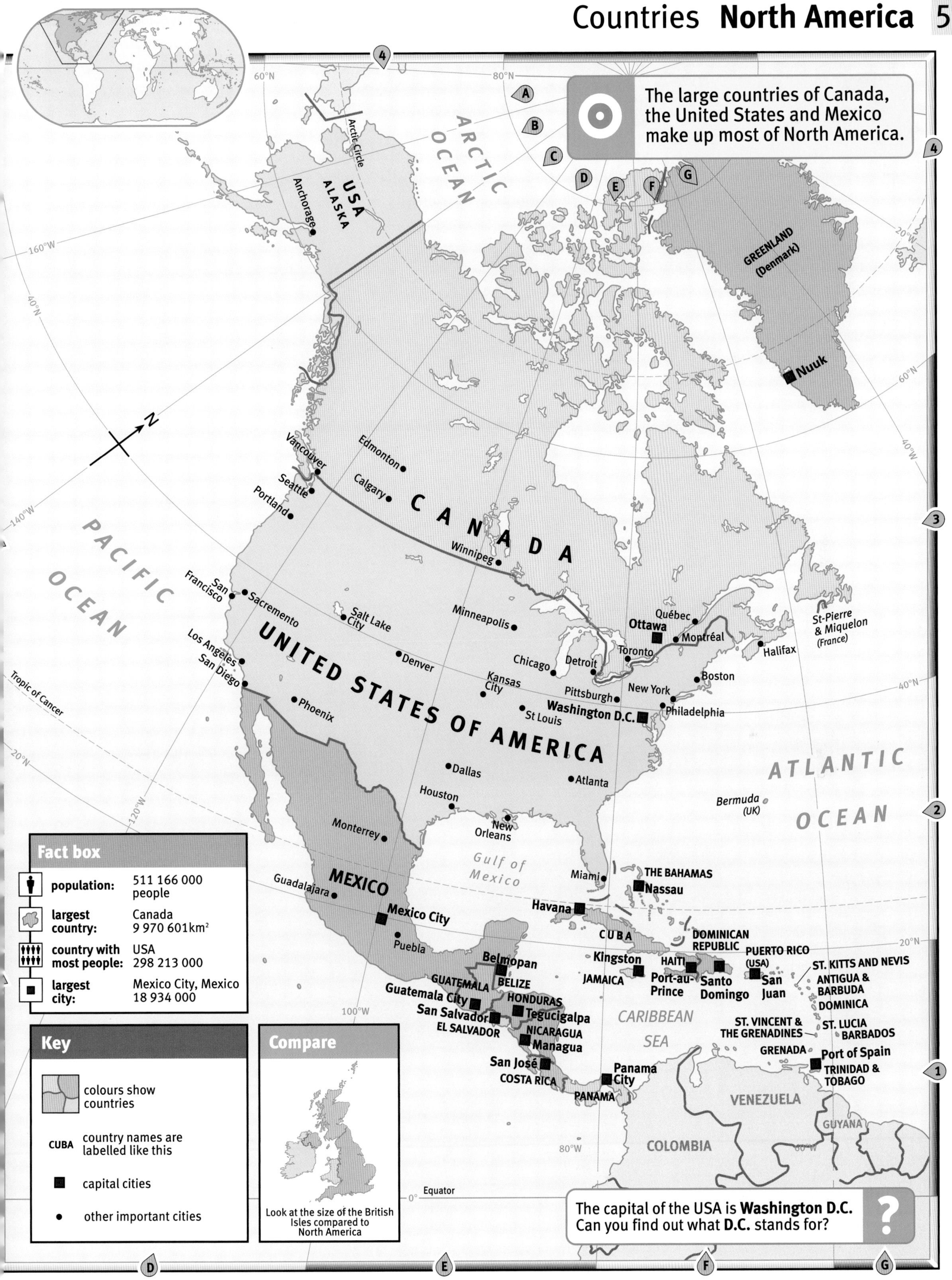

The large countries of Canada, the United States and Mexico make up most of North America.

ARCTIC OCEAN
PACIFIC OCEAN
ATLANTIC OCEAN
Gulf of Mexico
CARIBBEAN SEA
USA ALASKA
Anchorage
Arctic Circle
GREENLAND (Denmark)
Nuuk
CANADA
Vancouver
Edmonton
Calgary
Seattle
Portland
Winnipeg
Québec
Ottawa
Montréal
Toronto
Halifax
St-Pierre & Miquelon (France)
UNITED STATES OF AMERICA
San Francisco
Sacremento
Salt Lake City
Minneapolis
Los Angeles
San Diego
Denver
Chicago
Detroit
Boston
Kansas City
Pittsburgh
New York
Washington D.C.
Philadelphia
St Louis
Phoenix
Dallas
Atlanta
Houston
New Orleans
Bermuda (UK)
Miami
MEXICO
Monterrey
Guadalajara
Mexico City
Puebla
THE BAHAMAS
Nassau
Havana
CUBA
DOMINICAN REPUBLIC
PUERTO RICO (USA)
Kingston
JAMAICA
HAITI
Port-au-Prince
Santo Domingo
San Juan
ST. KITTS AND NEVIS
ANTIGUA & BARBUDA
DOMINICA
ST. LUCIA
BARBADOS
ST. VINCENT & THE GRENADINES
GRENADA
Port of Spain
TRINIDAD & TOBAGO
Belmopan
BELIZE
GUATEMALA
Guatemala City
HONDURAS
Tegucigalpa
San Salvador
EL SALVADOR
NICARAGUA
Managua
San José
COSTA RICA
Panama City
PANAMA
VENEZUELA
GUYANA
COLOMBIA
Tropic of Cancer
Equator
60°N
80°N
160°W
140°W
120°W
100°W
80°W
60°W
40°W
20°W
40°N
20°N
0°
N
A
B
C
D
E
F
G
1
2
3
4

Fact box

population:	511 166 000 people
largest country:	Canada 9 970 601km²
country with most people:	USA 298 213 000
largest city:	Mexico City, Mexico 18 934 000

Key

colours show countries

CUBA country names are labelled like this

capital cities

other important cities

Compare

Look at the size of the British Isles compared to North America

The capital of the USA is **Washington D.C.** Can you find out what **D.C.** stands for?

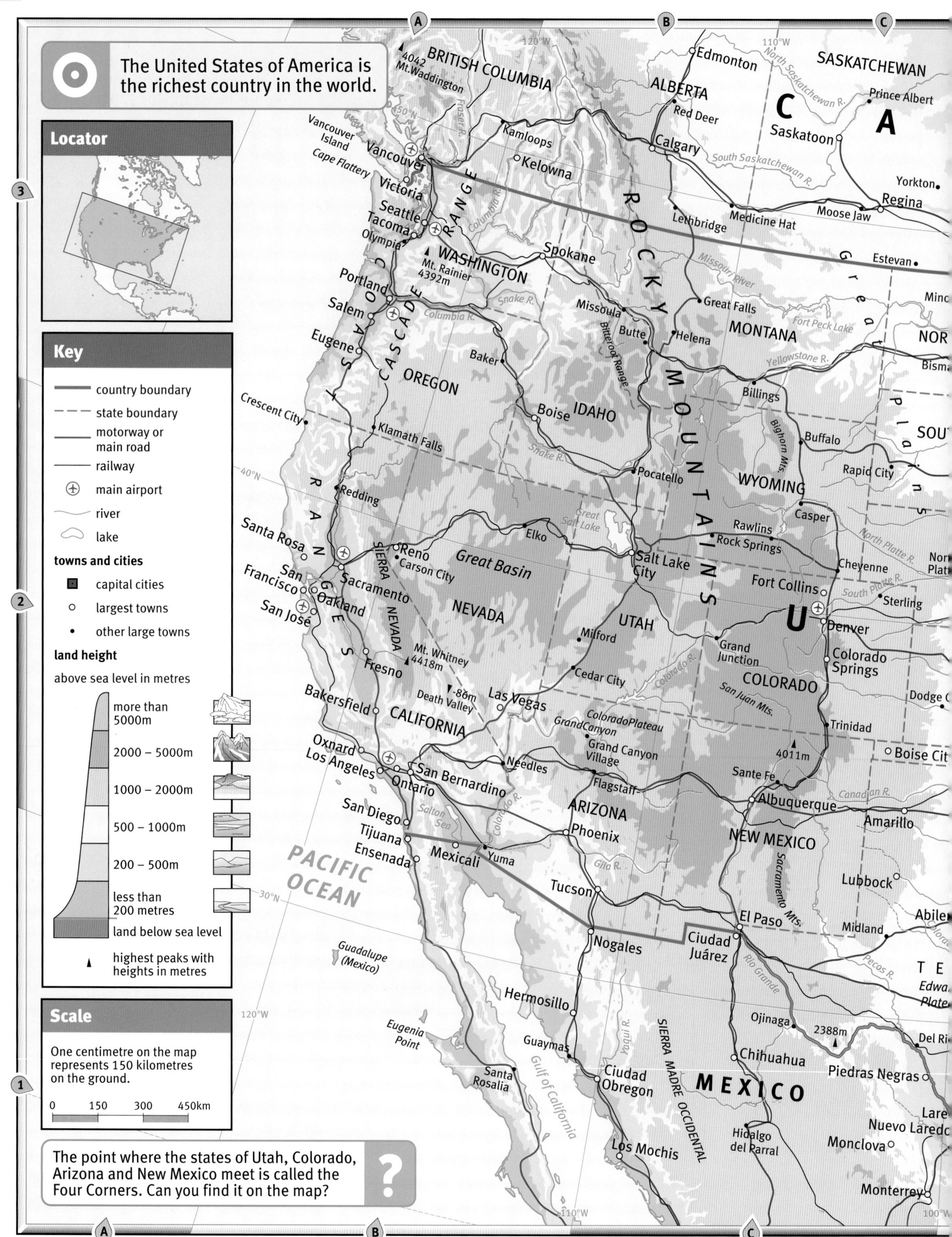
The United States of America is the richest country in the world.
Locator
Key
country boundary
state boundary
motorway or main road
railway
main airport
river
lake
towns and cities
capital cities
largest towns
other large towns
land height
above sea level in metres
more than 5000m
2000 – 5000m
1000 – 2000m
500 – 1000m
200 – 500m
less than 200 metres
land below sea level
highest peaks with heights in metres
Scale
One centimetre on the map represents 150 kilometres on the ground.
0
150
300
450km
The point where the states of Utah, Colorado, Arizona and New Mexico meet is called the Four Corners. Can you find it on the map?
?
A
B
C
3
2
1
120°W
110°W
100°W
50°N
40°N
30°N
BRITISH COLUMBIA
4042 Mt.Waddington
Fraser R.
ALBERTA
Edmonton
Red Deer
Calgary
SASKATCHEWAN
North Saskatchewan R.
South Saskatchewan R.
Prince Albert
Saskatoon
Yorkton
Regina
Moose Jaw
Medicine Hat
Lethbridge
Estevan
C
A
Vancouver Island
Cape Flattery
Vancouver
Victoria
Kamloops
Kelowna
Columbia R.
Seattle
Tacoma
Olympia
WASHINGTON
Mt. Rainier 4392m
Spokane
Snake R.
Portland
Salem
Eugene
Columbia R.
COAST RANGES
CASCADE RANGE
OREGON
Baker
Missoula
Bitterroot Range
Butte
Helena
Great Falls
Missouri River
MONTANA
Fort Peck Lake
Yellowstone R.
Billings
ROCKY MOUNTAINS
Crescent City
Klamath Falls
Boise
IDAHO
Snake R.
Pocatello
Bighorn Mts.
Buffalo
WYOMING
Rapid City
Casper
Great Plains
NOR
Bism
SOU
Redding
Santa Rosa
Great Salt Lake
Elko
Rawlins
Rock Springs
North Platte R.
Cheyenne
Nor Plat
Reno
Carson City
Great Basin
Salt Lake City
Fort Collins
South Platte R.
Sterling
San Francisco
Sacramento
SIERRA NEVADA
Oakland
San José
NEVADA
UTAH
U
Denver
Milford
Grand Junction
Colorado R.
Colorado Springs
Mt. Whitney 4418m
Fresno
Cedar City
COLORADO
San Juan Mts.
-86m Death Valley
Las Vegas
Bakersfield
CALIFORNIA
Colorado Plateau
Grand Canyon
Grand Canyon Village
Dodge C
Trinidad
4011m
Boise Cit
Oxnard
Los Angeles
Ontario
San Bernardino
Needles
Flagstaff
Santa Fe
Albuquerque
Canadian R.
Amarillo
San Diego
Salton Sea
Colorado R.
ARIZONA
Phoenix
NEW MEXICO
Tijuana
Ensenada
Mexicali
Yuma
Gila R.
PACIFIC OCEAN
Sacramento Mts.
Lubbock
Tucson
El Paso
Midland
Abile
Nogales
Ciudad Juárez
Rio Grande
Pecos R.
TE
Edwa Plate
Guadalupe (Mexico)
Hermosillo
Ojinaga
2388m
Del Ri
Eugenia Point
Guaymas
Yaqui R.
SIERRA MADRE OCCIDENTAL
Chihuahua
Piedras Negras
Santa Rosalia
Gulf of California
Ciudad Obregon
MEXICO
Hidalgo del Parral
Nuevo Laredo
Lare
Monclova
Los Mochis
Monterrey

Conical Orthomorphic Projection

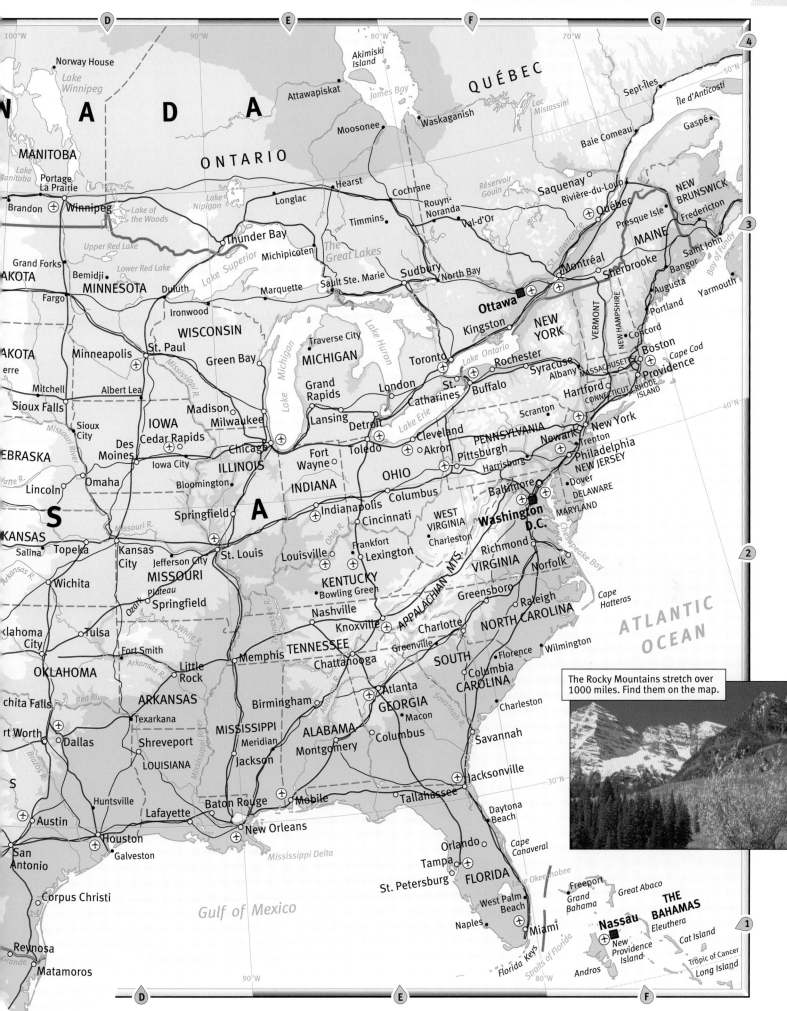

The Rocky Mountains stretch over 1000 miles. Find them on the map.

South America Land and rivers

The Andes are the longest mountain range in the world and stretch the whole length of South America.

Lake Maracaibo
Llanos
River Orinoco
River Magdalena
Mt. Roraima 2810m
GUIANA HIGHLANDS
Cocos Islands
Equator
Galapagos Islands
Cotopaxi 5896m
Chimborazo 6310m
ANDES
River Negro
River Amazon
Amazon Basin
River Tapajós
Selvas
River Ucayali
River Madeira
River Tocantins
River São Francisco
Mato Grosso
BRAZILIAN HIGHLANDS
ATLANTIC OCEAN
Rocas Island
PACIFIC OCEAN
Lake Titicaca
Lake Poopo
Atacama Desert
River Pilcomayo
River Paraguay
Gran Chaco
Tropic of Capricorn
6908m Ojos del Salado
Aconcagua 6960m
River Paraná
River Uruguay
Juan Fernández Islands
Pampas
Río de la Plata
R. Colorado
R. Negro
Valdés Peninsula
Chiloé Island
Patagonia
Falkland Islands
Tierra del Fuego
Cape Horn
South Georgia
SOUTHERN OCEAN
N
80°W
60°W
40°W
20°W
0°
20°S
40°S
60°S

Key

land height in metres above sea level

- more than 2000m
- 1000 – 2000m
- 500 – 1000m
- 200 – 500m
- less than 200 metres
- land below sea level
- highest peaks with heights in metres
- lake
- river

Fact box

area:	17 867 239km²
highest point:	Aconcagua 6 960m
lowest point:	Valdés Peninsula 40m below sea level
longest river:	River Amazon 6 516km

Scale

One centimetre on the map represents 350 kilometres on the ground.

0 350 700 850km

Can you find out which famous scientist studied plants and animals on the Galapagos Islands in 1835?

Oblique Mercator Projection

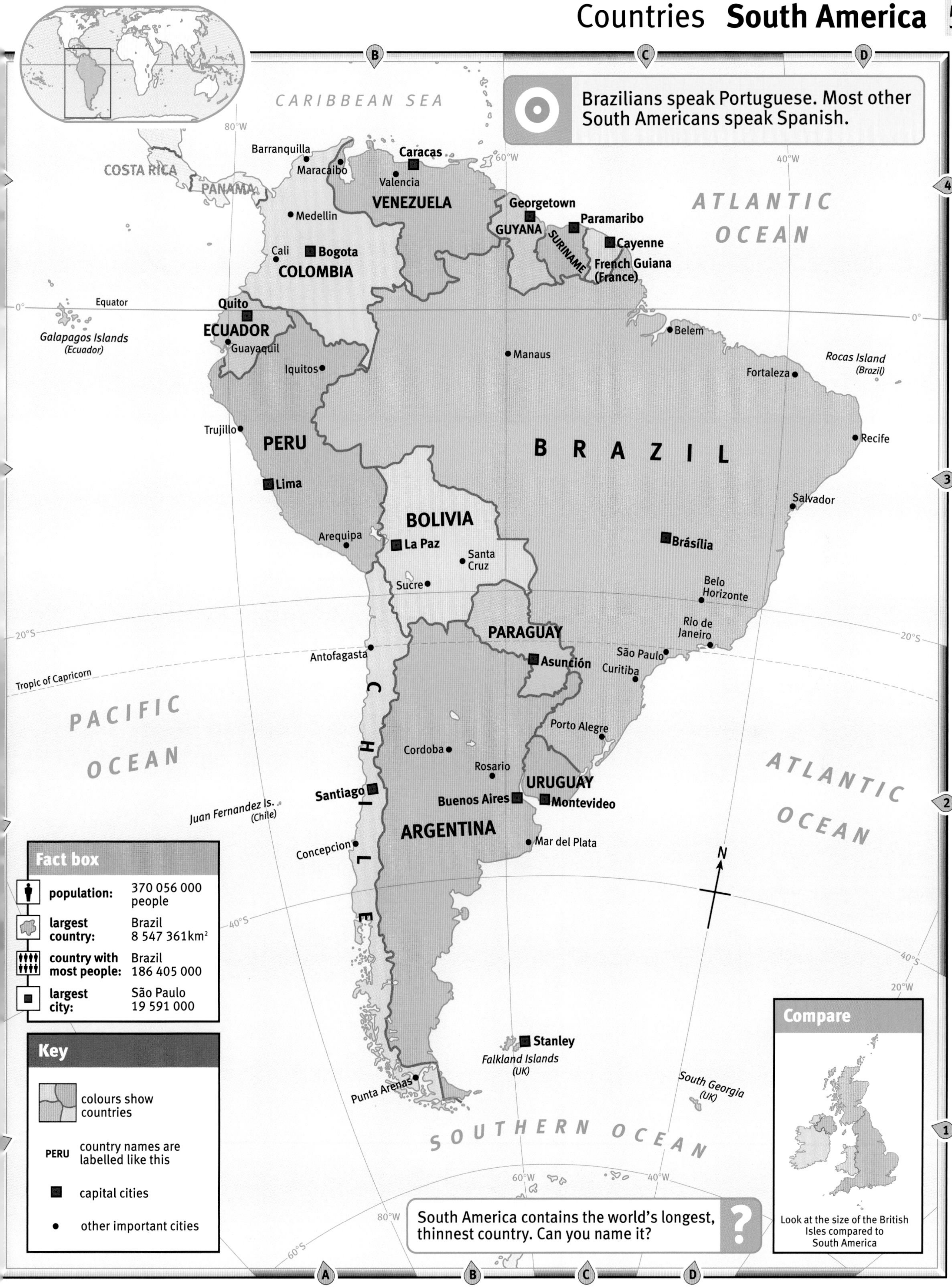

Brazilians speak Portuguese. Most other South Americans speak Spanish.

CARIBBEAN SEA
COSTA RICA
PANAMA
Barranquilla
Maracaibo
Caracas
Valencia
VENEZUELA
Medellin
Cali
Bogota
COLOMBIA
Georgetown
GUYANA
Paramaribo
SURINAME
Cayenne
French Guiana (France)
ATLANTIC OCEAN
Equator
Galapagos Islands (Ecuador)
Quito
ECUADOR
Guayaquil
Iquitos
Manaus
Belem
Fortaleza
Rocas Island (Brazil)
Trujillo
PERU
Lima
B R A Z I L
Recife
Salvador
BOLIVIA
La Paz
Arequipa
Santa Cruz
Sucre
Brásília
Belo Horizonte
Rio de Janeiro
PARAGUAY
Asunción
São Paulo
Curitiba
Antofagasta
Tropic of Capricorn
PACIFIC OCEAN
C H I L E
Porto Alegre
Cordoba
Rosario
URUGUAY
Santiago
Buenos Aires
Montevideo
Juan Fernandez Is. (Chile)
ARGENTINA
Mar del Plata
Concepcion
ATLANTIC OCEAN
N
Stanley
Falkland Islands (UK)
South Georgia (UK)
Punta Arenas
SOUTHERN OCEAN
80°W
60°W
40°W
20°W
0°
20°S
40°S
60°S

Fact box

population:	370 056 000 people
largest country:	Brazil 8 547 361km²
country with most people:	Brazil 186 405 000
largest city:	São Paulo 19 591 000

Key

- colours show countries
- PERU country names are labelled like this
- capital cities
- other important cities

South America contains the world's longest, thinnest country. Can you name it?

Compare

Look at the size of the British Isles compared to South America

Brazil, Peru, Bolivia

The Amazon rain forest contains half of all known plants and animals on Earth.

The Sugar Loaf Mountain, Rio de Janeiro. Find Rio on the map.

The capital of Brazil was built as a brand new city in 1960. Can you name it?

Key

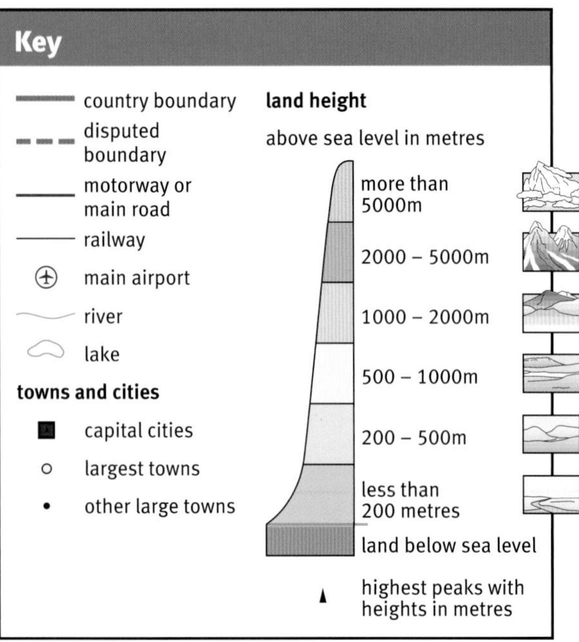
country boundary
disputed boundary
motorway or main road
railway
main airport
river
lake
towns and cities
capital cities
largest towns
other large towns
land height
above sea level in metres
more than 5000m
2000 – 5000m
1000 – 2000m
500 – 1000m
200 – 500m
less than 200 metres
land below sea level
highest peaks with heights in metres

Scale

One centimetre on the map represents 160 kilometres on the ground.

0 160 320 480km

Locator

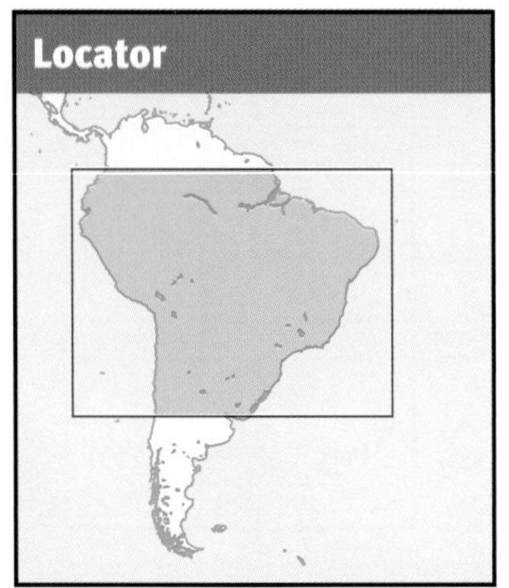

A
B
C
5
4
3
2
80°W
70°W
Equator
0°
10°S
20°S
30°S
Tropic of Capricorn
Bogota
Buenaventura
Cali
Neiva
COLOMBIA
River Guaviare
VENEZUE
Mitu
River Apaporis
Pasto
Uaupes
River Neg
River Caqueta
Quito
Cotopaxi 5896m
ECUADOR
Ambato
Manta
River Putumayo
River Napo
River Japura
Chimborazo 6310m
Guayaquil
Cuenca
River Amazon
Machala
Iquitos
Talara
Sullana
Piura
River Marañon
River Ucayali
River Yavari
River Jurua
Tarapoto
Cruzeiro do Sul
River Pu
Chiclayo
Trujillo
Chimbote
Pucallpa
Rio Branco
Cerro de Pasco
PERU
Callao
Lima
Ayacucho
River Madre de Dios
Cuzco
River Beni
Ica
Juliaca
Lake Titicaca
La Paz
Arequipa
Tacna
Arica
Lake Poopo
Oruro
PACIFIC OCEAN
Iquique
Atacama Desert
Tocopilla
Calama
Antofagasta
Chanaral
6908m Nevado Ojos de Salado
Copiapo
La Serena
Coquimbo
La Rioja
San Juan
CHILE
ANDES
Selva

Transverse Mercator Projection

D E F
50°W 40°W 60°W
French Guiana (France)
SURINAME
GUYANA
Boa Vista
ATLANTIC OCEAN
Serra Tumucumaque
River Branco
Mouths of the Amazon
Macapa
Barcelos
Balbina Reservoir
Ilha de Marajo
Braganca
Equator
0°
River Amazon
Belem
zon
Manaus
Santarem
R. Xingu
Cameta
São Luis
Manacapuru
Altamira
Parnaiba
4
5
Coari
Itaituba
Tucurui
River Iriri
sin
River Xingu
Bacabal
Caxias
Fortaleza
River Madeira
Maraba
Codo
Sobral
River Tapajos
Imperatriz
Teresina
Barra do Corda
Mossoro
Araguaina
Natal
River Aripuana
River Teles Pires
River Parnaiba
Porto Velho
Juazeiro do Norte
Campina Grande
Joao Pessoa
River Araguaia
River Tocantins
Recife
Ariquemes
Petrolina
Caruaru
River Juruena
BRAZIL
Maceio
10°S
Diamantina
Barreiras
Aracaju
River Guapore
Feira de Santana
Alagoinhas
Salvador
Mato Grosso
rinidad
River São Francisco
Chapada
Jequie
BRAZILIAN HIGHLANDS
Vitoria da Conquista
River Mamore
Cuiaba
Caceres
Brasilia
Ilheus
LIVIA
Rondonopolis
Anapolis
Goiania
Montes Claros
3
River Jequitinhonha
Santa Cruz
Rio Verde
River Paranaiba
cre
Teofilo Otoni
Corumba
Uberlandia
Mount Itambe 2033m
Governador Valadares
Sa. de Maracaju
Uberaba
São Jose do Rio Preto
Linhares
Tarija
Campo Grande
Ribeirao Preto
Belo Horizonte
Caratinga
Vitoria
Barbacena
Gran Chaco
Araraquara
20°S
Pedro Juan Caballero
Dourados
Bauru
Juiz de Fora
Campos
Campinas
Nova Iguacu
an Salvador e Jujuy
Maringa
Rio de Janeiro
PARAGUAY
São Paulo
Santo Andre
River Pilcomayo
Santos
Tropic of Capricorn
River Bermejo
alta
Asuncion
Foz do Iguacu
Ponta Grossa
Curitiba
Formosa
R. Paraguay
Paranagua
San Miguel de Tucuman
Resistencia
River Parana
2
GENTINA
Corrientes
Posadas
Itajai
Santiago del Estero
Florianopolis
River Salado
Passo Fundo
River Uruguay
ATLANTIC OCEAN
as Grandes
Santa Maria
Caxias do Sul
Uruguaiana
River Parana
Porto Alegre
Concordia
Lagoa dos Patos
Santa Fe
Parana
URUGUAY
Cordoba
Pelotas
50°W
40°W
30°S
60°W
C D E F
Rio Grande

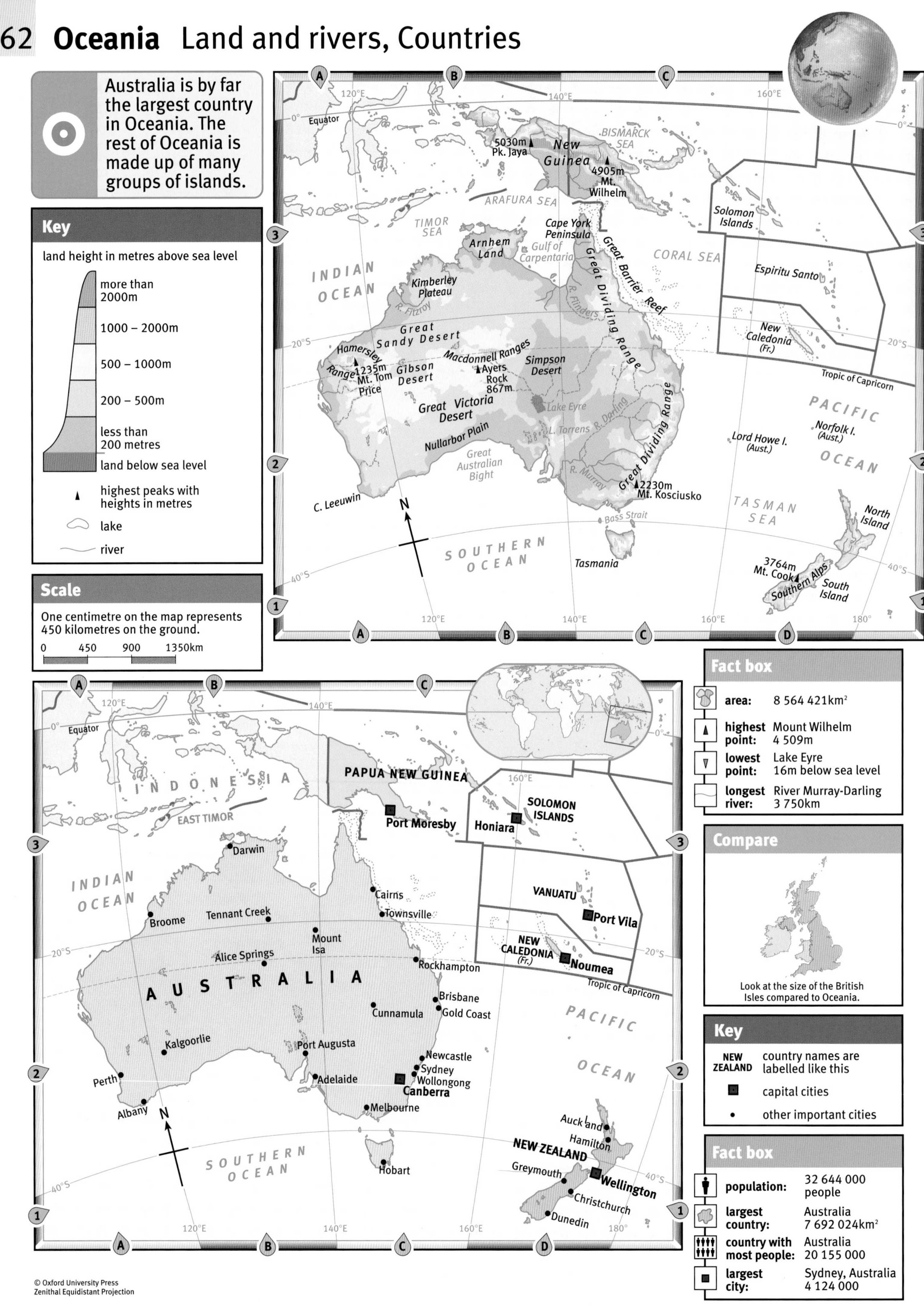
62 Oceania Land and rivers, Countries
Australia is by far the largest country in Oceania. The rest of Oceania is made up of many groups of islands.
Key
land height in metres above sea level
more than 2000m
1000 – 2000m
500 – 1000m
200 – 500m
less than 200 metres
land below sea level
highest peaks with heights in metres
lake
river
Scale
One centimetre on the map represents 450 kilometres on the ground.
0 450 900 1350km
Equator
120°E
140°E
160°E
20°S
40°S
180°
BISMARCK SEA
5030m Pk. Jaya
New Guinea
4905m Mt. Wilhelm
ARAFURA SEA
TIMOR SEA
Solomon Islands
Cape York Peninsula
Arnhem Land
Gulf of Carpentaria
CORAL SEA
Great Barrier Reef
INDIAN OCEAN
Kimberley Plateau
R. Fitzroy
R. Flinders
Great Dividing Range
Espiritu Santo
New Caledonia (Fr.)
Great Sandy Desert
Hamersley Range
1235m Mt. Tom Price
Gibson Desert
Macdonnell Ranges
Ayers Rock 867m
Simpson Desert
Tropic of Capricorn
Great Victoria Desert
Lake Eyre
L. Torrens
R. Darling
PACIFIC OCEAN
Norfolk I. (Aust.)
Lord Howe I. (Aust.)
Nullarbor Plain
Great Australian Bight
R. Murray
2230m Mt. Kosciusko
C. Leeuwin
N
Bass Strait
TASMAN SEA
North Island
SOUTHERN OCEAN
Tasmania
3764m Mt. Cook
Southern Alps
South Island
INDONESIA
PAPUA NEW GUINEA
EAST TIMOR
Port Moresby
SOLOMON ISLANDS
Honiara
Darwin
Cairns
Townsville
VANUATU
Port Vila
Broome
Tennant Creek
Mount Isa
NEW CALEDONIA (Fr.)
Noumea
Alice Springs
Rockhampton
AUSTRALIA
Brisbane
Gold Coast
Cunnamula
Kalgoorlie
Port Augusta
Newcastle
Sydney
Wollongong
Perth
Adelaide
Canberra
Albany
Melbourne
Auckland
Hamilton
NEW ZEALAND
Hobart
Greymouth
Wellington
Christchurch
Dunedin
Fact box
area: 8 564 421km²
highest point: Mount Wilhelm 4 509m
lowest point: Lake Eyre 16m below sea level
longest river: River Murray-Darling 3 750km
Compare
Look at the size of the British Isles compared to Oceania.
Key
NEW ZEALAND country names are labelled like this
capital cities
other important cities
Fact box
population: 32 644 000 people
largest country: Australia 7 692 024km²
country with most people: Australia 20 155 000
largest city: Sydney, Australia 4 124 000
© Oxford University Press
Zenithal Equidistant Projection

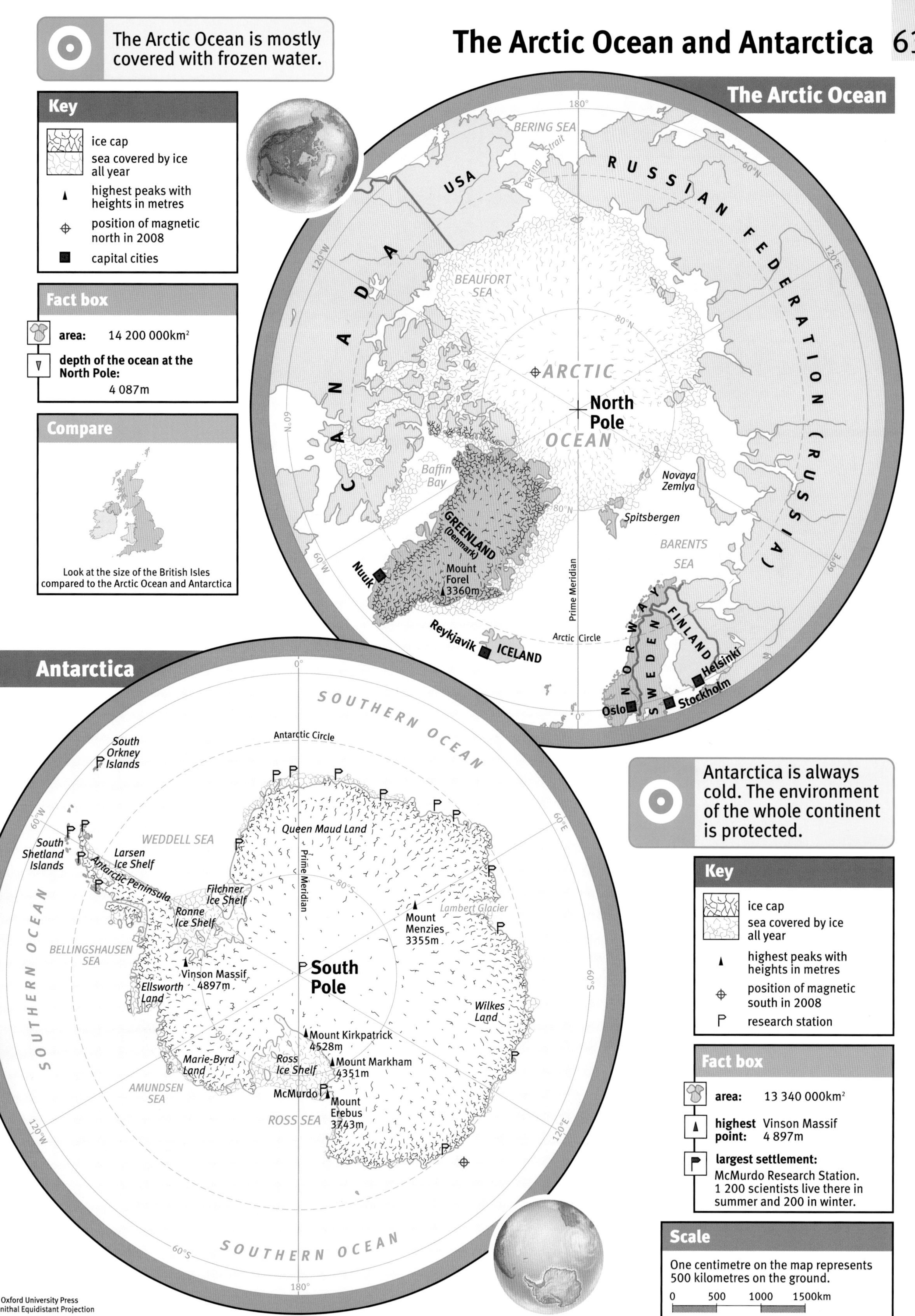
The Arctic Ocean is mostly covered with frozen water.
The Arctic Ocean
Key
ice cap
sea covered by ice all year
highest peaks with heights in metres
position of magnetic north in 2008
capital cities
Fact box
area: 14 200 000km²
depth of the ocean at the North Pole: 4 087m
Compare
Look at the size of the British Isles compared to the Arctic Ocean and Antarctica
180°
BERING SEA
Bering Strait
USA
CANADA
RUSSIAN FEDERATION (RUSSIA)
60°N
120°W
120°E
BEAUFORT SEA
80°N
ARCTIC OCEAN
North Pole
Baffin Bay
Novaya Zemlya
Spitsbergen
BARENTS SEA
GREENLAND (Denmark)
Nuuk
Mount Forel 3360m
60°W
60°E
Prime Meridian
Arctic Circle
Reykjavik
ICELAND
NORWAY
SWEDEN
FINLAND
Helsinki
Stockholm
Oslo
0°
Antarctica
SOUTHERN OCEAN
Antarctic Circle
South Orkney Islands
South Shetland Islands
WEDDELL SEA
Larsen Ice Shelf
Antarctic Peninsula
Queen Maud Land
Filchner Ice Shelf
Ronne Ice Shelf
BELLINGSHAUSEN SEA
Vinson Massif 4897m
Ellsworth Land
South Pole
Mount Menzies 3355m
Lambert Glacier
Wilkes Land
Mount Kirkpatrick 4528m
Marie-Byrd Land
Ross Ice Shelf
Mount Markham 4351m
McMurdo
Mount Erebus 3743m
AMUNDSEN SEA
ROSS SEA
60°W
60°E
80°S
120°W
120°E
60°S
180°
Antarctica is always cold. The environment of the whole continent is protected.
Key
ice cap
sea covered by ice all year
highest peaks with heights in metres
position of magnetic south in 2008
research station
Fact box
area: 13 340 000km²
highest point: Vinson Massif 4 897m
largest settlement: McMurdo Research Station. 1 200 scientists live there in summer and 200 in winter.
Scale
One centimetre on the map represents 500 kilometres on the ground.
0 500 1000 1500km
© Oxford University Press
Zenithal Equidistant Projection

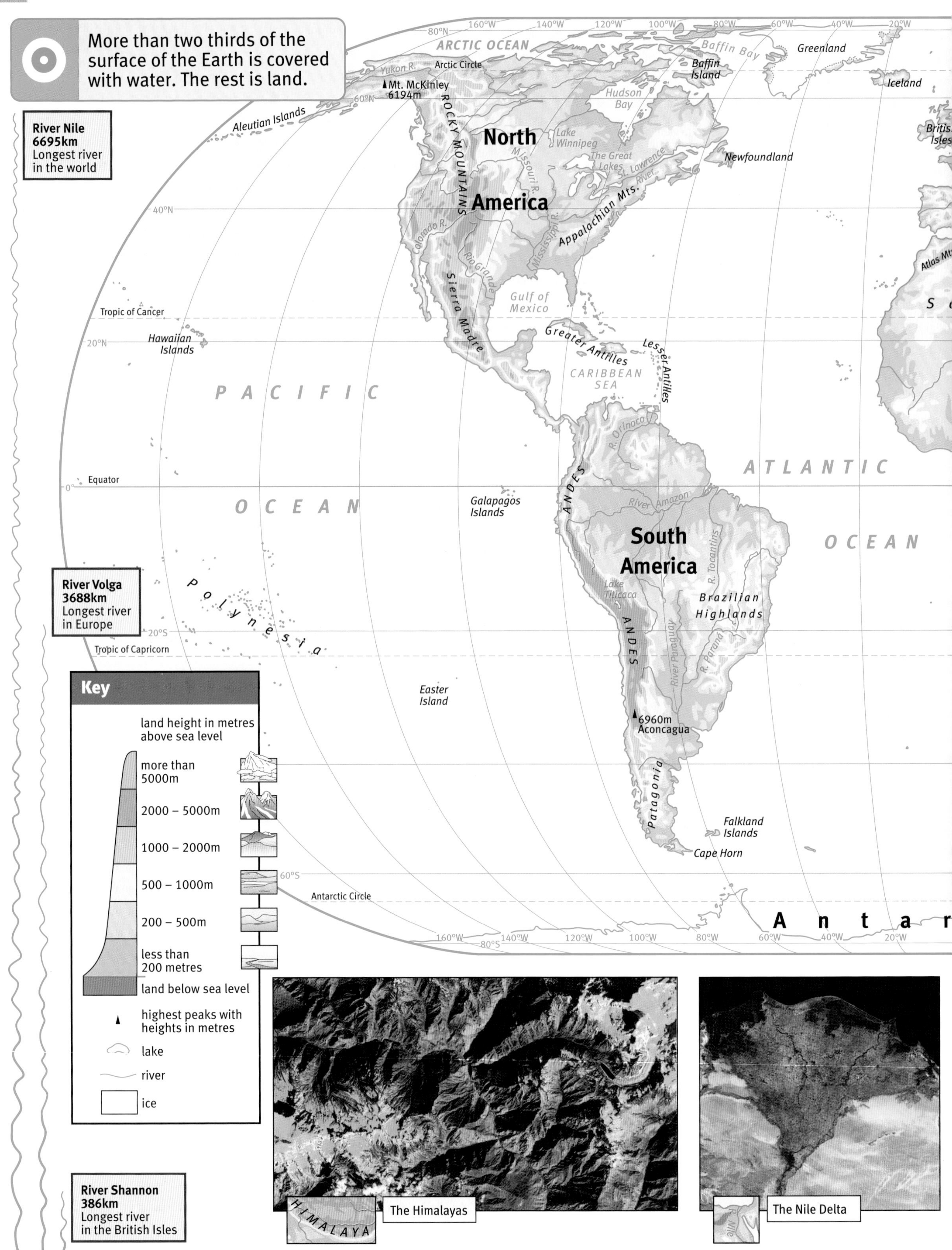
More than two thirds of the surface of the Earth is covered with water. The rest is land.
River Nile 6695km Longest river in the world
River Volga 3688km Longest river in Europe
River Shannon 386km Longest river in the British Isles
ARCTIC OCEAN
Arctic Circle
Yukon R.
Mt. McKinley 6194m
Aleutian Islands
ROCKY MOUNTAINS
North America
Lake Winnipeg
Hudson Bay
Baffin Bay
Baffin Island
Greenland
Iceland
British Isles
Newfoundland
The Great Lakes
St. Lawrence River
Missouri R.
Mississippi R.
Appalachian Mts.
Colorado R.
Rio Grande
Sierra Madre
Gulf of Mexico
Tropic of Cancer
Hawaiian Islands
Greater Antilles
Lesser Antilles
CARIBBEAN SEA
Atlas Mts
P A C I F I C
O C E A N
Equator
R. Orinoco
ANDES
River Amazon
Galapagos Islands
South America
R. Tocantins
A T L A N T I C
O C E A N
Lake Titicaca
Brazilian Highlands
Polynesia
Tropic of Capricorn
River Paraguay
R. Paraná
Easter Island
6960m Aconcagua
Patagonia
Falkland Islands
Cape Horn
Antarctic Circle
A n t a r
80°N
60°N
40°N
20°N
0°
20°S
60°S
80°S
160°W
140°W
120°W
100°W
80°W
60°W
40°W
20°W
Key
land height in metres above sea level
more than 5000m
2000 – 5000m
1000 – 2000m
500 – 1000m
200 – 500m
less than 200 metres
land below sea level
highest peaks with heights in metres
lake
river
ice
HIMALAYA
Nile

The Himalayas

The Nile Delta

Eckert IV Projection

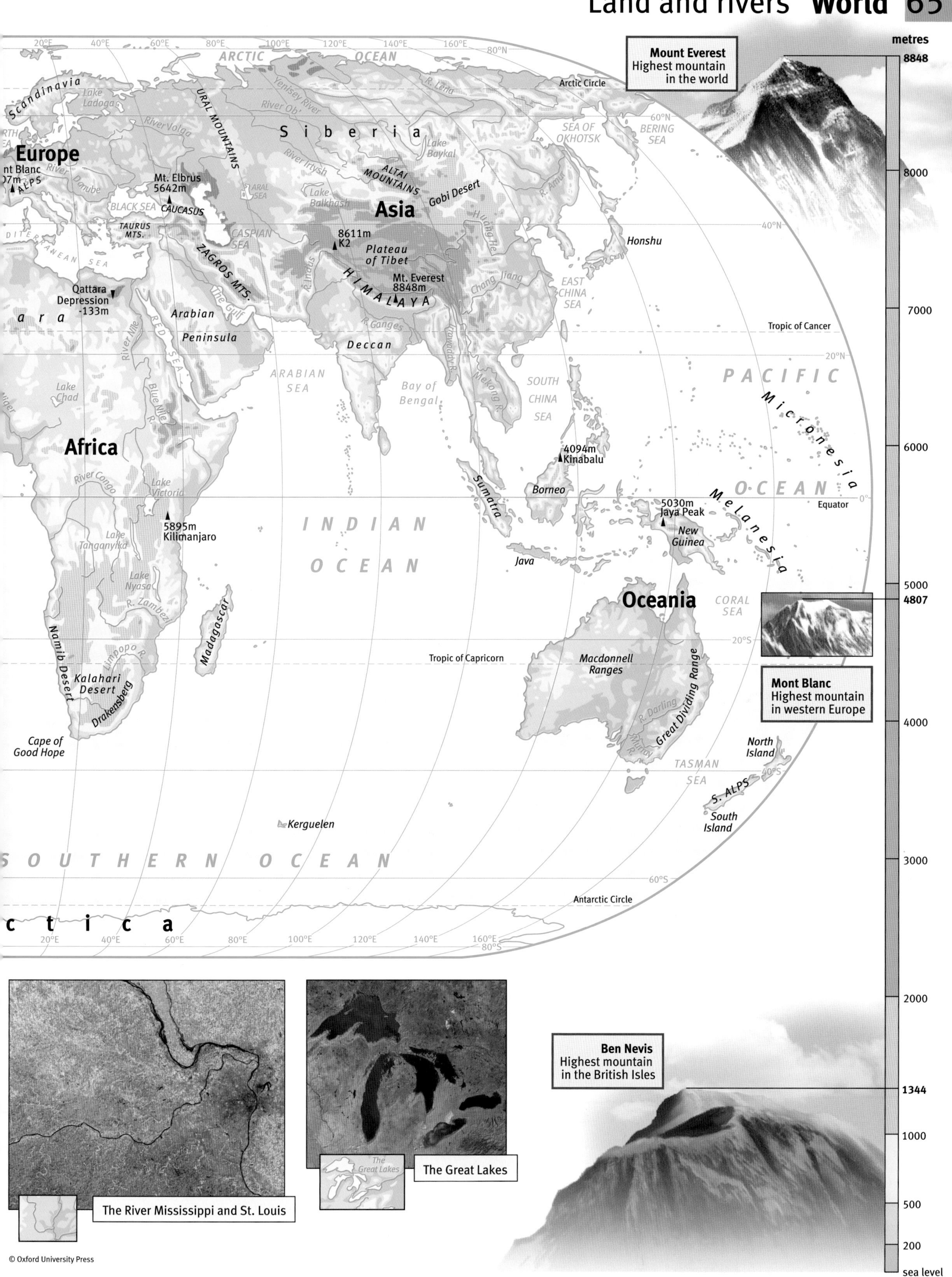

Mount Everest
Highest mountain in the world
metres
8848
8000
7000
6000
5000
4807
Mont Blanc
Highest mountain in western Europe
4000
3000
2000
Ben Nevis
Highest mountain in the British Isles
1344
1000
500
200
sea level
ARCTIC OCEAN
Scandinavia
Lake Ladoga
River Volga
URAL MOUNTAINS
River Ob'
Yenisey River
R. Lena
Arctic Circle
Siberia
Lake Baykal
SEA OF OKHOTSK
BERING SEA
Europe
River Danube
Mt. Elbrus 5642m
CAUCASUS
BLACK SEA
ARAL SEA
River Irtysh
ALTAI MOUNTAINS
Gobi Desert
Lake Balkhash
Asia
R. Amur
TAURUS MTS.
CASPIAN SEA
8611m K2
Plateau of Tibet
Huang He
Honshu
ZAGROS MTS.
HIMALAYA
Mt. Everest 8848m
R. Indus
Chang Jiang
EAST CHINA SEA
Qattara Depression -133m
Arabian Peninsula
The Gulf
RED SEA
River Nile
R. Ganges
Deccan
Tropic of Cancer
Irrawaddy R.
Mekong R.
SOUTH CHINA SEA
ARABIAN SEA
Bay of Bengal
PACIFIC OCEAN
Micronesia
Lake Chad
Blue Nile R.
Africa
4094m Kinabalu
River Congo
Lake Victoria
Sumatra
Borneo
Melanesia
Equator
5030m Jaya Peak
New Guinea
5895m Kilimanjaro
INDIAN OCEAN
Lake Tanganyika
Java
Lake Nyasa
R. Zambezi
Madagascar
Oceania
CORAL SEA
Namib Desert
Limpopo R.
Tropic of Capricorn
Macdonnell Ranges
Great Dividing Range
Kalahari Desert
Drakensberg
R. Darling
Murray R.
Cape of Good Hope
North Island
TASMAN SEA
S. ALPS
South Island
Kerguelen
SOUTHERN OCEAN
Antarctic Circle
Antarctica
The Great Lakes

The River Mississippi and St. Louis

The Great Lakes

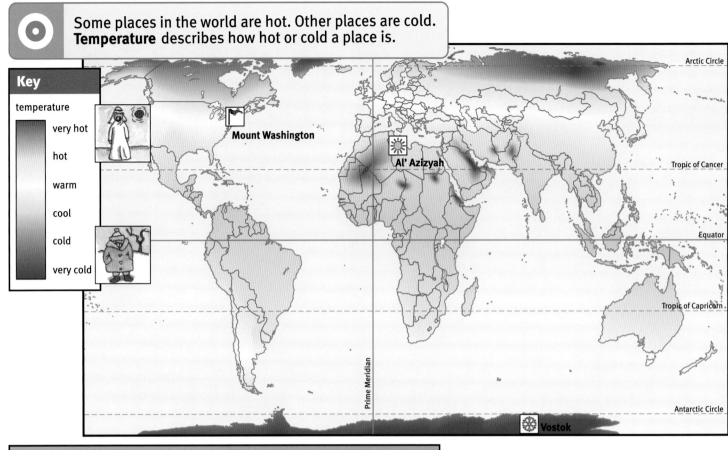

Some places in the world are hot. Other places are cold. **Temperature** describes how hot or cold a place is.

Key

temperature

very hot
hot
warm
cool
cold
very cold

Arctic Circle
Mount Washington
Al' Azizyah
Tropic of Cancer
Equator
Tropic of Capricorn
Prime Meridian
Antarctic Circle
Vostok

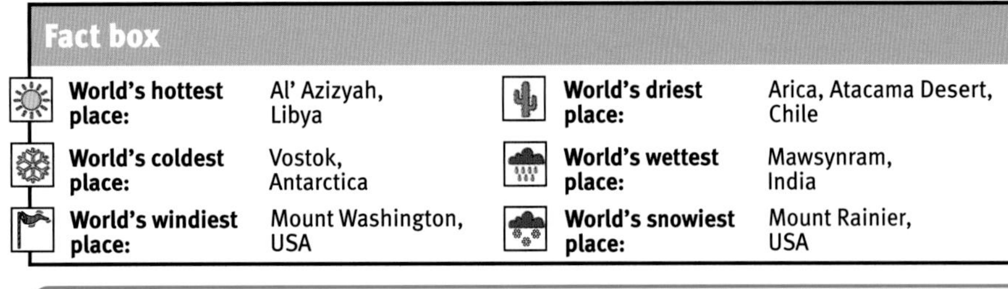

Fact box

World's hottest place:	Al' Azizyah, Libya	**World's driest place:**	Arica, Atacama Desert, Chile
World's coldest place:	Vostok, Antarctica	**World's wettest place:**	Mawsynram, India
World's windiest place:	Mount Washington, USA	**World's snowiest place:**	Mount Rainier, USA

Can you find each of these record breaking weather stations on the map?

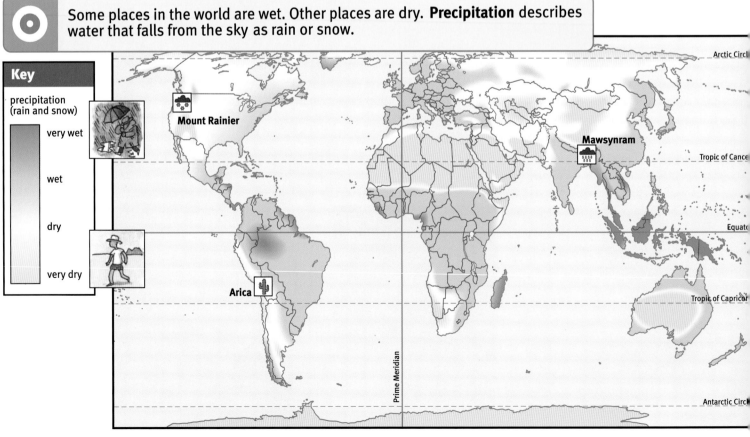

Some places in the world are wet. Other places are dry. **Precipitation** describes water that falls from the sky as rain or snow.

Key

precipitation (rain and snow)

very wet
wet
dry
very dry

Arctic Circl
Mount Rainier
Mawsynram
Tropic of Cance
Equat
Arica
Tropic of Capricor
Prime Meridian
Antarctic Circl

Patterns of temperature and precipitation throughout the year create different types of climate.

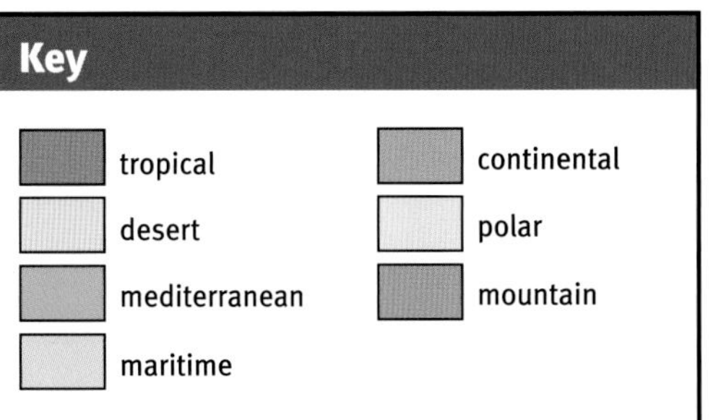
Key
tropical
desert
mediterranean
maritime
continental
polar
mountain

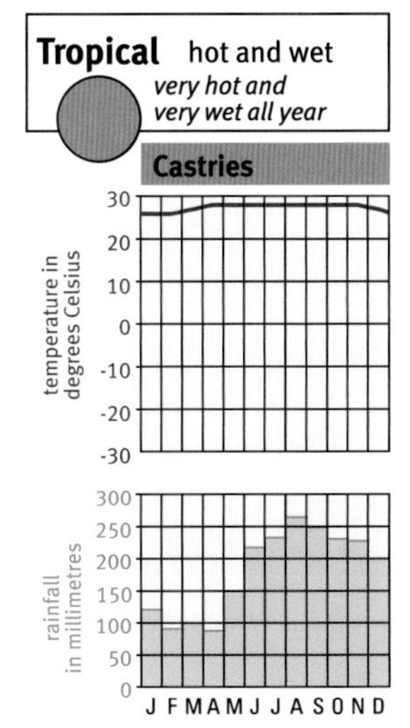
Tropical hot and wet
very hot and very wet all year
Castries
temperature in degrees Celsius
30
20
10
0
-10
-20
-30
rainfall in millimetres
300
250
200
150
100
50
0
J F M A M J J A S O N D

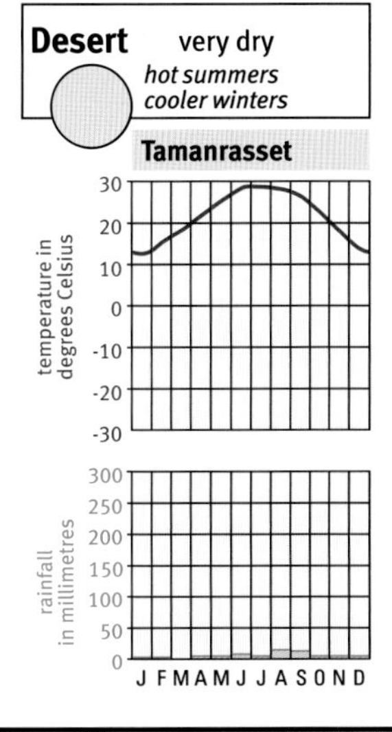
Desert very dry
hot summers cooler winters
Tamanrasset
temperature in degrees Celsius
30
20
10
0
-10
-20
-30
rainfall in millimetres
300
250
200
150
100
50
0
J F M A M J J A S O N D

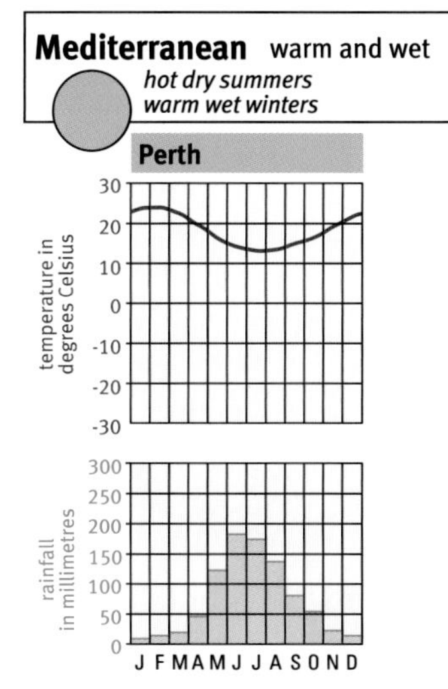
Mediterranean warm and wet
hot dry summers warm wet winters
Perth
temperature in degrees Celsius
30
20
10
0
-10
-20
-30
rainfall in millimetres
300
250
200
150
100
50
0
J F M A M J J A S O N D

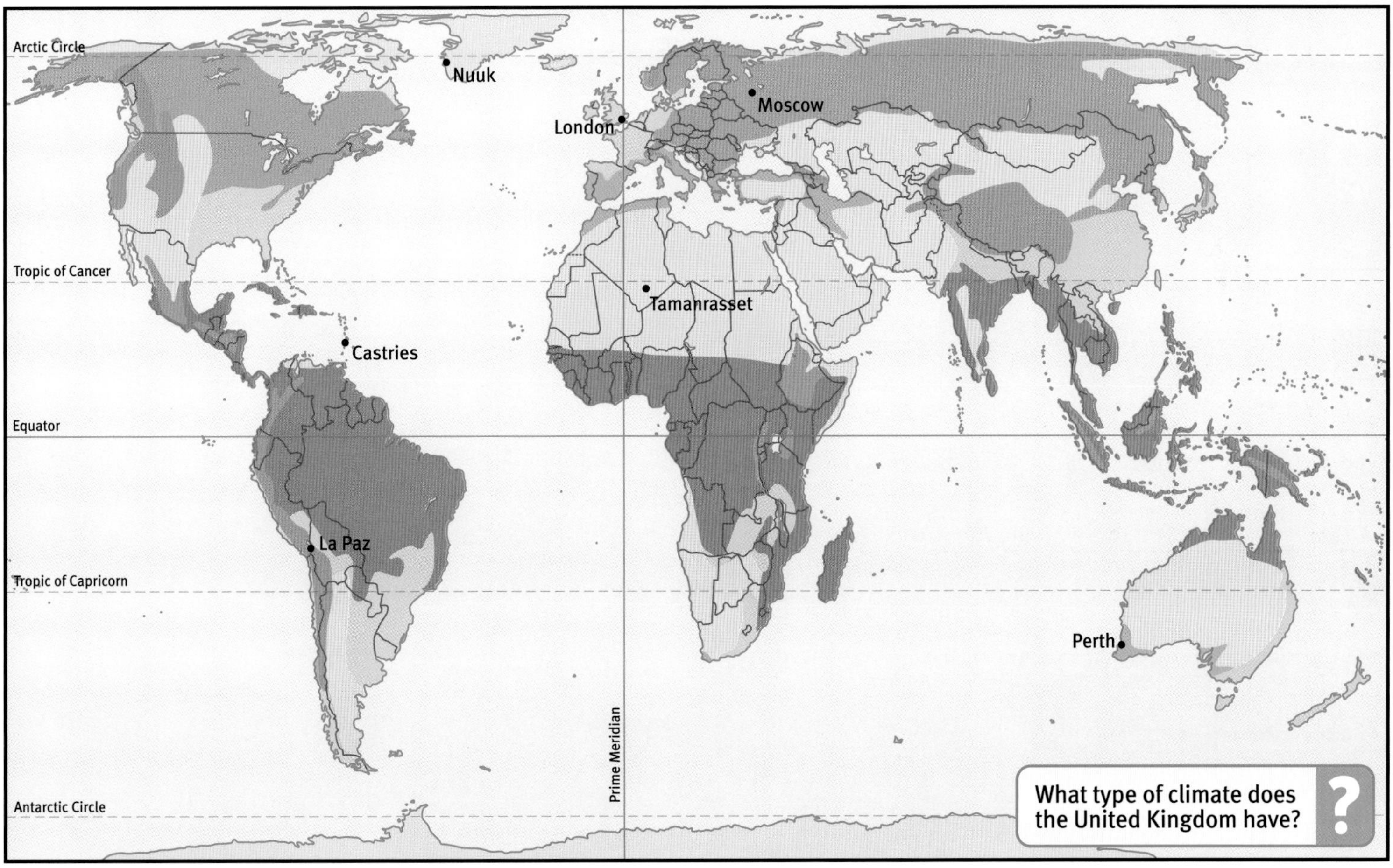

Arctic Circle
Nuuk
London
Moscow
Tropic of Cancer
Tamanrasset
Castries
Equator
La Paz
Tropic of Capricorn
Perth
Prime Meridian
Antarctic Circle

What type of climate does the United Kingdom have?

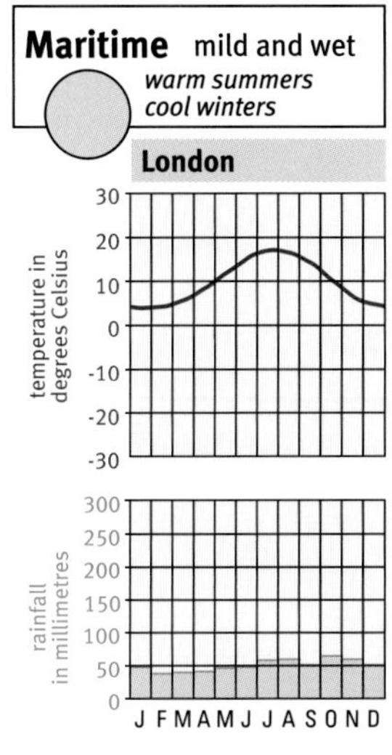
Maritime mild and wet
warm summers cool winters
London
temperature in degrees Celsius
30
20
10
0
-10
-20
-30
rainfall in millimetres
300
250
200
150
100
50
0
J F M A M J J A S O N D

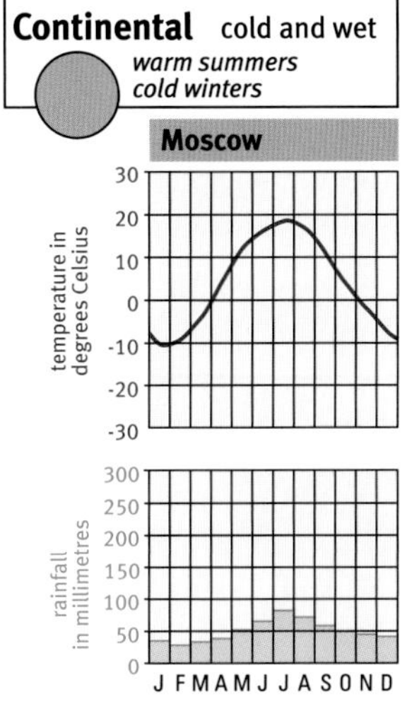
Continental cold and wet
warm summers cold winters
Moscow
temperature in degrees Celsius
30
20
10
0
-10
-20
-30
rainfall in millimetres
300
250
200
150
100
50
0
J F M A M J J A S O N D

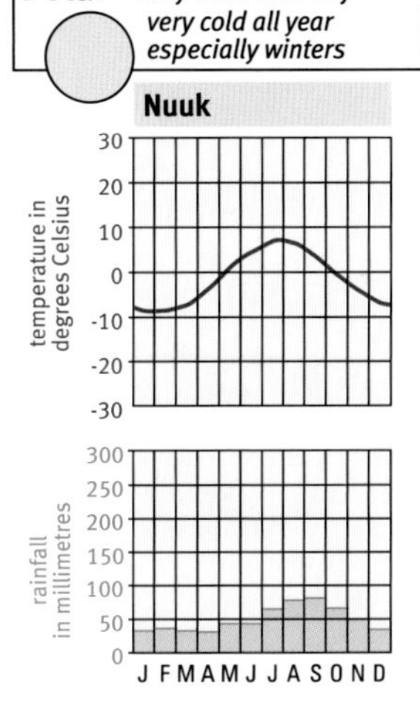
Polar very cold and dry
very cold all year especially winters
Nuuk
temperature in degrees Celsius
30
20
10
0
-10
-20
-30
rainfall in millimetres
300
250
200
150
100
50
0
J F M A M J J A S O N D

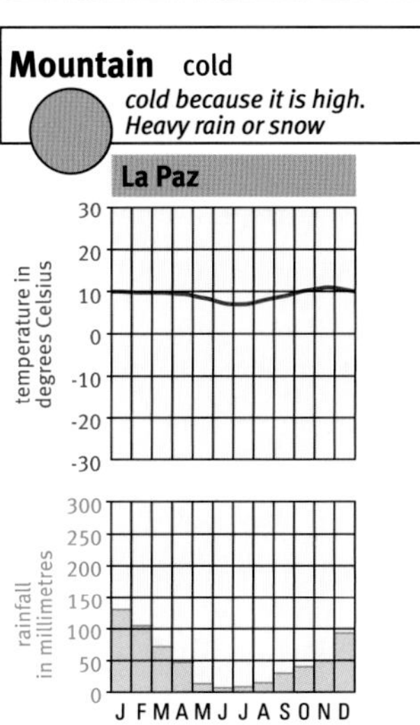
Mountain cold
cold because it is high. Heavy rain or snow
La Paz
temperature in degrees Celsius
30
20
10
0
-10
-20
-30
rainfall in millimetres
300
250
200
150
100
50
0
J F M A M J J A S O N D

World Environments

Each of the major world environments shown on the map has its own special climate, plant life and animals. Most natural environments have been influenced by people.

deciduous forest
coniferous forest
tropical forest
ARCTIC OCEAN
Arctic Circle
Tropic of Cancer
Equator
PACIFIC
OCEAN
ATLANTIC
OCEAN
Tropic of Capricorn
Antarctic Circle
80°N
60°N
40°N
20°N
0°
20°S
40°S
60°S
80°S
160°W
140°W
120°W
100°W
80°W
60°W
40°W
20°W
desert
semi desert

Key

- **coniferous forest** trees have leaves all year
- **deciduous forest** trees drop their leaves in winter
- **tropical forest** tall trees growing close together
- **savannah** tall grass and scattered trees
- **temperate grassland** prairies, steppes, pampas and veld
- **semi desert** short grass and small dry bushes
- **desert** sand and stones with few plants
- **tundra** moss and bog with some short trees
- **ice** no plants
- **mountains** thin soils and steep slopes

Eckert IV Projection

What type of environment is most common along the equator?

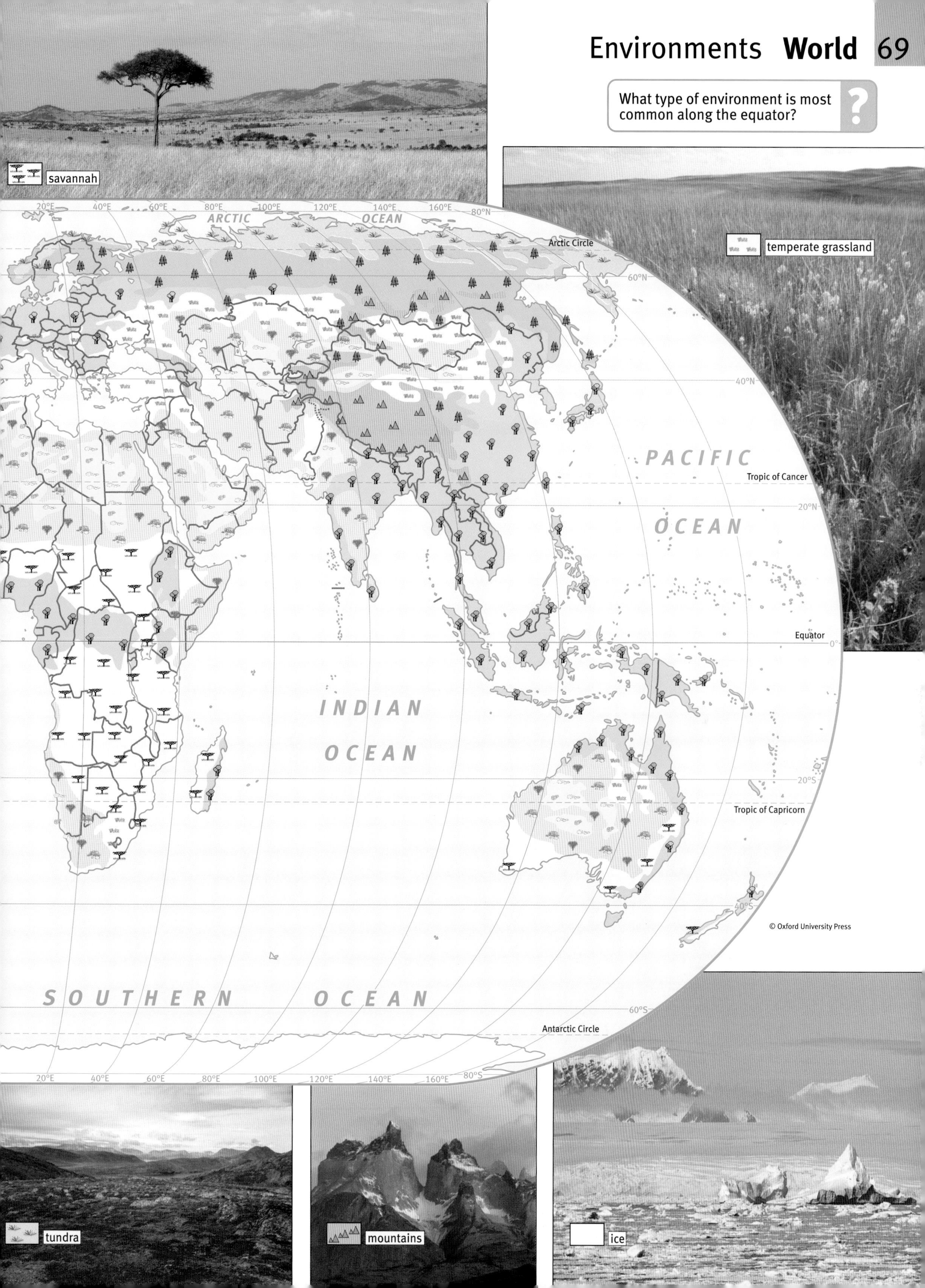

savannah
temperate grassland
ARCTIC OCEAN
Arctic Circle
PACIFIC OCEAN
Tropic of Cancer
Equator
INDIAN OCEAN
Tropic of Capricorn
SOUTHERN OCEAN
Antarctic Circle
20°E
40°E
60°E
80°E
100°E
120°E
140°E
160°E
80°N
60°N
40°N
20°N
0°
20°S
40°S
60°S
80°S
tundra
mountains
ice

World Environmental problems

People have damaged the environment in many parts of the world. Cutting down forests and burning fossil fuels affects the Earth's atmosphere and can cause **climate change**.

ARCTIC OCEAN

Arctic Circle

Gulf of Mexico

CARIBBEAN SEA

Tropic of Cancer

Equator

Tropic of Capricorn

Antarctic Circle

PACIFIC OCEAN

ATLANTIC OCEAN

80°N 160°W 140°W 120°W 100°W 80°W 60°W 40°W 20°W

40°N 20°N 0° 20°S 40°S 60°S 80°S

Key

- tropical rain forest
- areas where rain forest has been cut down
- desert
- areas that are becoming desert
- areas most affected by air pollution
- sea areas most affected by oil pollution
- areas where ice is melting

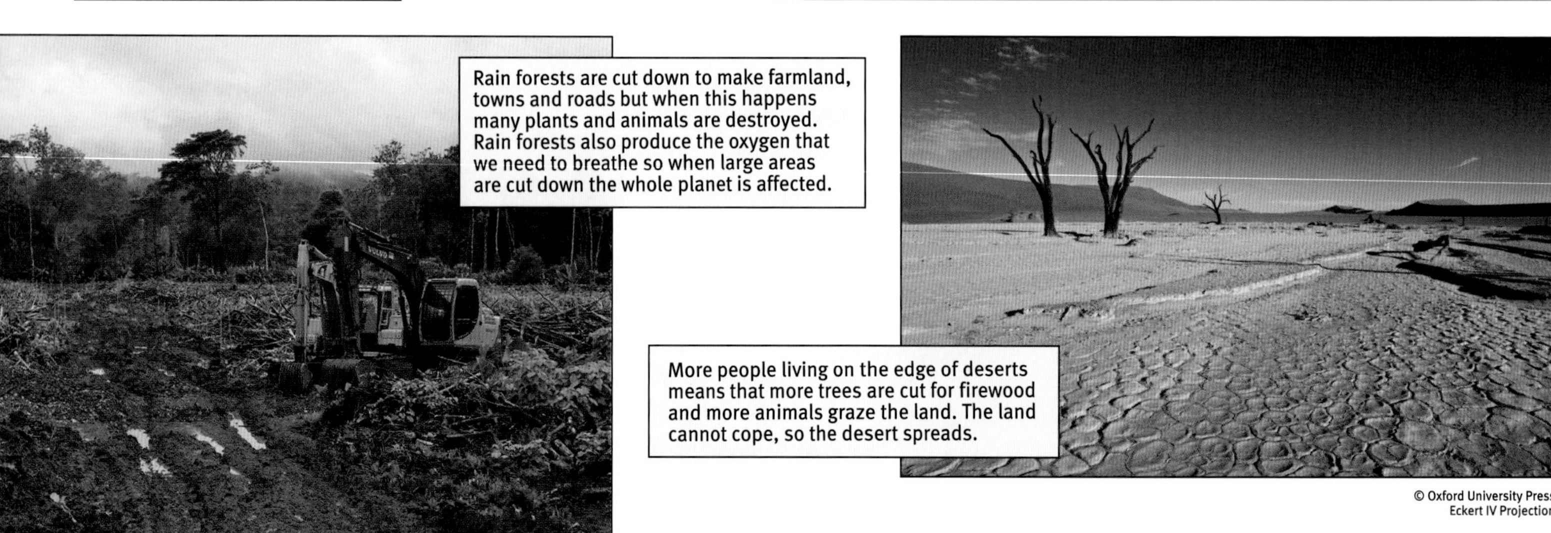

Rain forests are cut down to make farmland, towns and roads but when this happens many plants and animals are destroyed. Rain forests also produce the oxygen that we need to breathe so when large areas are cut down the whole planet is affected.

More people living on the edge of deserts means that more trees are cut for firewood and more animals graze the land. The land cannot cope, so the desert spreads.

Eckert IV Projection

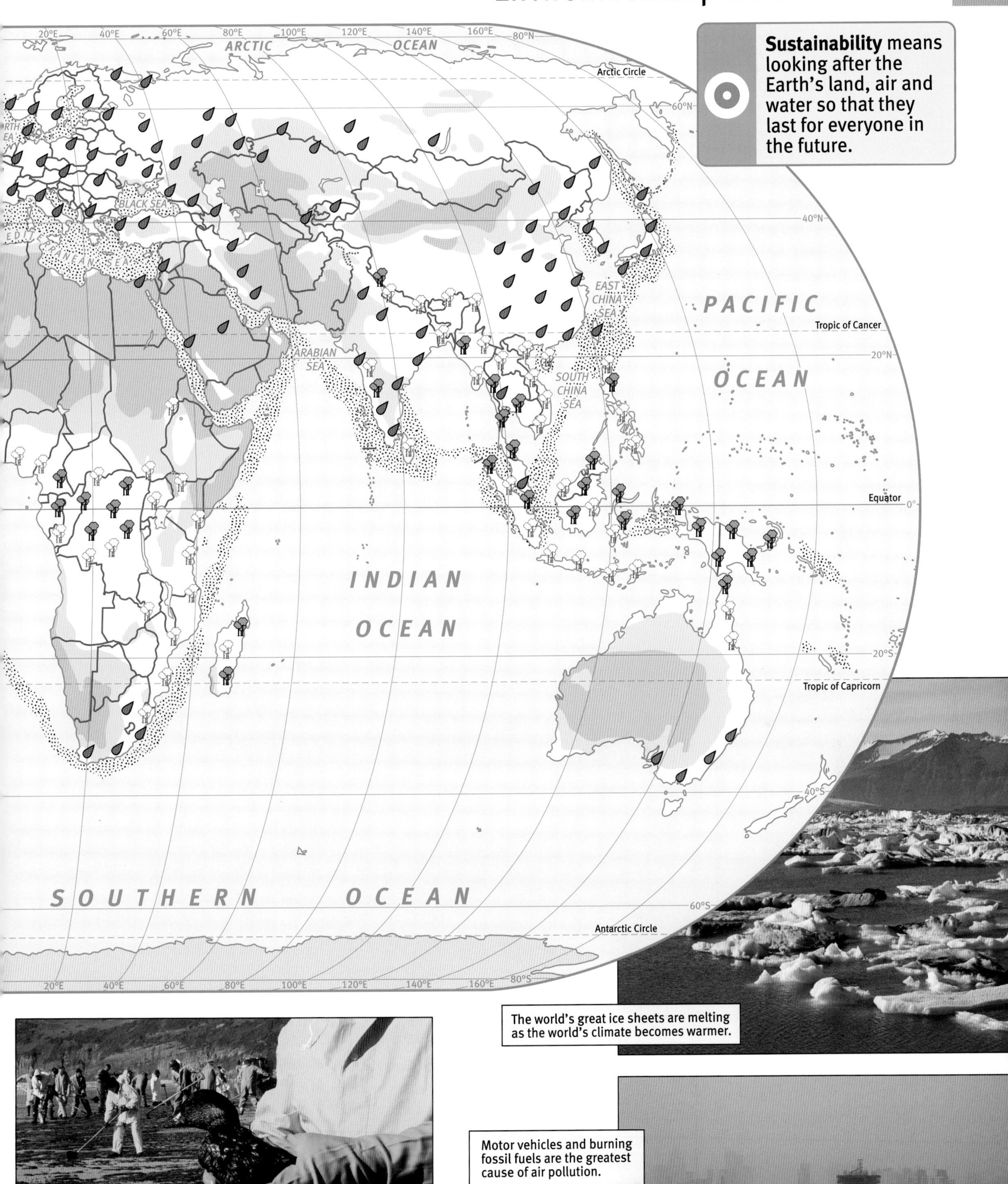
20°E
40°E
60°E
80°E
100°E
120°E
140°E
160°E
80°N
ARCTIC
OCEAN
Arctic Circle
60°N
40°N
BLACK SEA
MEDITERRANEAN SEA
ARABIAN SEA
EAST CHINA SEA
PACIFIC
Tropic of Cancer
20°N
SOUTH CHINA SEA
OCEAN
Equator
0°
INDIAN
OCEAN
20°S
Tropic of Capricorn
40°S
SOUTHERN
OCEAN
60°S
Antarctic Circle
80°S

Sustainability means looking after the Earth's land, air and water so that they last for everyone in the future.

The world's great ice sheets are melting as the world's climate becomes warmer.

Motor vehicles and burning fossil fuels are the greatest cause of air pollution.

Oil spilt from ships and oil rigs can damage beaches and wildlife. Birds with oil on their wings cannot fly.

World People and cities

There are about 6 500 000 people in the world. They are spread very unevenly. Some places are very crowded. Other places have very few people.

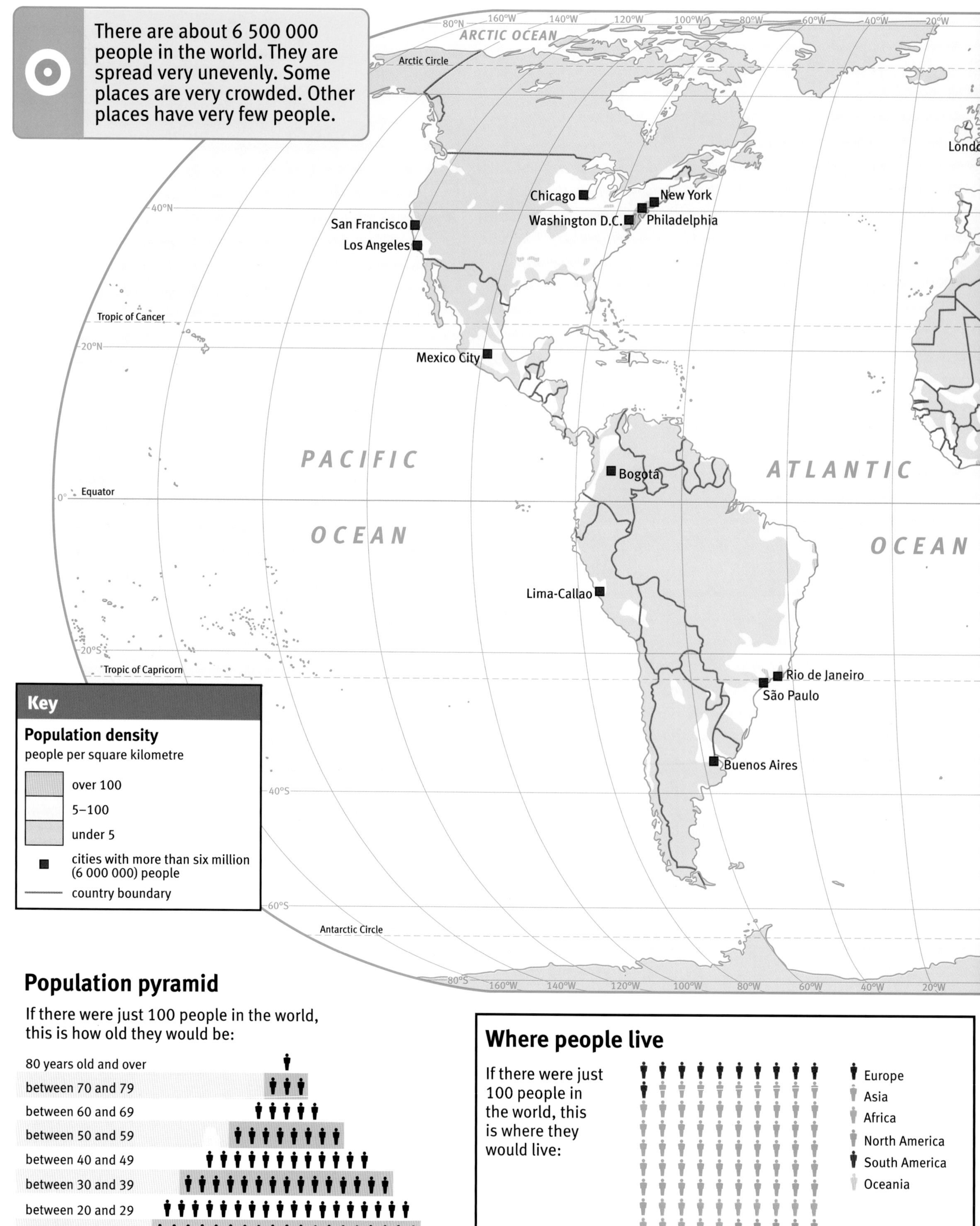
ARCTIC OCEAN
Arctic Circle
80°N
160°W
140°W
120°W
100°W
80°W
60°W
40°W
20°W
40°N
20°N
0°
Equator
Tropic of Cancer
20°S
Tropic of Capricorn
40°S
60°S
Antarctic Circle
80°S
PACIFIC OCEAN
ATLANTIC OCEAN
Chicago
New York
Philadelphia
Washington D.C.
San Francisco
Los Angeles
Mexico City
Bogotá
Lima-Callao
Rio de Janeiro
São Paulo
Buenos Aires
Londo

Key

Population density
people per square kilometre

- over 100
- 5–100
- under 5
- cities with more than six million (6 000 000) people
- country boundary

Population pyramid

If there were just 100 people in the world, this is how old they would be:

80 years old and over
between 70 and 79
between 60 and 69
between 50 and 59
between 40 and 49
between 30 and 39
between 20 and 29
between 10 and 19
9 years old and under

Where people live

If there were just 100 people in the world, this is where they would live:

Europe
Asia
Africa
North America
South America
Oceania

Eckert IV Projection

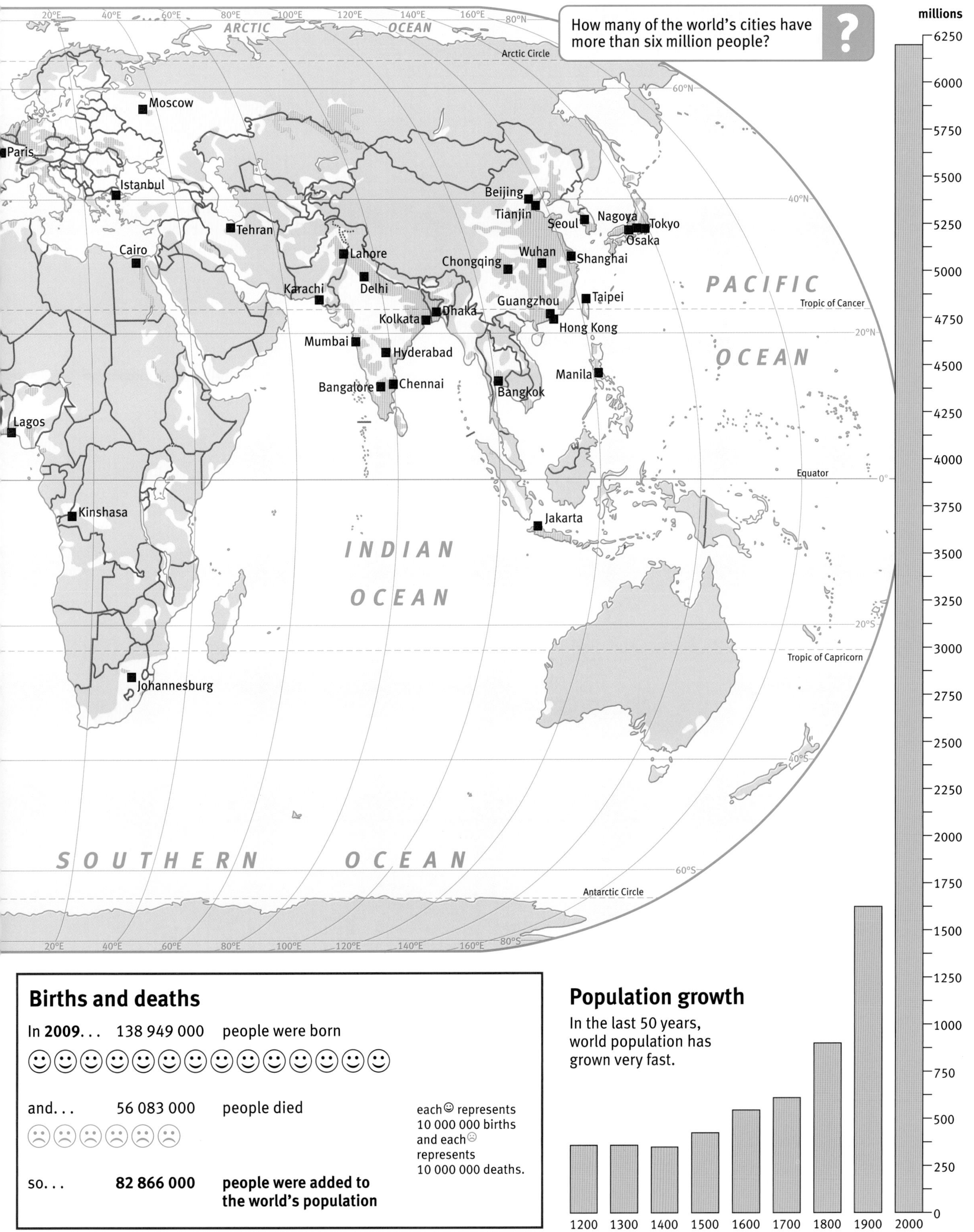
How many of the world's cities have more than six million people?
?
ARCTIC OCEAN
Arctic Circle
PACIFIC OCEAN
INDIAN OCEAN
SOUTHERN OCEAN
Tropic of Cancer
Equator
Tropic of Capricorn
Antarctic Circle
Moscow
Paris
Istanbul
Tehran
Cairo
Lahore
Delhi
Karachi
Kolkata
Dhaka
Mumbai
Hyderabad
Bangalore
Chennai
Beijing
Tianjin
Seoul
Nagoya
Tokyo
Osaka
Shanghai
Wuhan
Chongqing
Guangzhou
Hong Kong
Taipei
Manila
Bangkok
Jakarta
Lagos
Kinshasa
Johannesburg
20°E
40°E
60°E
80°E
100°E
120°E
140°E
160°E
80°N
60°N
40°N
20°N
0°
20°S
40°S
60°S
80°S
millions
6250
6000
5750
5500
5250
5000
4750
4500
4250
4000
3750
3500
3250
3000
2750
2500
2250
2000
1750
1500
1250
1000
750
500
250
0
1200
1300
1400
1500
1600
1700
1800
1900
2000

Births and deaths

In **2009**... 138 949 000 people were born

☺☺☺☺☺☺☺☺☺☺☺☺☺☺

and... 56 083 000 people died

☹☹☹☹☹☹

so... **82 866 000** **people were added to the world's population**

each ☺ represents 10 000 000 births and each ☹ represents 10 000 000 deaths.

Population growth

In the last 50 years, world population has grown very fast.

World Connections

Travel and communication around the world are becoming faster but some places are better connected than others.

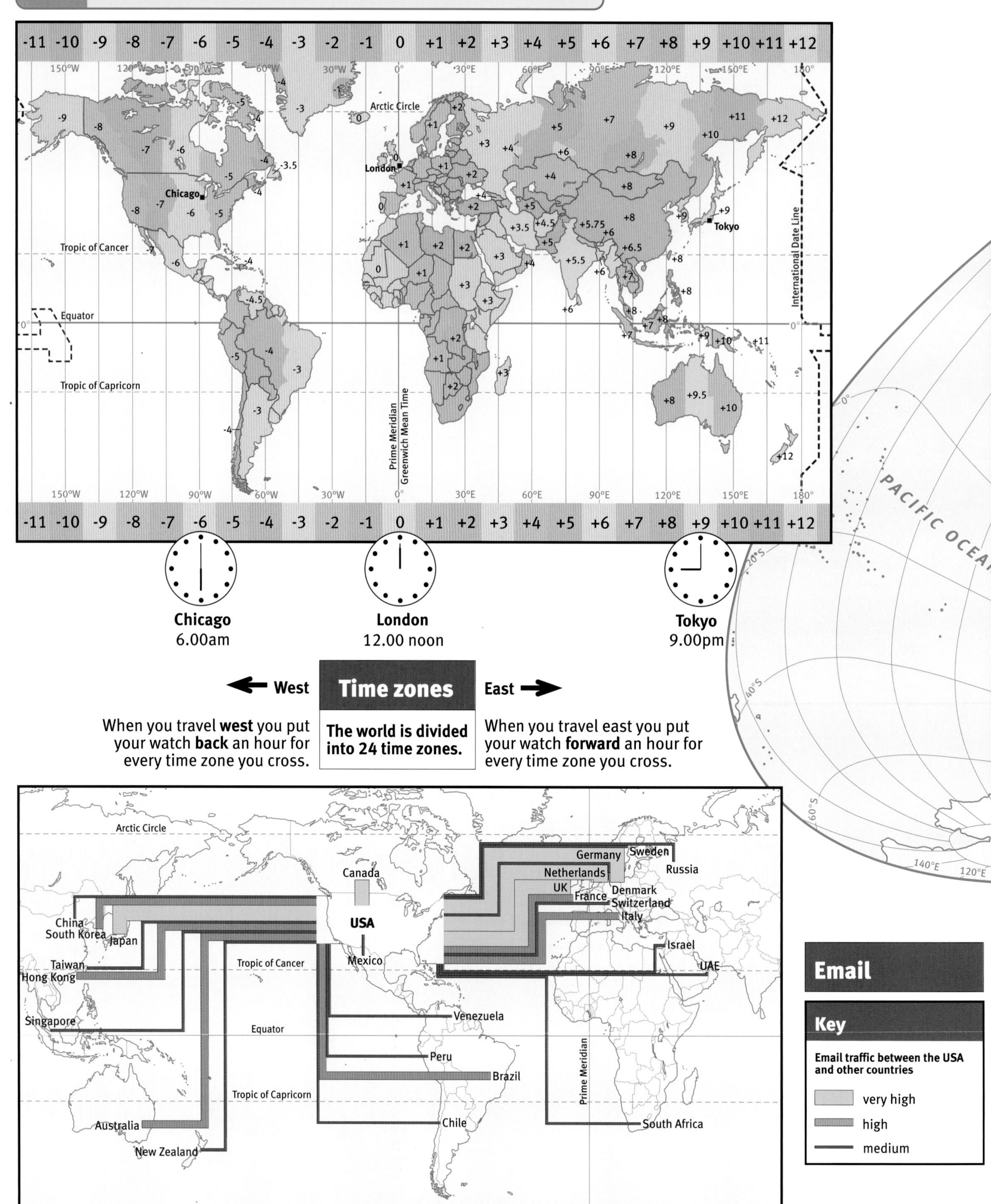

-11 -10 -9 -8 -7 -6 -5 -4 -3 -2 -1 0 +1 +2 +3 +4 +5 +6 +7 +8 +9 +10 +11 +12
Arctic Circle
London
Chicago
Tokyo
Tropic of Cancer
Equator
Tropic of Capricorn
Prime Meridian
Greenwich Mean Time
International Date Line
PACIFIC OCEAN
Chicago
6.00am
London
12.00 noon
Tokyo
9.00pm
West
Time zones
East
When you travel **west** you put your watch **back** an hour for every time zone you cross.
The world is divided into 24 time zones.
When you travel east you put your watch **forward** an hour for every time zone you cross.
Arctic Circle
Canada
USA
Mexico
Germany
Sweden
Russia
Netherlands
UK
France
Denmark
Switzerland
Italy
Israel
UAE
China
South Korea
Japan
Taiwan
Hong Kong
Singapore
Australia
New Zealand
Venezuela
Peru
Brazil
Chile
South Africa
Tropic of Cancer
Equator
Tropic of Capricorn
Prime Meridian
Email
Key
Email traffic between the USA and other countries
very high
high
medium

Gall Projection

The distance round the Earth at the Equator is 40 075 kilometres (24 846 miles)

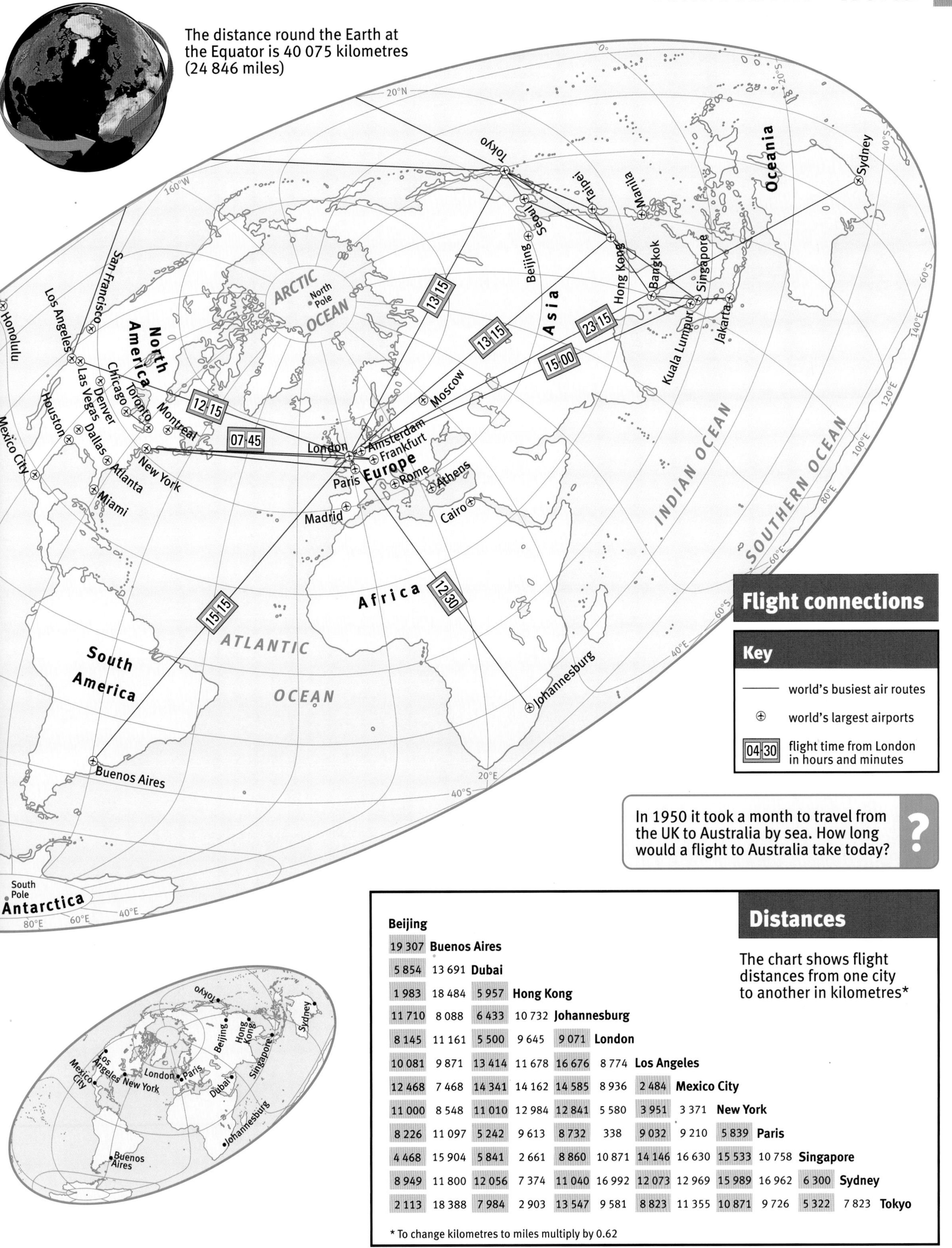
ARCTIC OCEAN
North Pole
North America
South America
Europe
Asia
Africa
Oceania
Antarctica
South Pole
ATLANTIC OCEAN
INDIAN OCEAN
SOUTHERN OCEAN
Honolulu
Los Angeles
San Francisco
Las Vegas
Denver
Chicago
Toronto
Montreal
Houston
Dallas
Atlanta
New York
Miami
Mexico City
Buenos Aires
London
Amsterdam
Frankfurt
Paris
Rome
Athens
Madrid
Cairo
Moscow
Johannesburg
Beijing
Seoul
Tokyo
Taipei
Manila
Hong Kong
Bangkok
Singapore
Kuala Lumpur
Jakarta
Sydney
12 15
07 45
13 15
13 15
23 15
15 00
15 15
12 30
Dubai
20°N
0°
20°S
40°S
60°S
20°E
40°E
60°E
80°E
100°E
120°E
140°E
160°W

Flight connections

Key

- world's busiest air routes
- world's largest airports
- 04 30 flight time from London in hours and minutes

In 1950 it took a month to travel from the UK to Australia by sea. How long would a flight to Australia take today? ?

Distances

The chart shows flight distances from one city to another in kilometres*

	Beijing	Buenos Aires	Dubai	Hong Kong	Johannesburg	London	Los Angeles	Mexico City	New York	Paris	Singapore	Sydney
Buenos Aires	19 307											
Dubai	5 854	13 691										
Hong Kong	1 983	18 484	5 957									
Johannesburg	11 710	8 088	6 433	10 732								
London	8 145	11 161	5 500	9 645	9 071							
Los Angeles	10 081	9 871	13 414	11 678	16 676	8 774						
Mexico City	12 468	7 468	14 341	14 162	14 585	8 936	2 484					
New York	11 000	8 548	11 010	12 984	12 841	5 580	3 951	3 371				
Paris	8 226	11 097	5 242	9 613	8 732	338	9 032	9 210	5 839			
Singapore	4 468	15 904	5 841	2 661	8 860	10 871	14 146	16 630	15 533	10 758		
Sydney	8 949	11 800	12 056	7 374	11 040	16 992	12 073	12 969	15 989	16 962	6 300	
Tokyo	2 113	18 388	7 984	2 903	13 547	9 581	8 823	11 355	10 871	9 726	5 322	7 823

* To change kilometres to miles multiply by 0.62

Oblique Aitoff Projection

Country data files

Choose two countries. Using the information on these pages, can you say how your countries are the same and how they are different? ?

Country area in square kilometres

Population estimated number of people in 2009 — represents 10 million people

Family size number of children in an average family — one child

Years of life number of years people can expect to live — represents 10 years

Work if there were 100 people in the country, this is where they would work — farms, factories, offices and services

Rich and poor the average amount each person spends in a year, converted into US dollars — $1000, $500

Health the number of doctors for every 10 000 people — one doctor

Country	Area	Population	Family size	Years of life	Rich and poor	Health
Australia	7 741 000km²	21 852 000 people	2 children	81 years	$37 250	25 doctors
Bangladesh	144 000km²	162 221 000 people	2.5 children	65 years	$1450	3 doctors
Brazil	8 547 000km²	191 481 000 people	2 children	73 years	$10 008	12 doctors
China	9 598 000km²	1 331 398 000 people	1.6 children	73 years	$6010	14 doctors
Ethiopia	1 104 000km²	82 825 000 people	5.3 children	53 years	$870	less than 1 doctor

Country area in square kilometres

Population estimated number of people in 2009 — represents 10 million people

Family size number of children in an average family — one child

Years of life number of years people can expect to live — represents 10 years

Work if there were 100 people in the country, this is where they would work — farms, factories, offices and services

Rich and poor the average amount each person spends in a year, converted into US dollars — $1000, $500

Health the number of doctors for every 10 000 people — one doctor

Country	Area	Population	Family size	Years of life	Rich and poor	Health
France	552 000km²	62 621 000 people	2 children	81 years	$33 280	34 doctors
India	3 288 000km²	1 171 029 000 people	2.7 children	64 years	$2930	6 doctors
Kenya	580 000km²	39 070 000 people	4.9 children	54 years	$1560	1 doctor
United Kingdom	245 000km²	61 823 000 people	1.9 children	79 years	$36 240	23 doctors
USA	9 364 000km²	306 805 000 people	2.1 children	78 years	$46 790	26 doctors

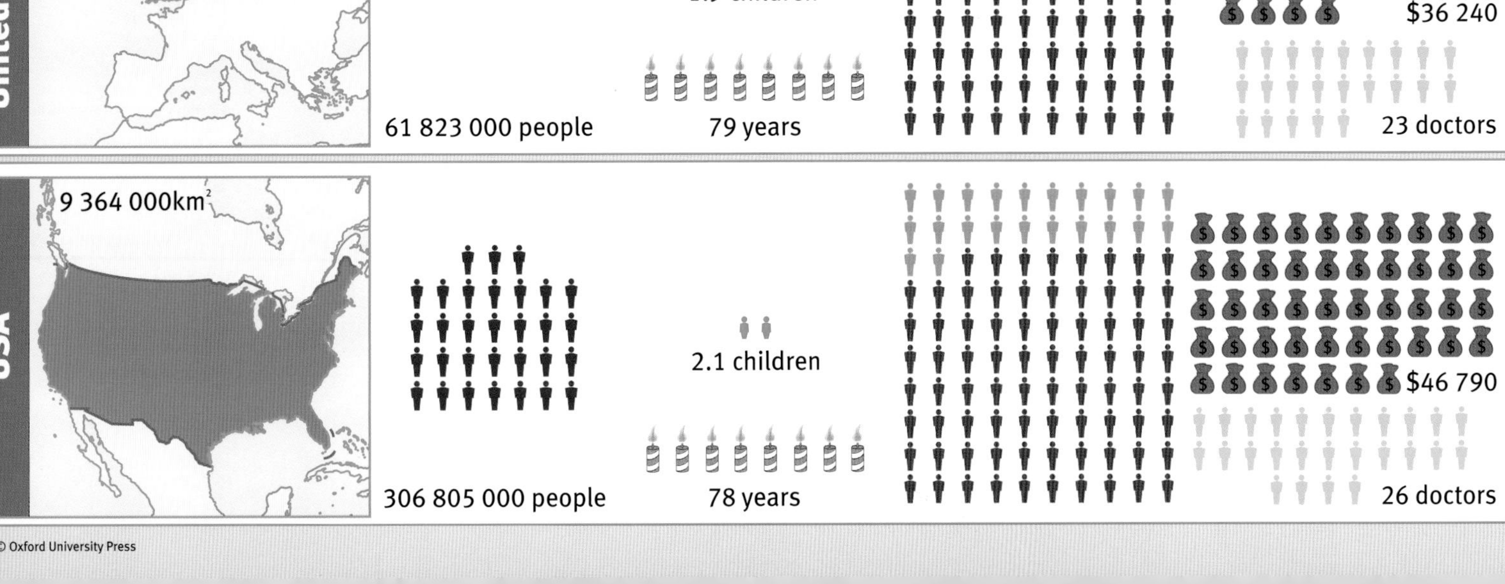

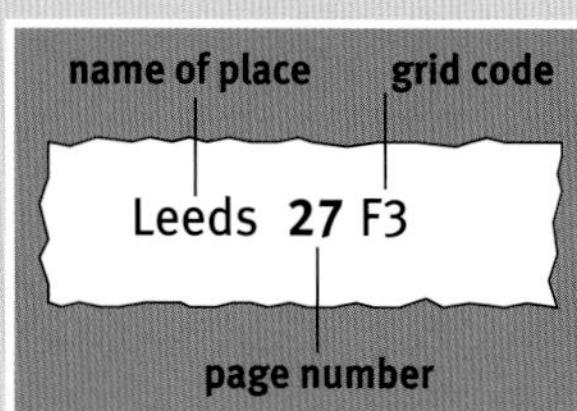
name of place
grid code
Leeds 27 F3
page number